O.S. NOCK'S POCK.

BRITISH STEA.   ᴧAYS
& LOCOMᴏTIVES

O.S. NOCK'S POCKET ENCYCLOPAEDIA OF
BRITISH STEAM RAILWAYS
& LOCOMOTIVES

by
O.S. Nock
B.Sc., M.I.C.E., M.I. Mech E., M.I. Loco E.

&B Bounty
Books

First published in Great Britain in 1983 by Blandford Press
Poole, Dorset

New edition published in 2009 by Bounty Books,
a division of Octopus Publishing Group Ltd

This paperback edition published in 2013 by Bounty Books,
a division of Octopus Publishing Group,
Endeavour House, 189 Shaftesbury Avenue,
London WC2H 8JY
www.octopusbooks.co.uk

An Hachette UK Company
www.hachette.co.uk

ISBN: 978-0-753726-34-1

The Pocket Encyclopaedia of World Railways

STEAM RAILWAYS
OF BRITAIN
IN COLOUR

by
O.S. NOCK
B.Sc., M.I.C.E., M.I. Mech E., M.I. Loco E.

Illustrated by
CLIFFORD and WENDY MEADWAY

Bounty
Books

First published in Great Britain in 1967
by Blandford Press
Poole, Dorset

Reprinted 1970, 1975 and 2009

An Hachette UK Company
www.hachette.co.uk

A CIP catalogue record for this book is available from the British Library

Printed in China

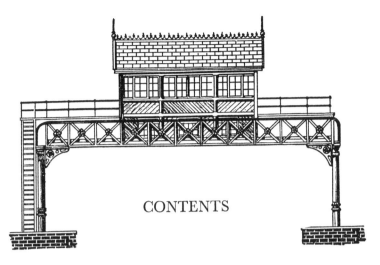

CONTENTS

PREFACE

From the very inception of steam railways it was perhaps inevitable that the locomotive itself should form the centrepiece of popular interest. For it was the locomotive and its prowess that made possible the striking developments in social evolution in Great Britain that followed the building of railways.

In an earlier volume in this series the process of technical development in the design of locomotives was traced, and the artistic adornment of the machines themselves portrayed in 192 coloured illustrations; but while it was not possible in that first volume to picture more than a typical selection from the multifarious types that have run the rails in Great Britain, it was realized only too well that in these days interest in the steam railways is by no means confined to locomotives. The growth of the skilled and fascinating hobby of railway modelling has drawn the keen interest of many enthusiasts upon the design and embellishments of passenger carriages, while equally the desire to preserve, even if in no more than a miniature form, the authentic atmosphere of the old steam railways has emphasized the vast field of study represented by the sema-phore signalling practice of the individual railways.

In preparing this book I have had once again the expert and delight-ful assistance of Charles Rickitt and his artists Clifford and Wendy Meadway.

I am grateful to British Railways for much valuable help in looking out drawings and photographs and to my one-time colleague in the Westinghouse Brake and Signal Company, Douglas Wilkinson, whose sketches of picturesque semaphore signal arrangements have formed the basis of some of the coloured illustrations. I am also indebted to John H. Scholes, Curator of Historical Relics, British Railways Board, for his help in connection with the coats of arms.

Lastly, as always, my special thanks are due to Olivia, my wife, for her advice and help, and for typing the MSS.

Brock

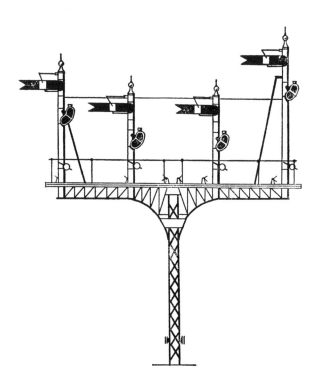

HISTORICAL INTRODUCTION

In the earlier volume of this series, *The Pocket Encyclopaedia of British Steam Locomotives*, the origins and development of this great invention were described, and its influence upon the social evolution of this country emphasised. In the rapid development of railways the steam locomotive, which alone made possible the tremendous nineteenth-century speed-up in communications, naturally claimed most of the limelight. Those who began to take more than a passing interest in this new mode of travel were naturally drawn to the gaily painted machines that trundled the early trains along, and they were fascinated by the manifestations of power evidenced by the puffing of the exhaust, the escape of steam through the safety valves; and those early enthusiasts realized that steam locomotives had for them an emotional as well as a scientific appeal.

In this second volume a further selection of historical steam locomotives are illustrated in colour, including a few specially adorned for great occasions like the London and North Western compounds *Greater Britain* and *Queen Empress*, gorgeously painted in honour of the Diamond Jubilee of Queen Victoria's reign. But in this book other aspects of the British steam railways are noticed. There is, for example, the development in carriage design. This is a deeply interesting subject which provides a reflection upon social conditions of the times, and how the travel habit gradually spread and led to a greatly improved standard of comfort for people travelling at the very lowest fares. The earliest first class carriages were built exactly in the style of a stagecoach. Those who had travelled 'inside' on the old mail coaches expected, and received, the same standards of comfort on the new railways. The stage coach builders of old applied their craft to the building of first class carriages for the railways, and whereas the stage coaches had but a single compartment the new railway carriages had at least three.

Travel in separate compartments was considered the normal standard of luxury, and it is a form of carriage design that has persisted throughout the steam railway age in this country. Just as on the old stage coaches many passengers had to travel outside and brave the elements in bad weather, so, on the earliest railways, open carriages were provided for second and third class passengers. The 'seconds' had a canopy over the top, but were completely open at the sides, while the thirds were just open trucks. At first no one thought anything of it. Many people had always travelled 'outside', some for very long distances. But as the travel habit began to grow, so there grew also an agitation for better carriages for the third class passengers. By the end of the eighteen-thirties railway speed was passing far beyond the fastest of mail coaches on the road; while on the road the outside passengers had only the elements to brave, on railways there were smuts, cinders, and smoke from the engines – not to mention the unpleasant conditions when passing through the tunnels.

In 1844 when W. E. Gladstone was President of the Board of Trade, the celebrated 'Regulation of Railways Act' was passed by Parliament, and all railways were bound by law to provide covered-in carriages for third class passengers at the statutory fare of one penny per mile. Some of the early rolling stock used to comply with this regulation was forbidding in the extreme, and consisted of little more than closed-in boxes, with the merest slits to provide light and ventilation. Furthermore some of the railway companies ran the so-called 'Parliamentary' trains only at night, when their presence and slow progress would be least likely to delay first class and mail traffic. Although things became vastly better for the third class passenger as railway travel increased, on some suburban lines in London third class carriages with bare boards for seats survived even until the nineteen-thirties.

The book illustrates the development of passenger carriages from these primitive and spartan types to the first introduction of dining and sleeping cars, and to the gradual superseding of four- and six-wheeled stock by smooth-riding bogie coaches. At the same time there have been many interesting vehicles that were not available to the general public, yet becoming familiar to regular travellers. Of these the Travelling Post Office vans must be specially mentioned, most of which were equipped with apparatus for picking up and dropping mail bags at full speed. It is interesting to recall that this apparatus was introduced as long ago as 1838 on the Grand Junction Railway – later a section of the London and North Western Railway. The network of railway postal services worked by T.P.O. vans reached its zenith shortly after World War I, and on some of the more important services mail bags would be picked up and set down at a great number of intermediate stations en route, where the train itself did not stop.

Today, however, mail bag exchange on the T.P.O. trains is on a very much reduced scale. The postal authorities now find it more convenient to concentrate mail traffic at a few large centres and distribute from such centres by road, than to collect and deliver small consignments at wayside stations. The Midland route from Bristol to the north is a case in point. At one time mail bags were exchanged at small stations like Wickwar and Charfield, but now there is no mail bag exchange at speed on the Midland T.P.O.; all the traffic is dealt with at the large stopping stations, such as Gloucester and Birmingham. Thus a very interesting and picturesque aspect of railway working is tending to disappear.

In Great Britain the vehicles used on passenger trains have mostly been as distinctive and colourful as the locomotives themselves. In this respect British railways have always stood out distinctly from the steam railways on the continent of Europe, which for the most part were uniformly drab in outward appearance. The technique of railway carriage building, as in the physical style of the compartments had its origins in coaching days. The indigenous materials familiar to the coach builders of old were used in railway vehicles, and until well into the twentieth century the bodies of lengthy main line corridor carriages were constructed in wood, even though steel was coming into general use for the underframing. The use of timber for the bodies perpetuated a picturesque form of construction in which the sides and ends were elaborately panelled; and with that same pride of finish, that was manifested in the gay liveries applied to locomotives, carriages were not only beautifully finished so far as basic painting was concerned, but were elaborately lined out, and usually adorned with the company's coat of arms. Some highly decorative examples of railway heraldry are illustrated in this book, and points about the individual designs are discussed in the descriptive matter relating to particular illustrations.

The railways of this country, in their choice of colour schemes, displayed a rare artistic taste in adopting combinations of locomotive and carriage liveries that blended harmoniously together. Only three companies painted engines and coaches the same colour, yet in other cases the combinations were not only pleasing in themselves, but were suited to those instances where on long through runs a change of locomotive introduced no jarring note in colour combinations. In this book the illustrations have in many cases been grouped so as to show contemporary locomotive and carriage styles together, such as the black engines, and chocolate and white coaches of the London and North Western; the beautiful green, and varnished teak of the Great Northern, and the crimson-lake of both engines and carriages on the Midland. On all routes to Scotland harmony continued when the trains crossed the border, and the Midland trains were taken forward from Carlisle on one route by the rich brown engines of the North British, or on the other by the handsome dark green engines of the Glasgow and South Western. On the West Coast Route the blue Caledonians were natural successors to the black North Westerns.

Perhaps the most remarkably colourful effects were to be seen on the Highland Railway where it was not unusual to find through carriages from all three Anglo-Scottish routes from London marshalled in the same train from Perth to Inverness: chocolate and white North Western; crimson-lake Midland, and varnished teak Great Northern, interspersed with some of the local Highland green carriages, maybe a travelling post-office van, and hauled by a green Highland engine. The soft moss-green of the Highland engines blended remarkably well with the harlequin effects along the trains themselves, and might almost have been chosen for the very purpose!

Another phase in the evolution of railways that recalls a step in the gradual development of transport facilities in this country is represented by a group of four rail motor cars illustrated in this book. Early in the present century railways were already feeling the effects of high costs involved in working branch lines where traffic was light; and to reduce operating costs the conventional locomotive and carriage combination was replaced by very picturesque little combined units, in which a tiny locomotive was mounted on the main frames of a bogie coach. There were very few British railways that did not try this expedient, and in days when public transport by road in country districts consisted of nothing larger or faster than one-horse buses these rail motor cars filled a useful, if short-lived niche. They were rather slow; but then branch line services were generally slow in years before World War I.

The signals require a special word of commendation. The actual semaphores depicted in the coloured illustrations in this book form no more than the outward and visible signs of the great edifice of safety regulations, and ingenious mechanism that had been built up in the course of more than a hundred years of railway operation in this country. Travel at speeds of 80 m.p.h. or more is a common experience of countless persons today who drive, or ride in modern motor cars; and while road signs and traffic lights are becoming more frequent than they used to be the road user may sometimes be puzzled by the elaborate methods of signalling that are used on railways, when traffic does not appear to be so intense as on many a modern highway, and certainly travelling at no higher speeds. This is no place to discuss the relative merits, in the social conditions of today, of road and railway travel. Instead it is necessary to look back into the nineteenth century and to the first years of the present century, when railways were incomparably the fastest means of travel known to man.

Fundamentally the whole art of signalling on railways is linked up with the distances in which a train can be stopped. Exactly the same principles are naturally being used in connection with road traffic. On an ordinary road a motorist needs no more than 100 yards warning of a 'HALT SIGN' or traffic lights ahead; but on the motorways, where the fastest vehicles may be travelling at 100 m.p.h. or more, the first advice of junctions or changes in road conditions is given a mile in advance. On railways, even with the most modern of appliances, the process of braking steel wheels, running on smooth steel rails, must necessarily be more gradual than with a road vehicle; nor would very rapid deceleration be accepted as part of the usual standards of railway comfort. Signals were erected to give drivers ample warning that a stop or a deceleration was necessary, and at the same time the highly specialized science of interlocking was built up, whereby it was rendered a physical impossibility for a signalman to set points, or lower signals in such a way as to cause a collision at a junction. There did, of course, remain certain loop-holes, where a man could, in a moment of forgetfulness, omit to carry out a point of procedure in the regulations. The human element could still enter into things – albeit to a very limited extent; nevertheless it was a policy on the part of many railway administrations to sustain the high sense of responsibility manifested by the very great majority of all railwaymen concerned with the running of the trains. The wonderful safety record of the British railways in steam days – incomparably the finest in the world – provided ample justification for this policy.

As with locomotive and carriage design, and in the distinctive liveries, the old steam railways of Great Britain developed some very distinctive patterns of semaphore signals, and some of these are shown among the coloured illustrations in this book. While the basic semaphore indications were the same the details differed widely. But in the devices used for subsidiary movements individuality ran riot, and it has not been possible to illustrate more than a few of the varied styles that were once used. Another feature that contributed greatly to the picturesque aspects of the steam railways was the vast multiplicity of semaphore arms to be seen in the approaches to large stations. This was due to the need, in former days, of having a separate arm for each alternative route. In later years, even with semaphore arms, such elaboration was obviated by the use of route indicators; but the development of a really satisfactory form, that could be read and recognized equally well by day or night was a lengthy process, and one that was not finally solved until the nineteen-thirties, by which time the semaphore signal was definitely, if gradually, on the way out.

A full description of the colour
illustrations which follow
appears between
pages 109-190

1 **Richard Trevithick's locomotive, 1804**; winner of the Pne-y-daren prize.

2 **Cauldron Wagon**; used on early railways for transport of coal. From these were developed the first third-class carriages.

3 **First class carriage "Traveller"**; Liverpool and
Manchester Railway.

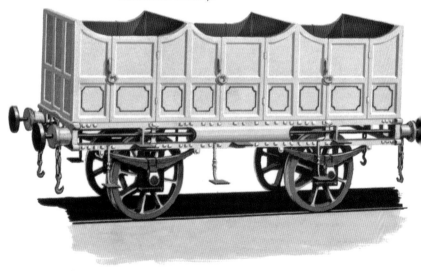

4 **Third class carriage**; Liverpool and Manchester
Railway.

5 **First class carriage**; North Union Railway.

6 **Tri-composite four-wheeler of Monmouth-shire Railway design**; Great Western Railway.

7 **Stirling 7 ft 7 in. 2-2-2**; Great Northern Railway.
1886 design.

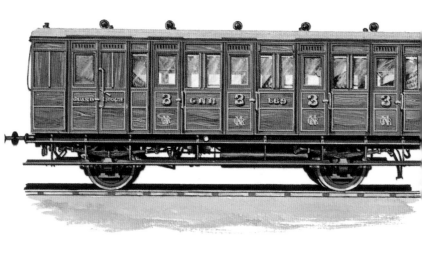

8 **Four-wheeled brake-third carriage**; Great
Northern Railway.

9 **Coniston branch 2-2-2 tank engine**; Furness
Railway. Built 1866.

10 **Sir James Ramsden's Inspection Car**; Furness
Railway.

11 **Suburban Tank Engine**; London, Chatham and Dover Railway.

12 **The celebrated 4–2–2 single No. 123**; Caledonian Railway. Built 1886.

13 **Rebuilt Cudworth 2-4-0 express locomotive;**
South Eastern Railway.

14 **Midland and Great Northern Joint Railway;**
2-4-0 passenger engine.

15   **London Suburban Carriage**; Midland Railway.

16   **Second-class Suburban Carriage**; Great Eastern
Railway.

17 **Local Train Carriage**; Great Western Railway.

18 **Four-wheeled Coach**; North London Railway.

19 **Webb eight-wheeled Radial Coach**; London and North Western Railway.

20 **T. G. Clayton's twelve-wheeled "brake-third"**; Midland Railway.

21 **Broad gauge composite carriage**; Great Western
Railway.

22 **Boat Train six-wheeler**; South Eastern Railway.

23 **London and North Western Railway**; coat of arms.

24 **Midland Railway**; coat of arms.

25 **Lancashire and Yorkshire Railway**; coat of arms.

26 **North London Railway**; coat of arms.

27 **The** *Greater Britain* **engine**; London and North Western Railway, built 1891.

28 **West Coast Joint Stock Coach.**

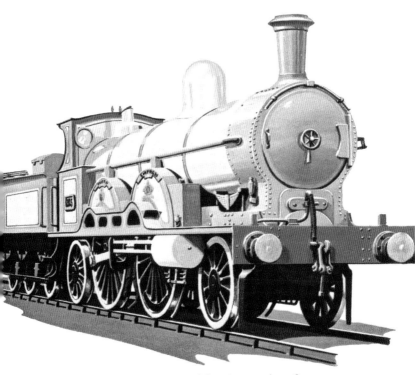

29 **Diamond Jubilee celebration engine** *Queen Empress*; London and North Western Railway, 1897.

30 **One of the first dining cars**; London and North Western Railway, built 1889.

31 **Six-coupled 0–6–0 mineral engine**; North
Eastern Railway, originally built 1866.

32 **Kirtley 2–4–0 No. 158A**; Midland Railway.

33 **Caledonian mixed traffic 2-4-0**; built 1877.

34 **"River" class 2-4-0** *Teign*; Great Western Railway.

35 **East Coast Joint Stock Sleeping Car.**

36 **Llandudno Club Carriage**; London and North Western Railway.

37 **Morecambe Club Carriage**; Midland Railway.

38 **Ocean Liner Sleeping Car**; London and South
Western Railway.

39 **Caledonian Railway**; coat of arms.

40 **North British Railway**; coat of arms.

41   Highland Railway; coat of arms.

42   **Glasgow and South Western Railway**; coat of arms.

43 **Picnic Saloon**; London and North Western
Railway.

44 **Chariot-ended, first class carriage**; Highland
Railway.

45 **Composite four-wheeled carriage**; Somerset and Dorset Joint Railway.

46 **Family Saloon**; London, Chatham and Dover Railway.

47 **"L" class 4-4-0 locomotive**; South Eastern and
Chatham Railway, built 1914.

48 **A Continental Boat Train Carriage**; South
Eastern and Chatham Railway.

49 **Drummond's 4-cylinder "double-single" engine No. 720**; London and South Western Railway, built 1897, at first with smaller boiler.

50 **Main-line non-corridor carriage**; London and South Western Railway.

51–52 **Early semaphore signals and box**; Stewarts
Lane Junction.

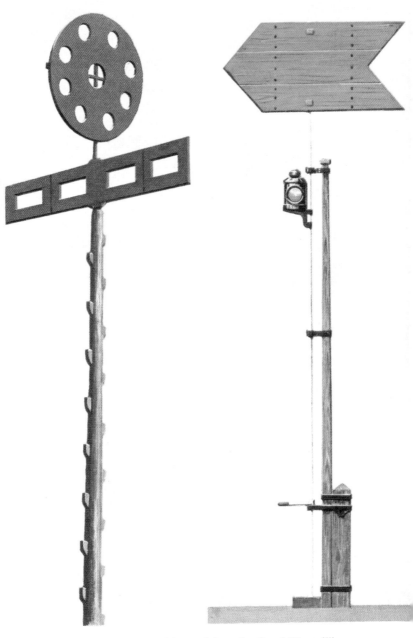

53-54 **Brunel's "Disc and Crossbar" and "Fantail" signals**; Great Western Railway.

55 **West Coast Joint Stock**; coat of arms.

East Coast Joint Stock;
coat of arms.

57 **The Royal Mail coat of arms**; used on Travelling Post Offices.

58 **Great North of Scotland Railway**; coat of arms.

59 **The "1020" class 4-4-0 locomotive**; Great
Central Railway, built 1901.

60 **Vestibuled clerestory carriage**; Great Central
Railway.

61 **Ivatt 4-2-2 locomotive, 1898**; Great Northern
Railway.

62 **Clerestory brake-composite carriage**; Great
Northern Railway.

63　**12-wheeled dining car**; West Coast Joint Stock.

64　**Third class dining car**; Midland Railway.

65 **Bow-ended elliptical-roofed dining car**; Great
Northern Railway.

66 **Composite 70 ft dining car**; Great Western Railway.

67 **Hughes 4–6–4 tank engine**; London, Midland
and Scottish Railway, built 1924.

68 **Adams 0–6–2 radial tank engine**; North
Staffordshire Railway, built 1903.

69 **4-6-2 Express tank engine**; London and North Western Railway, built 1910.

70 **0-4-4 Passenger tank engine**; Midland Railway. introduced in 1875.

71 **Great Northern Railway**; coat of arms.

72 **Great Eastern Railway**;
coat of arms.

73 **Great Central Railway**; coat of arms.

North Eastern Railway;
coat of arms.

75 **Webb Four-cylinder compound 4-4-0**; London
and North Western Railway, of 1901 design.

76 **45 ft Corridor brake-first**; West Coast Joint Stock.

77 **"Duke of Cornwall" class 4–4–0 engine**; Great Western Railway, 1895 design.

78 **Narrow-gauge clerestory coach**; Great Western Railway.

79 **6 ft "Castle" class 4–6–0 of 1917**; Highland Railway.

80 **Composite Corridor Carriage**; Highland Railway.

81 **"Scott" class 4-4-0 locomotive**; North British Railway, 1914 design.

82 **Non-corridor first class carriage**; North British Railway.

83 **0–6–4 Passenger tank engine**; Midland Railway 1907 design.

84 **Pickersgill 4–6–2 tank engine**; Caledonian Railway, 1917 design.

85 **Robinson's 4-6-2 passenger tank engine**;
Great Central Railway, built 1910.

86 **Reid 4-4-2 tank engine**; North British Railway,
1915 design.

87 **Dynamometer Car**; Great Western Railway.

88 **North Eastern Railway**; dynamometer car in L.N.E.R. livery.

89 **Dynamometer Car of 1908**; London and North Western Railway.

90 **A Modern Dynamometer Car;** London Midland and Scottish Railway No. 3, of 1948.

91 **London and South Western Railway**; coat of arms.

92 **South Eastern Railway**; coat of arms.

93 **London Chatham and Dover Railway**; coat of arms.

94 **London Brighton and South Coast Railway**; coat of arms.

95 **Travelling Post Office Van**; Highland Railway.

96 **Combined T.P.O. and passenger coach**; Great
Western Railway.

97 **Tri-composite corridor brake coach**; South Eastern and Chatham Railway.

98 **Tri-composite lavatory carriage**; Cambrian Railways.

99 **"Experiment" class 4–6–0 locomotive**; London
and North Western Railway, 1905.

100 **57 ft Corridor composite carriage**; London and
North Western Railway.

101 **A "Barochan" class 4–6–0**; Caledonian Railway, 1906.

102 **A "Grampian" corridor carriage**; Caledonian Railway.

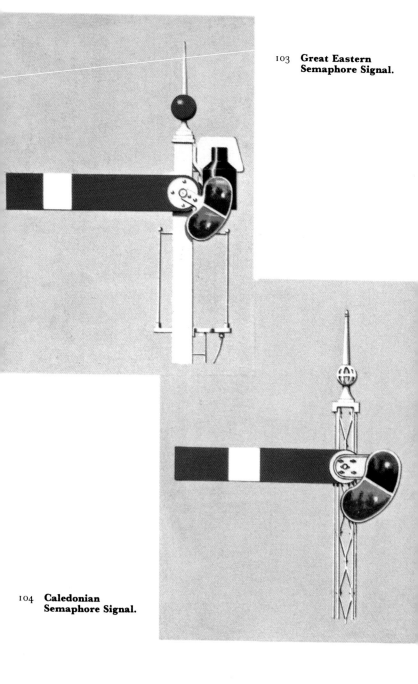

103 **Great Eastern Semaphore Signal.**

104 **Caledonian Semaphore Signal.**

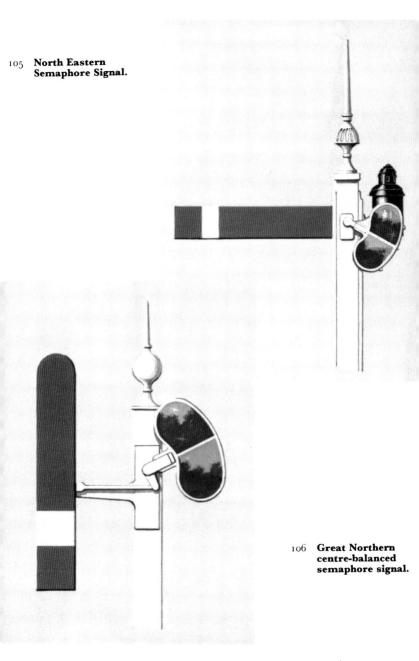

105 **North Eastern Semaphore Signal.**

106 **Great Northern centre-balanced semaphore signal.**

107   **Ocean Mail Stowage Van**; Great Western Railway.

108   **Six-wheeled Travelling Post Office**; Great Northern Railway.

109 **T.P.O. Van for the Postal "Special"**; West Coast Joint Stock.

110 **Six-wheeled Travelling Post Office**; Midland Railway.

111 **Robinson's o–6–o Goods engine**; Great Central
Railway.

112 **Composite slip-brake carriage**; Great Central
Railway.

113 **Bogie third-class carriage**; London Brighton and South Coast Railway.

114 **L. Billinton's 2–6–0 express goods engine;** London Brighton and South Coast Railway.

115 **Rebuilt non-superheater 4–4–0, No. 2 class**; Midland Railway.

116 **David Bain's design of "brake-first"**; Midland Railway.

117 **Wilson Worsdell's "V" class "Atlantic"**; North
Eastern Railway.

118 **Elliptical-roofed corridor carriage**; North
Eastern Railway.

119 Shunt-ahead signal, Great Western Railway.

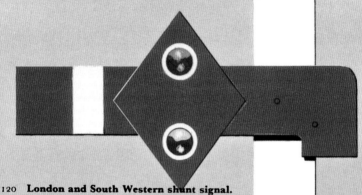

120 London and South Western shunt signal.

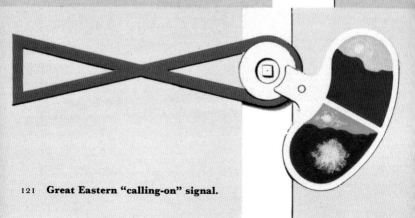

121 Great Eastern "calling-on" signal.

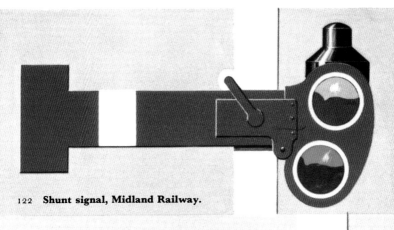

122 **Shunt signal, Midland Railway.**

123 **Subsidiary signal, London Brighton and South Coast Railway.**

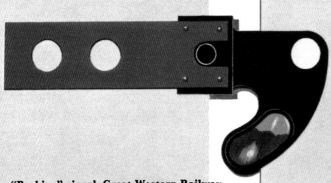

124 **"Backing" signal, Great Western Railway.**

125 **Taff Vale Railway**; coat of arms.

126 **Rhymney Railway**; coat of arms.

127 **Cambrian Railways**; coat of arms.

128 **Festiniog Railway**; coat of arms.

129 **Ocean Special Saloon**; Great Western Railway.

130 **David Bain's design of Royal Saloon**; Midland Railway.

131   **Saloon Carriage, No. 1**; Furness Railway.

132   **Open Saloon third class**; Great Central Railway.

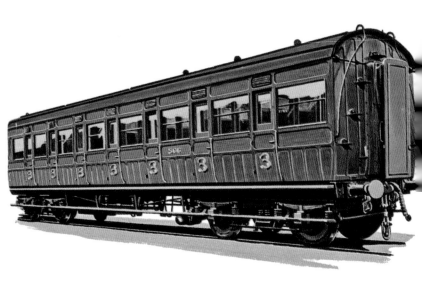

133 **Corridor third class carriage**; Great Eastern Railway.

134 **Twelve-wheeled dining car**; Midland Anglo-Scottish Joint stock.

135 **Non-corridor bogie composite carriage**; Somerset and Dorset Joint Railway.

136 **Open "brake-third" corridor carriage**; Lancashire and Yorkshire Railway.

137 **Churchward's "County" class 4-4-0 of 1904**;
Great Western Railway.

138 **70 ft Corridor Carriage, 1908 design**; Great
Western Railway.

139 **Hawksworth's "County" class 4–6–0 of 1945**;
Great Western Railway.

140 **Bow-ended corridor carriage of 1947**; Great
Western Railway.

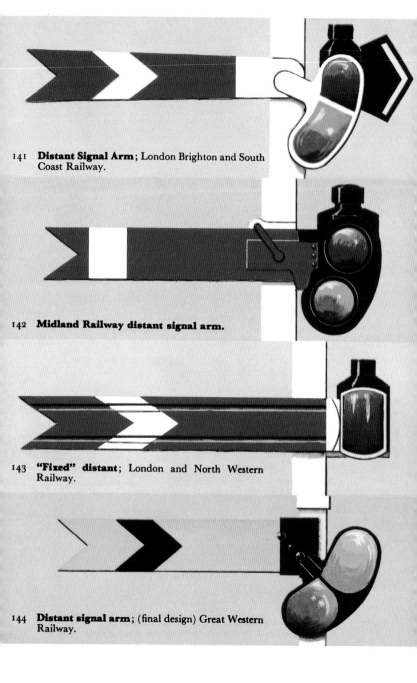

141 **Distant Signal Arm**; London Brighton and South Coast Railway.

142 **Midland Railway distant signal arm.**

143 **"Fixed" distant**; London and North Western Railway.

144 **Distant signal arm**; (final design) Great Western Railway.

145
Tall Semaphore Signal, with co-acting lower arms; Great Western Railway

146
Tall Semaphore Signals, for 4-track lines; London and North Western Railway.

147 **Large-boilered "Claughton" class** 4–6–0;
London Midland and Scottish Railway.

148 **Open-third saloon carriage**; London Midland
and Scottish Railway.

149 **Rebuilt "Lord Nelson" class 4–6–0**; Southern
Railway.

150 **Standard corridor coach**; Bulleid era, Southern
Railway.

151 **Furness Railway**; rail motor and trailer.

152 **Rail Motor, Edgware branch**; Great Northern
Railway.

153 **Lancashire and Yorkshire rail motor.**

154 **70 ft rail motor coach**; Great Western Railway.

155 *Maid of Morven* **observation car**; Caledonian Railway.

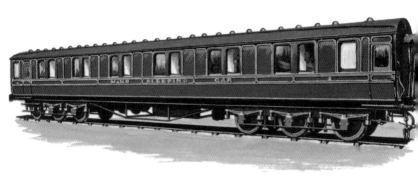

156 **Waverley Route sleeping car**; M. & N.B. joint Scotch stock.

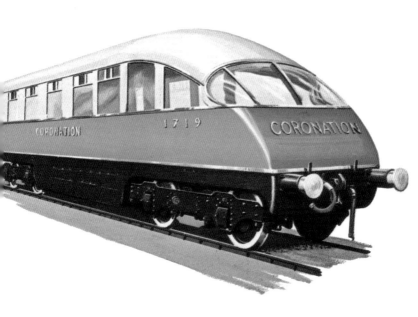

157 **The Coronation beaver-tail observation car**; London and North Eastern Railway, 1937.

158 **The "Centenary Riviera" stock**; Great Western Railway, 1935.

159 **The first Gresley streamlined Pacific**; No.
2509 *Silver Link*, built 1935.

160 **2-car articulated coach set**; "Silver Jubilee"
train, London and North Eastern Railway, 1935.

161 **Stanier streamlined Pacific**; in "red" livery as
used for these engines from 1939 on the L.M.S.R.

162 **"Coronation Scot" coach**; for New York World's
Fair, 1939.

163 **Great Western Railway**; coat of arms.

164 **London Midland and Scottish Railway**; coat of arms.

165 **London and North Eastern Railway**; coat of arms.

166 **The Pullman coat of arms.**

167 **E. Thompson's "A2" class Pacific**; London and
North Eastern Railway, 1947.

168 **Bulleid's Austerity 0–6–0 goods**; Class "Q1"
Southern Railway.

169 **"Schools" class 4–4–0 in wartime livery**; Southern Railway.

170 **L.M.S.R. Class "5" 4–6–0**; with Caprotti valve gear.

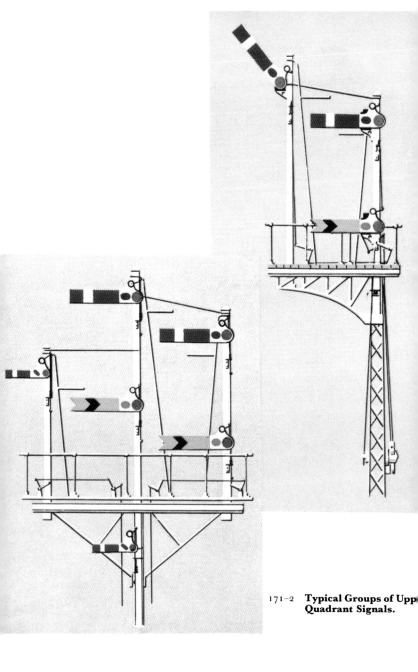

171-2   **Typical Groups of Upp[er] Quadrant Signals.**

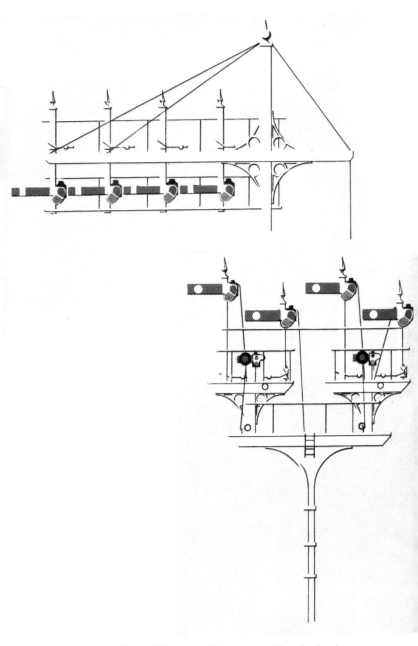

173–4 **Typical Groups of Semaphore Signals**; South Eastern and Chatham Railway.

175 **Fowler 2–6–4 fast passenger tank engine**;
London Midland and Scottish Railway.

176 **Thompson's 2–6–4 tank engine, Class "L1" for
mixed traffic**; London and North Eastern Railway.

177 **Heavy Mineral 2–8–2 tank engine**; "72XX" class Great Western Railway.

178 **"BR4" Standard 2–6–4 tank engine**; British Railways.

179 **Furness Railway**; coat of arms.

180 **Somerset and Dorset Joint Railway**; coat of arms.

181 Hull and Barnsley Railway;
coat of arms.

182 North Staffordshire Railway;
coat of arms.

183 **The** *Princess Elizabeth* **engine, in black**; British Railways London Midland Region.

184 **"Merchant Navy" class 4–6–2 in standard blue**; British Railways, Southern Region.

185 **A Gresley "A3" Pacific in experimental dark blue**; British Railways, Eastern and North Eastern Regions.

186 **A "Castle" class 4–6–0 in experimental light green**; British Railways Western Region.

187 **Double-chimneyed "King" class 4–6–0**; British Railways, Western Region.

188 **Standard main line coaching stock**; in first style of painting, British Railways.

189 **Rebuilt "Royal Scot" 4–6–0 in "standard" green**; British Railways.

190 **Standard main line coaching stock, with Commonwealth bogies**; British Railways.

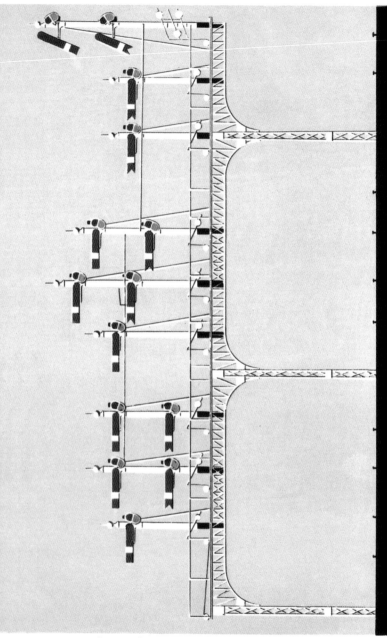

191 **Large signal gantry, with somersault type arms**; Great Northern Railway.

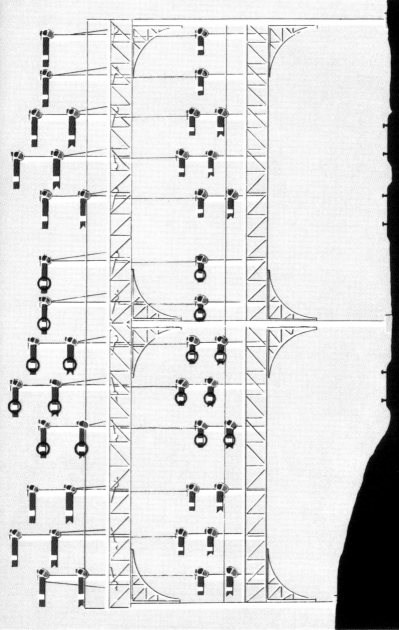

192 **The great signal gantry at Rugby**; London and
North Western Railway.

193   **"BR6" Pacific "Clan" class**; British Railways.

194   **"BR9" 2–10–0 with Franco-Crosti boiler**; British Railways.

1 Richard Trevithick's locomotive, 1804; winner of the Pen-y-daren prize. At one time there was much controversy over the question of who was the true originator of steam railways. While it was certain that George Stephenson built the first public railway in 1825, and had the vision and the keen practical outlook to set the railway industry firmly on its way, there were many men before him who had been experimenting with steam engines – not necessarily for the purpose of locomotion. Of these none was more daring in his ideas nor achieved a greater measure of success than the great Cornish mining engineer, Richard Trevithick. Yet his greatest triumph with steam locomotives was secured not in Cornwall but in Wales. Samuel Homfray, a prominent iron-master, was greatly interested in Trevithick's work and in 1804 proposed to use a steam locomotive on the 'plate-way' that existed from his two works at Pen-y-daren to the canal at Abercynon. One of his fellow ironmasters challenged him, with a bet of 500 guineas, that the locomotive would not haul a load of 10 tons over that distance. Trevithick entered into the spirit of the wager with tremendous enthusiasm, and when the appointed day came they carried 10 tons of iron, 5 wagons and 70 men riding on them the whole way. It is true that they took 4 hr. 5 min. to do the journey of 9 miles; but apparently the suitability of the line had been surveyed less carefully than the locomotive had been prepared, and they had to stop several times to cut down trees that blocked the way, and at one point some rocks had to be removed! Nevertheless, on clear sections the engine travelled at 5 m.p.h. and Homfray won his bet. Trevithick's locomotive contained many imperfections, and a vast amount of experimenting had to be done with steam between the year 1804 and Robert Stephenson's triumph with the *Rocket* at Rainhill, in 1829. But the Pen-y-daren locomotive can be set down as the very first to haul a good load successfully.

2 Cauldron Wagons; early railways. On the ever-famous journey of Trevithick's locomotive along the 9 miles of the Pen-y-daren 'plate-way', 70 men were carried, partly to make up the load, and equally to share in the excitements and triumphs of the day. One can imagine that none of them minded any discomfort or inconvenience from riding in trucks designed for conveyance of coal or iron. It was the same at the opening of the Stockton and Darlington Railway in 1825. That line, the first public railway in the world, was built primarily for the conveyance of coal, and for that the cauldron wagons were the standard form of vehicle. The passenger services were operated by single vehicles drawn by a horse, and these coaches were in the style of a stage coach. But as the popularity of the railway increased, and more and more people of humble means wanted to travel, accommodation was provided for them in open trucks. On the Stockton and Darlington Railway the cauldron wagons were adapted for the purpose, and as time went on special carriages for passengers paying the lowest fares were built. These 'carriages' were nothing more than enlarged wagons, with nothing in the way of seats or protection from the weather. It sounds a little crude; but passengers of the lowest orders expected no different in those early days. Hitherto, if such folk had required to make a journey there had been nothing for it but to walk!

3 First-class carriage, 'Traveller'; Liverpool and Manchester Railway. While the Stockton and Darlington Railway, opened in 1825, was the first public railway, the Liverpool and Manchester, opened in 1830, was one of the first to rely also entirely upon steam traction, and one whereon passenger traffic was reckoned as important as, if not more important than, goods. Accommodation was provided for first-, second- and third-class passengers, and our picture illustrating one of the earliest first-class carriages on the line clearly shows how the earliest designs were based upon the traditional style of a stage coach. The experienced coach builders were called upon to provide railway carriages, and one can readily imagine the 'Traveller' carriage as three stage-coach bodies in one. The principal difference between road and rail coaches is that in the latter no accommodation was provided for outside passengers – somewhat naturally, in view of the smoke and sparks emitted by the early locomotives; but tradition was continued in that outside seats were provided for the guard, and luggage was loaded on to the roof. This latter practice was combined for many years on railways; but it became recognized as a source of considerable danger, in that sparks from the engines could lodge among the various packages and cause fires. The earliest railways had no station platforms as we know them today and passengers had to clamber up from ground level by the rather primitive steps. As crinolines were still in vogue at the time of the earliest railways, climbing up must have been something of a feat for the ladies.

4 **Third - class carriage;** Liverpool and Manchester Railway.
In the earliest days of railways there was little encouragement for third-class passengers to travel – rather the reverse. Accommodation was provided in open trucks, but to those orders of society who had been accustomed to walk if they wished to travel anywhere, a ride in an open third-class carriage, even in the depths of winter, was no great hardship. The only change from braving the elements was that one had to brave the smoke and exhaust fumes from the loco-motives. The amenities for second-class

passengers lay midway between those of the 'firsts' and the 'thirds'. The carriages were open at the sides, but had a canopy over the top to keep out some of the weather. As the travelling habit began to grow, and many people who had never travelled in their lives began to venture on to the railways, the cry arose for better third-class carriages. One hears of coaches having holes drilled in the floors to let the water out, and on the other hand of a riotous company flinging empty bottles at men working on the line. Many a cherished top hat was lost when gusts of wind caused by the speed of the train caught its owner unprepared; though to be sure there was a certain clergyman who said he always travelled third class on the railway because there was not a fourth class! There were some seats in the open trucks; but more often than not there were far more passengers than seats and the earliest third-class trains bore a striking resemblance in the way passengers were huddled together to present-day rush-hour traffic on the London Underground.

5 **First-class carriage;** North Union Railway.
As railway travelling became more popular the amenities of travel gradually increased and the particular illustration shows an interesting development of the stage-coach type of first-class carriage. But before referring more particularly, a word is necessary about the railway itself. The system of railways extending from London up the western side of England owes a great deal to the far-sightedness and enterprise of the central partner – the Grand Junction, which linked the London and Birmingham with the Liverpool and Manchester, at a point about midway between the two last-mentioned cities. But the management of the Grand Junction had visions of an enterprise of much greater extent, one which eventually took the metals of its partners as far

north as Aberdeen. The Lancaster and Preston Junction was another link in the chain, and to connect the latter with the Grand Junction proper the North Union Railway was projected from Preston, through Wigan to Newton. This North Union had one coupé compartment at the end, with observation windows, while beneath the windows the body was chariot-shaped. There was a close compartment for luggage, the buffers were stuffed with horse hair, and a notable amenity is to be seen in the oil lamps. Lighting was at one time considered quite unnecessary. A complaint was once made to Brunel about the darkness of Box Tunnel. He replied that the tunnel was no darker than the rest of the line was at night!

6 Tri-composite four-wheeler of Monmouthshire Railway design;
Great Western Railway.

This carriage, primitive though it looks, represented a great advance upon early railway standards. In 1844 W. E. Gladstone was President of the Board of Trade, and he piloted through Parliament a Bill that required all railways to provide covered-in carriages for third-class passengers to serve all stations, at a standard fare of one penny per mile. Some of the less progressive railways took unkindly to this legislation and provided nothing more than forbidding closed-in boxes for third-class passengers, and ran the so-called 'Parliamentary' trains at night. For many years the term Parliamentary, or Parley as they were more often called among railwaymen, was applied to any stop-at-all-stations slow train. The tri-composite coach shown in our picture reveals the lingerings of stage-coach design styles in the windows of the first- and second-class compartments, while in the 'thirds' windows were provided only in the doors, as though to keep passengers of more lowly orders concealed out of sight. This coach was

designed in 1851 for the Monmouthshire Railway, a line later absorbed by the Great Western Railway. The builder was J. Wright, a noted coach manufacturer of the period. The coach is shown in our picture in the traditional chocolate and cream of the G.W.R., which dates from the very early days of that railway.

7 Stirling 7 ft. 7 in. 2-2-2 Single;
Great Northern Railway.

Patrick Stirling, Locomotive Superintendent of the G.N.R. from 1866 to 1895, will always be remembered by his beautiful bogie 8 ft. single express locomotives, with outside cylinders. But these engines were in a class apart, in that they were the only ones he built having outside cylinders. All the rest, goods engines, suburban tanks, mixed traffic and express passenger alike, had inside cylinders, and an extremely neat exterior, with all the machinery discreetly hidden. The very handsome engine illustrated was one of a class introduced in 1886 for working turn and turn about with the bogie 8-footers on the fastest express duties. They were very successful engines, and ran freely at really high speeds. The Great Northern passenger services of those days were among the fastest anywhere in the world. In the great railway race of 1895 one of this class, No. 874, took the 8 p.m. Aberdeen express from Kings Cross to Grantham $105\frac{1}{2}$ miles in $112\frac{3}{4}$ min. with a load that would be considered heavy for so fast a run – 190 tons. The 27 miles from Hitchin to Huntingdon were covered in $24\frac{1}{2}$ min., and the maximum speed was just short of 80 m.p.h. Unfortunately, these engines were introduced at a time when train loads were very much on the increase, and by the early years of the twentieth century they were outclassed. Of the 21 engines built to this design, the majority had a life of less than 20 years, which was very short for a well-designed and efficient locomotive of that period.

8 Four-wheeled brake-third carriage; Great Northern Railway.
The Great Northern had, both for its locomotives and its passenger stock, one of the most pleasing liveries to be seen anywhere. Behind the light-green engines, always so immaculately turned out, there ran trains of coaches in which the teak of their construction was given no other finish than varnish. But it was done so well that the effect was superb. The Great Northern, like its age-old rival on the West Coast route from Euston, was a convinced user of non-bogie coaches, even for the fastest main-line expresses, and the Aberdeen 'racer' of 1895, although making average speeds in excess of 60 m.p.h. was composed entirely of 6-wheeled stock. The coach illustrated is one used in a set of close-coupled London suburban vehicles, as will be appreciated from the truncated buffer at the right-hand end in the picture. If coupling and uncoupling had to be done regularly, as in the case of some main-line formations, these short buffers would have been most inconvenient; but the suburban trains were kept in close-coupled sets, and in a long train there was some saving in overall length. The Great Northern suburban coaches, although cramped by modern standards, were considerably less spartan than some of their neighbours, and the partitions between compartments were taken up to the roof. The roofs themselves, when newly turned out of the shops, were white. This may have seemed a most impractical colour, but there was no intention of trying to keep them so. The white lead paint used was found to be excellent in its lasting qualities, and it soon 'weathered' to a pleasing grey, as shown in this picture.

9 Coniston branch 2-2-2 tank engine; Furness Railway.
The Furness Railway, although isolated by geography from the major arteries of through railway traffic in Great Britain, came to have a notably high tradition in engineering matters. Its association with the iron and steel industry in its own neighbourhood, and with the great works of Messrs. Vickers, at Barrow-in-Furness, naturally brought its men into contact with the latest developments in heavy engineering production, and the outcome was a particularly fine range of steam locomotives for all classes of duty, albeit on a scale limited by the size and traffic of the railway. The dainty little 2-2-2 tank engine illustrated belongs nevertheless to an earlier period, when the position of the Furness Railway was being consolidated. It was built by Sharp Stewart and Co. Ltd., in 1866, specially for working on the picturesque branch line from Foxfield to Coniston. Although this line, in climbing into the mountains overlooking Coniston Lake, is heavily graded, the traffic was light in early days and a locomotive with cylinders no larger than 15 in. diameter by 18 in. stroke; driving wheels of 5 ft. 6 in. diameter, and a boiler pressure of 120 lb. per sq. in. was quite adequate. The water supply was carried in a well tank – invisible in the picture – having a capacity of 500 gallons. This illustration shows admirably the beautiful locomotive livery of the Furness Railway – a very appropriate iron-ore red – and characteristic of the colour of the soil in many parts of the country through which the railway ran.

10 Sir James Ramsden's Inspection Car; Furness Railway.
The higher management of the Furness Railway was, so far as can be traced, unique in Great Britain, in that the directors gave their services entirely free, regarding this work as a social service to the districts served by the railway. The supreme command again was unusual in being vested in a Managing Director, in the person of Sir James Ramsden – a very prominent figure in Barrow. In 1865 Wright Brothers built the picturesque

little coach illustrated specially for Sir James to use during inspections of the line. There were two compartments inside; but one was made narrow so that one could see both fore and aft from the other. The picture shows the open platform at the back, which was used for outside observation, if necessary. This vehicle was in constant use by Sir James Ramsden for upwards of thirty years, indeed up to the time of his retirement. The colour of the vehicle, as shown in the illustration, is that of the first carriages of the Furness Railway, a rich varnished wood closely matching that of the locomotives; but in later years, as shown in subsequent pictures in this book, a beautiful two-colour scheme of Royal blue and white was adopted. It is pleasant to recall that the management of the Furness Railway was always historically minded, and this inspection vehicle was included among a series of picture postcards issued in years before World War I; this series also included a picture of the Duke of Devonshire's private carriage – another quaint old four-wheeler dating from the 1850s.

11 **Suburban Tank Engine;** London, Chatham and Dover type.
The London, Chatham and Dover Railway, in the complexity of its lines in the London suburban area, was one of the most difficult of systems to manage, and reference was made in the *Pocket Encyclopaedia of British Steam Locomotives* to the 0-4-2 tank engines of the 'Scotchmen' series introduced by William Martley. These were splendid little machines, and although introduced as long ago as 1866 they were still hard at work in 1898, when the company was brought into association with its old rival, the South Eastern Railway, under a Managing Committee, and locomotives of both companies thenceforth bore the initials S.E.&C.R. Legally and financially there was never such a concern as the 'South Eastern and

Chatham Railway', and close scrutiny of the heraldic device carried on the express locomotives revealed the reference to the Managing Committee. But under the new working arrangement all the locomotives of both companies were decked in a very bright and gay livery of fresh green, plentifully ornamented with polished brass, and much attractive lining. The 'Scotchmen' 0-4-2 tank engines had by that time been reboilered and, as our picture shows, acquired a more modern look than in their original form of 1866. In S.E.&C.R. days, nevertheless, they were among the smartest and prettiest little tank engines working in and around London.

12 **The 'Single' No. 123;** Caledonian Railway.
This celebrated engine, a completely isolated specimen built by Neilson & Co. and exhibited at the Edinburgh Exhibition of 1886, has in 80 years achieved a fame that would have astonished her builders had they lived to witness it. Dugald Drummond was building powerful new 4-4-0 locomotives for the heavily graded routes of the Caledonian Railway; and it was remarkable in the first place that they should have ordered also a single-wheeler, with the same boiler and machinery. No. 123 was greatly admired at the Edinburgh Exhibition, but two years later, in 1888, it was shown that she was no mere ornament. In the Race to the North she had the task of hauling the racing train from Carlisle to Edinburgh, and her fastest journey gave an average speed of 60 m.p.h., even though the 1,014 ft. altitude of Beattock summit had to be surmounted and a second heavy climb from Carstairs to Cobbinshaw also made. In later years No. 123 was set aside by the Caledonian Railway to haul the Directors' Inspection Saloon; but after the grouping of the railways in 1923, and the inclusion of the Caledonian in the

L.M.S. system, this duty was no longer required, and No. 123, by that time renumbered 14010, returned to ordinary passenger service, chiefly on local trains between Perth and Dundee. As such she became the last single-wheeler in Great Britain to remain in revenue earning service. After her eventual withdrawal she was saved from the scrapheap and restored to the Caledonian livery for preservation. In recent years she has been further renovated to full working order, and has done much excellent working in the haulage of enthusiasts' special trains in many parts of the country. As preserved now she has the later type of small Caledonian boiler, with plain dome, and Ramsbottom safety valves over the firebox. She is also in the bright blue livery, familiar to travellers in Scotland in the twentieth century. Our picture shows her in original condition, as she ran in the Race of 1888; the safety valves were then on the dome, in the traditional Drummond style, and the livery was the very distinguished Prussian blue.

13 Rebuilt Cudworth 2-4-0 locomotive; South Eastern Railway.

The trunk route from London to Dover had a most curious and complicated origin. One might have imagined that in the projecting of railway communication over a route that had connections across the English Channel to all parts of Europe, and by the overland route to India and the Far East, would have involved nothing more nor less than a direct line. Instead such were the initial pecuniary difficulties that use was made of the Brighton railway as far as Redhill, and there the line to Dover swept round sharply at right angles, and then ran almost dead straight for Ashford, before turning towards Folkestone. Cudworth built some good engines for the line, but other circumstances precluded any chance of really fast running. The engine shown in our picture is one of his numerous

2-4-0 passenger class, but as rebuilt by James Stirling. This was an interesting example of a rebuild in which the second version was really a prettier machine than the original. The colours are those in vogue in the latter part of the Victorian era, when these engines were used on branch-line passenger trains, and on lighter express trains. No fewer than 124 of them were originally built, between 1857 and 1875, and at the latter date they formed roughly half the entire locomotive stock of the South Eastern Railway. In their rebuilt form as illustrated quite a number of them survived after 1899 to bear the colours of the South Eastern and Chatham Managing Committee.

14 Midland and Great Northern Joint Railway; 2-4-0 passenger engine.

A glance at the picture of this pretty little engine immediately suggests a strong connection with Alexander Allan in the form of the front-end framing and the spacing of the wheels. It certainly is an Allan engine, but the connection with the designer, so far as the 'M.&G.N.' was concerned, was exceedingly indirect. The Midland and Great Northern Joint Railway was a somewhat 'indirect' affair itself, and a note on its origins will help to explain how it came to possess two Allan engines. Despite the weight of Great Eastern influence in East Anglia, one or two local railways in North Norfolk tried to pursue independent careers, such as the Yarmouth and North Norfolk, and the Lynn and Fakenham. With some lines west of Kings Lynn, these fragments were at first gathered together under the title of the Eastern and Midlands Railway, in 1883, and then the whole concern came under the joint ownership of the Midland and the Great Northern Railways. Between them, the two large companies worked the joint line up into a very creditable, if not very profitable, business, and in the summer they handled a very heavy Saturday holiday traffic from the Midlands to East Anglia. But in days before the joint ownership the 'Eastern and Midlands' was constantly in financial difficulties, and they were compelled to buy what locomotives they could pick up cheaply – second, third or even fourth hand. Naturally a somewhat heterogeneous collection assembled in East Anglia, and the two Allan 2-4-os were bought from the London and North Western Railway, in 1883. They had originally been allocated to the Lancaster and Carlisle section, and one of the two was employed as a slow-train engine on the Ingleton branch, working between that town and Tebay. The 'M.&G.N.' made it look very smart in their mustard yellow livery, and as illustrated it bore the initials in full on the tender. In later days the initials were just 'M.&G.N.'

15 London Suburban Carriage; Midland Railway.

In pre-grouping days the Midland Railway had one of the most distinctive liveries of any company, with engines and carriages alike in a rich shade of crimson lake. In more recent years this colour, or a modern synthetic version of it, became much more familiar to the travelling public as the livery of the L.M.S., and it has now been adopted as standard for British Railways. The little four-wheeler illustrated may seem a rather primitive thing, but in late Victorian days the Midland, by abolishing second-class carriages into thirds, provided much better accommodation for the third-class passenger than was to be found on most other lines. The seats were cushioned, and if the head-rests were plain boards at least the partitions extended up to the ceilings. The carriage illustrated was used on the service into the heart of the City of London, over the so-called 'widened lines' of the Metropolitan Railway from Kings Cross to Moorgate. Over this section of the Inner Circle there were then, as now,

four tracks, and the steam-hauled trains of the Midland and of the Great Northern descended to the level of the Underground by steeply-graded and sharply-curved tunnels from their own lines. While the Great Northern tunnels came to the surface adjacent to Kings Cross station, the Midland lines surfaced about half-way between St. Pancras and Kentish Town.

16 Second-Class Suburban Carriage; Great Eastern Railway.

The steam-hauled suburban service of the Great Eastern, worked from its terminal stations at Liverpool Street and Fenchurch Street, was one of the phenomena of the railway network of London. Most of the trains were made up of entirely four-wheeled coaches, close-coupled as can be inferred by the design of the buffers shown in our illustration, and including first-, second- and third-class carriages. The 'firsts' were quite luxurious in their seating, though they rode rather 'hard'. The 'seconds' were much more cramped, and although having cushioned seats were straight-backed, and gave little room for the knees. The 'thirds' sat on bare boards, and the partitions extended only to shoulder-height. A third-class carriage was thus virtually open, and one could easily climb over the partition from one section to another. But although the accommodation was spartan for the majority of travellers, the service was very smartly run. There were literally swarms of trains, and to see them follow each other out of Liverpool Street in the evening rush-hour was an object lesson as to what could be done when efficient steam locomotives were backed by a superb operating organization. Stopping times at intermediate stations were reckoned in seconds rather than minutes, and to enable passengers of the three classes to recognize their compartments quickly the doors were at one time painted in bright distinctive colours. This led to the nickname 'Jazz Trains', but while the coloured doors are now long forgotten by the public the Liverpool Street suburban service has ever since been known to railwaymen as 'the jazz', even now that it is changed out of all recognition, and worked by electric multiple unit trains.

17 Local Train Carriage; Great Western Railway.

In contrast to the majority of railways that worked into London the G.W.R. never developed an intensive suburban service of its own. This was partly due to geography, in that during the nineteenth century the busiest and most populous suburbs grew up in the north-eastern and in the south of London, and partly due to one of those dramatic pieces of inter-railway warfare that enlivened the development of the transport network of this country in mid-Victorian times. The original line of the underground Metropolitan Railway ran from Farringdon Street to a junction with the Great Western, adjoining Paddington station, and it was originally laid mixed gauge. The passenger service was in fact provided in broad gauge carriages by the Great Western. But a sharp disagreement over the frequency of service led to the withdrawal of Great Western stock, and for a time this potentially lucrative traffic was lost. The carriage illustrated is typical of those used on the numerous country branch services of the G.W.R., on which the tempo of life was the very opposite of the rush and bustle of London suburban trains. Station stops were leisurely, during which the driver, fireman and guard greeted their friends among the local railwaymen and residents, and when a train would be held waiting if a regular passenger, however humble his or her status, was late in arriving at the station. The mileage worked daily by the coaching stock was in keeping with the spacious air of the

general proceedings and the coach illustrated was one of a small set allocated to the 5 p.m. train from Bala to Ruabon. Apparently it had little other duty, because that train was duly painted on the solebars.

18 Four-wheeled coach; North London Railway.

This busy and prosperous little railway was in many ways a smaller counterpart of the Great Eastern, in the character and operation of its passenger traffic. Its terminal station, at Broad Street, in the City of London, was adjacent to the great Liverpool Street terminus of the G.E.R., and its coaching stock was similar, both in colour and in the agility with which vast numbers of passengers were packed into incredibly small compartments. From Dalston Junction its lines fanned out into three directions, and the centre one of these climbed over the 'northern heights' to serve Hampstead. The days when those cramped little four-wheeled coaches disgorged city workers in their hundreds, and even quite humble clerks would be wearing tall hats and morning coats, take some imagining today. But in addition to the services of its own the North London had running powers over the Great Northern Railway, which was reached at Finsbury Park through a connection by Canonbury Tunnel. The little North London 4-4-0 tank engines, and their long trains of close-coupled four-wheeled coaches, used to work out to Potters Bar, on the main line, and up the steep gradients of the High Barnet branch. The further ramifications of the North London are referred to under reference 26, wherein its coat of arms is described.

19 Webb eight-wheeled radial coach; London and North Western Railway.

In the nineteenth century there was considerable reluctance among British railway managements to adopt longer passenger vehicles. Most main-line express trains were composed of six-wheeled coaches, and not infrequently included some four-wheelers. It is true that the clearances existing in some sidings and platforms precluded the use of longer vehicles, but in many ways the introduction of bogie vehicles had been retarded by the excellence of British permanent way. In America, where bogie vehicles were in regular service, the standards of track maintenance were not so high, and the greater flexibility of the bogie coach provided some compensation against irregularities in the line and level of the track. The introduction of bogie coaches were resisted nowhere more strongly than on the London and North Western; but the advantage of longer coaches was equally realized, and F. W. Webb, the celebrated Chief Mechanical Engineer, designed an eight-wheeled coach in which flexibility in the wheelbase was provided by making two of the axles capable of radial movement to suit the curves of the line. On a route so relatively free from sharp curves these coaches with radial axles were quite successful, and provided a very smooth ride. The 'racing' train of 1888 which ran at unprecedented speeds between Euston and Edinburgh was composed of four of these vehicles, though the smooth riding was partly due to the care taken to see that all the coaches were tightly coupled at the ends with the spring buffers slightly compressed together.

20 T. G. Clayton's twelve-wheeled 'brake-third'; Midland Railway.

The opening of the Settle and Carlisle line in 1876 and the inauguration of through express services to Glasgow and Edinburgh marked a very important stage in the development of the Midland Railway. For the new trains Clayton built some twelve-wheeled carriages that for comfort and smooth riding were marvels for that period. They had high clerestory roofs,

but these were not entirely a success, and condensation from the small windows in the clerestory led to the dripping of moisture on passengers. In the next batch of main-line coaches the clerestory roof was abandoned, from 1877 onwards, and our picture shows a typical Midland main-line carriage of the period between then and about 1900. Its great length will be noted, and no less the generous width of compartment inside, evident from the wide spacing of the windows. The wheels had wooden centres, and this resulted in very quiet riding. The Midland was a pioneer in providing very comfortable carriages for third-class passengers, and for the period these could certainly be considered as the finest 'ordinary' carriages running in Great Britain. So far as the Scotch services were concerned, the company was breaking in upon the established business of the London and North Western and Great Northern Railways, neither of which was over-generous in its accommodation at that time. Passengers had to be tempted away, by the magnificence of the Midland trains.

21 Broad-gauge composite carriage; Great Western Railway.

The era of the broad gauge on the Great Western Railway will always remain one of the greatest epics, romances, and tragedies of British railway history. The company's first Chief Engineer, the great Isambard Kingdom Brunel, felt that the rail gauge of the old colliery tramways in the north of England, which George Stephenson was perpetuating in the passenger-carrying railways he was constructing, imposed far too great a limitation on future development; and not without a great deal of opposition he persuaded the Great Western Board to sanction his use of the seven-foot gauge, as against the northern standard of 4 ft. 8½ in. There is no doubt he imagined that once a magnificent line like the original

Great Western Railway from London to Bristol was in operation, its advantages would be so obvious that everyone else would change to the broad gauge. And when the Great Western commenced working it would certainly not have been too late to do so. Unfortunately for Brunel he remained the 'odd man out'; but between the incorporation of the Great Western Railway by Act of Parliament in 1835, and the final conversion of the gauge in 1892, the 'broad gauge' built up its remarkable aura of romance and epic struggle. One of the claims strongly put forward in its favour by Brunel was the spaciousness of the carriages, and our picture shows one of these exceptional vehicles. The third-class compartments seated no fewer than 9-aside. As the time for final conversion drew near, many coaches used on the broad-gauge lines were built with narrow bodies, so that when the time of conversion came these bodies could be transferred, with little trouble, from broad gauge to narrow-gauge frames; but our picture shows one of the maximum width broad-gauge carriages. The tragedy of the broad gauge was two-fold: that the opportunity was lost of a more spacious railway system that would have been a godsend in dealing with the tremendous problems of city commuter traffic, and that the personal tragedy for Brunel greatly shortened his brilliant life.

22 **Boat Train six-wheeler;** South Eastern Railway.

Coaching stock was not the strongest feature of the railways running south-eastwards from London. The South Eastern itself had an extraordinarily heterogeneous collection of rolling stock of all shapes and sizes, so much so that a wit once described their trains as looking like a moving castellated caravan – no two adjacent coaches being of the same height. Furthermore, the need for economy in expenditure led to these coaches falling into a somewhat decrepit condition, and the old two-tone colour scheme of pink upper panels and brown bodies could look woebegone in the extreme. But if the passengers in local trains, and also in the mid-week 'Cheap fasts' to the seaside, had to put up with vehicles that became nicknamed 'dog-boxes', there was nothing parsimonious about the stock provided for the Continental boat trains, even before the introduction of bogie coaches. Our picture shows a very smart carriage that was typical of the boat trains in late Victorian times. In this respect the trains of the South Eastern and of its rival the London Chatham and Dover were an excellent advertisement for Great Britain. They were vastly superior to the carriages used at that time in France and Belgium, which were not only dingy in outward appearance, both in their basic colour and the state of their upkeep, but also in their interior appointments and general comfort.

23 **Coat of Arms;** London and North Western Railway.

Some of the most interesting and colourful points of detail connected with the old railways of Britain were centred upon their 'Coats of Arms'. In calling them coats of arms, however, it must be admitted that in many cases the devices displayed on locomotives and carriages had no heraldic justification, and were not railway counterparts of the crest and coat of arms, in the heraldry of old English families. The crest of the London and North Western Railway was a case in point. It is true that this great joint-stock corporation claimed to be the oldest established firm in the railway business, and that its sphere of activity extended far beyond the territory suggested by its name. But its crest had as its centrepiece Britannia herself, and the British lion. It was surrounded by a profusion of ornamental scrolls, but with nothing in the way of a motto, or other explanation. Although an earlier version of this device had been used for various purposes, its first use as an item of decoration for locomotives did not occur till the 1880s, when it was put on to the Webb 18-inch express goods o-6-o engines. For a time these engines were known as the 'Crested Goods'; but before long the enginemen had found a much more homely nickname which has lasted ever since. They called the engines the 'Cauliflowers', and one had to agree that seen at a little distance, when the detail became a little blurred, that 'crest' could look uncommonly like a cauliflower! Although the crest was subsequently applied to all express passenger engines, the 18-inch 'Crested Goods' were always known as the 'Cauliflowers'.

24 Coat of Arms; Midland Railway.

There were many points of strong contrast between the London and North Western and the Midland Railways, and in the coat of arms adopted in the early years of the twentieth century the Midland had a device that was not only very beautiful in itself but which had a strong historical significance. In its origins no railway was more aptly named. It was born out of an amalgamation between the Midland Counties Railway, the Birmingham and Derby, and the North Midland. It had not extended north of Leeds nor south of Rugby. When its new coat of arms was designed it had extended enormously: the main line ran from London to Carlisle, and south-westwards to Bath and Bristol; while its through carriages penetrated to Bournemouth and Torquay, to Glasgow and Edinburgh, and in the high season to Inverness. Nevertheless, in its heraldic device the Midland remained faithful to its origin. Its crest was the Wyvern of Mercia, and the shield incorporated those of six of the largest centres of activity in the original orbit of the company: Birming-

ham, with the chains, screws and other insignia of manufactories; Derby; Bristol, with its association with the Merchant Venturers; Leicester, Lincoln, and Leeds. The inclusion of Lincoln might perhaps be questioned, but the cross-country line from Derby through Nottingham and Newark was an important feature of Midland strategy to cut across and deeply into the territory of the rival Great Northern Railway. As such the arms of the city of Lincoln had to occupy a centrepiece on the shield as prominent as that of Derby, which latter place always remained the headquarters of the Midland, even after the London extension had been completed.

25 Coat of Arms; Lancashire and Yorkshire Railway.

This beautiful device, which was carried on engines and carriages alike, was one of the simplest of railway emblems for the travelling public to understand. For it included the red and white roses of the Royal Houses of Lancaster and York, surmounting the shields of those two ancient cities. Curiously enough, however, the Lancashire and Yorkshire Railway did not reach either Lancaster or York on its own tracks. Its engines and trains worked into York over the metals of the North Eastern Railway, but so far as Lancaster was concerned its traffic associations extended to no more than the through services worked from Liverpool and Manchester to Scotland. These were hauled through Lancaster by London and North Western locomotives. The Lancashire and Yorkshire Railway was a line of the teeming industrial regions clustered around what could be termed the Liverpool-Manchester-Leeds 'axis'. The old Manchester and Leeds Railway was indeed one of its major constituents, and from that origin branches and subsidiary main lines penetrated into the hilly, highly industrialized country on both sides of the Pennines. Although it did not reach Lancaster itself and the fringes of the Lake District, nor the wide-open spaces of the North and East Riding, as a thoroughgoing industrial concern no railway was more aptly named than the Lancashire and Yorkshire.

26 Coat of Arms; North London Railway.
The group of coats of arms illustrated under references 23 to 26 all relate to concerns that were eventually included in the London Midland and Scottish Railway. Two were great trunk lines that extended from London to Carlisle, usually in strong competition with each other. The third, although a local enterprise, became one of great influence and prestige. Nevertheless, to judge by its coat of arms, in the beauty of its design and colouring, one could well imagine the North London could hold its own with the best! And among the four quarters of its shield will be noticed with some surprise that of Birmingham. How could this purely local London railway claim any connection with Birmingham? This line was originally known as 'The East and West India Docks and Birmingham Junction Railway'. From its inception, however, it was closely associated with the London and North Western, and one of the lines radiating from Dalston Junction ran almost due west to join the North Western at Chalk Farm, at the eastern end of Primrose Hill Tunnel. It was not until the twentieth century that this connection was used for anything more than purely local service. Then the interesting 'City to City' express service was introduced between Birmingham and Broad Street, thus after many years fulfilling the ambitions of the North London in having Birmingham on its coat of arms. The quarterings were as follows: top left, the shield of the East India Dock Company; top right, Birmingham; bottom left, the City of London;

and bottom right, the entrance gateway to the West India Import Dock.

27 The *Greater Britain* **engine of 1891;** London and North Western Railway.
For some years prior to the building of this remarkable engine F. W. Webb, Chief Mechanical Engineer of the L.& N.W.R., had been using three-cylinder compound locomotives for the heaviest express passenger work. All these engines were six-wheelers, with two high-pressure cylinders outside the frames and a single low-pressure cylinder inside. These drove on to the rear and leading pairs of driving wheels respectively, and as can be seen in the illustration, the two pairs of driving wheels were not coupled. This sometimes led to differential slipping, and some difficulty in starting a heavy train. But in developing the three-cylinder compound system from the 'Teutonic' class of 1889 Webb designed a very much larger boiler, making it longer rather than increasing the diameter, so as to avoid too great a concentration of dead weight. To avoid the disadvantage of very long flue tubes he used an intermediate combustion chamber, so that the exhaust gases from the firebox passed through one set of tubes; then through the combustion chamber, and then through a further set of tubes before reaching the smokebox. To accommodate the extra length of boiler a pair of trailing wheels was provided under the firebox, and as thus built the *Greater Britain* was one of the longest engines yet to appear in this country. Its unusual livery is referred to later, under reference 29, relating to the *Queen Empress*.

28 West Coast Joint Stock coach.
Up to the time of the grouping of the railways in 1923 the express services between London and the Scottish cities were operated by a number of independent railways working in partnership.

Thus, from Kings Cross one travelled over the tracks, successively, of the Great Northern, the North Eastern, and of the North British Railway to reach Edinburgh, while from Euston it was the London and North Western and the Caledonian that were in partnership in providing services from London to both Edinburgh and Glasgow. Similarly, on the Midland route from St. Pancras, that railway was associated with both the North British and the Glasgow and South Western, in Scotland. On all these routes 'joint' rolling stock, reserved specially for the regular Anglo-Scottish expresses, was provided. The West Coast vehicles, working from Euston, carried the initials 'W.C.J.S.', and a special crest, illustrated under reference 55. At the time of their introduction it was a remarkable coincidence that those initials were also those of the general managers of the London and North Western and Caledonian Railways, namely William Cawkwell and James Smithells. The carriages of the West Coast Joint Stock were always built to London and North Western designs, at Wolverton works, and in general followed standard North Western practice, of which the coach illustrated was a typical example.

29 **The Diamond Jubilee celebration engines;** London and North Western Railway.
In the year 1891, when Webb's large 2-2-2-2 compound express locomotives were introduced, the growth of the British Empire was an increasing source of national pride and satisfaction. In the year 1877 Queen Victoria had assumed the title of Empress of India, and the name *Greater Britain* applied to the first of the new engines was a natural expression of popular sentiment at the time. For two years it remained an isolated engine, while extensive trials were in progress. It ran in the standard L.&N.W.R. colours, glossy black, with red, cream and light grey lining; but in 1893 a second engine was built, the *Queen Empress*, and again in the standard 'black' sent to the Chicago Exhibition. Eight more engines of the class were built in 1894. In the year of the Diamond Jubilee however, 1897, the engines *Greater Britain* and *Queen Empress* were specially painted in celebration of the event. *Greater Britain* was decked in scarlet, with the Royal Arms on one of the driving-wheel splashers and on the tender, while *Queen Empress* was painted in *white*! At the time it was thought that there were eventually to be three specially painted engines: one red; one white; and one blue. But actually the 'red, white and blue' were all incorporated on the *Greater Britain*, which had the smokebox and wheel centres blue, and white wheel rims. The *Queen Empress* carried an extraordinarily beautiful, but somewhat impracticable livery, of a soft creamy white, with lavender edging and thus symbolical of the elderly lady after whom the engine was named. Somewhat naturally the standard L.&N.W.R. livery was restored soon after the period of the Diamond Jubilee celebrations had passed.

30 **One of the first dining cars;** London and North Western Railway.
The reluctance of the North Western authorities to depart from six-wheeled coaches has been referred to earlier in connection with Webb's radial axles, reference 19; but having obtained such good riding from the West Coast Joint Stock used in the racing train of 1888, it is not a little surprising that when dining cars were first introduced, on the Liverpool and Manchester expresses from London in 1889, a reversion to six-wheelers should have been made. They were available only to first-class passengers, and seated no more than 14 passengers, with only one chair on either side of the gangway. They were run in pairs, connected to each other, but without any

connection to the rest of the train, so that once in the dining car one stayed there for the rest of the journey. The companion car contained the so-called 'dining and smoking saloon', which seated 8 passengers; also the kitchen, and what was described on the original drawing as the 'butler's pantry'. Our picture of one of these cars was prepared from a copy of the original drawing still preserved at Wolverton works, and this drawing helps to recreate something of the spacious atmosphere of the period, not only in the exquisite draughtsmanship, but in the use of 'Old English' lettering in the titles. Imagine a modern engineering drawing office having time for such adornment of its documents.

31 Short-coupled 0-6-0 mineral engine; North Eastern Railway.
In bringing under one management the locomotives of four such individual concerns as the York and North Midland, the Leeds Northern, the York, Newcastle and Berwick and the Stockton and Darlington, the responsible engineers had an almost insuperable task when it came to the first attempts at standardization. Edward Fletcher never really seriously attempted it; but by his own skill and kindly nature he brought a high degree of efficiency and reliability to this exceeding diverse stud of locomotives as well as imparting to them an exceedingly picturesque appearance. Our picture shows a coal engine of 1866 as 'modernized' by Mr. Fletcher. It is astonishing to recall that engines engaged in heavy mineral traffic, between the mining areas and the ports from which coal was exported, should have had such a highly decorative finish. Not only so, but that they were kept spotlessly clean. Technical features of these engines were the very long boilers, which were well suited to the job of working the mineral trains; the picturesque outside frames, and outside cranks,

and the double safety valves, so frequently to be seen on many nineteenth-century locomotives. One set, of the Salter-type spring-balance type, was on the dome, and the other was contained in the brass column over the firebox. These engines did excellent work and many survived into the twentieth century.

32 Kirtley 2-4-0 No. 158A; Midland Railway.
Matthew Kirtley, Locomotive Superintendent of the Midland Railway from 1844 to 1873, was one of the most successful of mid-Victorian engine designers. He was no scientist, or man of theory; but a practical engineer who had risen from the ranks, and knew precisely what was needed to work a heavy traffic with reliability, and a remarkable degree of efficiency. In 1866 he built the '156' class of 2-4-0s at Derby, and in them he achieved one of his greatest successes. The original engines were good enough, but it was their massive construction that enabled them to be twice rebuilt, and their cylinders enlarged from the original 16½ in. by 22 in. up to 18 in. by 24 in. Our picture shows the third engine of the class, No. 158, as numbered on the duplicate list – 158A, and as such she still exists today, carefully preserved, and of the ripe old age of 100 years. But much happened to her since she was renumbered No. 2 of the Midland Railway, in 1907. Fifteen years later she was still going strong and she became No. 2 of the L.M.S.R. – still handsomely painted in Derby red. Then she became 20002, and served all through World War II, painted plain black, and still in active service in 1945. She was taken out of traffic in 1948, after 82 years' service, and then most beautifully restored to her condition of the 1900–1907 period, and preserved. In this form she is a blend of the Kirtley and Johnson styles of engine designing: Kirtley frames and machinery, and a Johnson boiler.

33 Mixed traffic 2-4-0 engine of 1877;
Caledonian Railway.
Until the appointment of Dugald Drummond as Locomotive Superintendent, in 1882, all Caledonian engines, passenger and goods alike, had outside cylinders. They had also the characteristic double framing at the front end, whereby the cylinders were snugly and massively ensconced; stove-pipe chimneys were the rule, and the driving-wheel splashers were slotted like the paddle-box of most packet steamers of the age. Under the superintendence of Benjamin Conner 2-2-2 singles with 8 ft. driving wheels had been built for the express traffic and when the loads became too great for single-wheelers Conner built 2-4-0s, with 7 ft. 2 in. wheels. The engine shown in our picture belongs to the intermediate class, with 6 ft. 2 in. coupled wheels, designed for stopping-train duties and branch-line work. They were excellent, sturdy little things, and survived on secondary work well into the twentieth century. A few of them were rebuilt by Dugald Drummond with larger boilers, as a stop-gap main-line passenger class pending the construction of his own very successful 4-4-0 engines. But many of the Conner engines, like No. 52 illustrated, remained unaltered. Some of them could be seen at Carlisle in the early 1900s, and although then relegated to the lightest of stopping trains they were still immaculately turned out, and as perfect little period pieces they stood out, among the very large 4-4-2 and 4-6-0 engines that were then being introduced on several of the railways running into Carlisle.

34 'River' class 2-4-0 *Teign*; Great Western Railway.
These beautiful little engines, which in the form illustrated date from 1895, could be described as engines with a dual identity. There were eight of them in all, with numbers running from 69 to 76, and they originated in their first condition in

1872. At that time the broad gauge was still in full operation in the West of England, but the Great Western was also operating a considerable mileage on the standard gauge and these eight engines were built at Wolverhampton, as 2-2-2 singles for fast express working between Wolverhampton, Birmingham and Paddington. They did excellent work, but as with all engines the time came when they were no longer capable of working their original duties, and they were transferred to Swindon to help in the working of narrow-gauge expresses to Paddington. After the abolition of the broad gauge there was a general rearrangement of train services and they were no longer needed at Swindon. But their frames and machinery were still in excellent condition, and the eight engines were rebuilt as 2-4-0s in the very handsome style illustrated, and it was then that they received the added dignity of names – all after rivers in the West Country: *Avon, Dart, Dee, Exe, Isis, Stour, Teign,* and *Wye*. With their sandwich frames, and their profusion of brass and copperwork, they too were period pieces in the early 1900s; but they were sufficiently robust and serviceable engines for the last of them was to survive until 1918.

35 East Coast Joint Stock sleeping-car.
The 'joint stock' vehicle shown in this illustration dates from the early years of the twentieth century, and was one built by the North Eastern Railway, at York. Unlike the West Coast Joint Stock the East Coast was built variously by the Great Northern, North Eastern and North British Railways, and exhibited the design characteristics of the different works. Until the years 1905–6, high clerestory roofs had been used for large bogie vehicles, providing additional natural lighting and ventilation. But these were expensive to build – although very handsome in appearance (see reference

62) – and the North Eastern built sleeping-cars representing an attempt to get a simpler and cheaper form of construction. The panelled sides were quite flat, and the roofs elliptical. Like the traditional style of the East Coast Joint Stock, the finish was in varnished teak. The vehicle illustrated is of interest in that it was a 'composite' including both first- and third-class accommodation. Only the first-class passengers had proper sleeping-berths. There were only six single berths in the carriage, and two ordinary compartments for third-class passengers. It was not a very large vehicle, as East Coast Joint Stock went, measuring 56 ft. 5 in. over the end vestibule connections, but it represents a very interesting stage in the gradual evolution of accommodation for night travel between England and Scotland. Full berth accommodation for third-class passengers did not come till the late nineteen twenties.

36 Llandudno Club Carriage; London and North Western Railway.

In these days of private motor cars and the rapid development of very fast travel on trunk roads it is a little difficult to imagine the conditions in which the business tycoons in the first years of the present century travelled to and from their offices. Many magnates of the cotton industry whose activities were centred upon Manchester lived in the coastal resorts, such as Blackpool, Southport, and even as far away as towns on the North Wales coast. For them it was not enough to travel in first-class comfort, in fast non-stop trains; they must have club facilities on the journey, and in co-operation with the railway companies concerned some very interesting facilities were provided. Travelling clubs were formed, and special carriages provided to which only members were admitted. The accommodation was of the most luxurious kind, with each member having his own

particular leather padded armchair, and the journey to and from the city could be a congenial and pleasant occasion. The Lancashire and Yorkshire Railway was one of the pioneers of this particular form of luxury service, and it became so popular that the so-called 'Club Trains' conveyed many more than one carriage for club members. The example chosen for illustration is one of the London and North Western Railway, operating between Manchester and Llandudno, and serving the resorts of Rhyl and Colwyn Bay en route.

37 Morecambe Club Carriage; Midland Railway.

The Midland was a railway of unbounding enterprise. Looking at a map of the system as it existed in the early years of the present century, one would hardly imagine it could emulate the practice of the Lancashire and Yorkshire, and London and North Western Railways in running attractive residential services from great centres of industry and commerce to seaside resorts. From Manchester it had no outlet to the Lancashire coast, or to North Wales, and while the North Eastern ran residential expresses from Leeds to Bridlington and Scarborough, the nearest resort to Leeds or Bradford on the Midland system was Morecambe. Sure enough, even though the route was not an easy one, and several intermediate points had to be catered for, the Midland developed a first-class residential service from Leeds and Bradford to Morecambe, and at the height of its enterprise put on a Club Carriage, running from Bradford. This handsome vehicle, reserved of course for club members only, made a daily journey of some 60 miles each way, with a journey time of about $1\frac{1}{2}$ hours morning and evening, travelling over the Anglo-Scottish main line of the Midland Railway between Shipley and Settle Junction, and then through Giggleswick and the moorland Clapham Junction to Lancaster, and so to journey's end on the shores of Morecambe Bay. Compared with the 35-mile run of the L.&Y.R. Manchester–Southport 'club' train, or even the fast 50-mile run of the Blackpool club train, it was a lengthy journey to make daily. But many people, quite apart from club members, travelled daily from Morecambe to both Bradford and Leeds.

38 Ocean Liner Sleeping-Car; London and South Western Railway.

In the early years of the present century liners of several nations, eastbound from the United States to Europe, called at Plymouth. By landing passengers there for British destinations considerable time could be saved over the more usual call at Southampton. Great importance was attached to this traffic by both the Great Western and the London and South Western Railways, and although there was a great rivalry between the two in respect of speed, there was agreement that the Great Western should take the mails, and the South Western the passengers. Special new train-sets were built, incorporating the most luxurious appointments considered desirable in the years 1900–5; but a further consideration was that the liners might arrive at any time during the 24 hours. While night running was not normally scheduled, a steamer could be delayed by fog or bad weather. Consequently the L.S.W.R. built some sleeping-cars specially for the ocean liner traffic, so that if a night run had to be made sleeping-berths were available. This service came to encounter a great tragedy in 1906, when one of these trains, for some quite unexplained reason, ran through Salisbury station at greatly excessive speed and was completely wrecked. In this disaster, coming suddenly in the dead of night, 24 out of the 43 ocean liner passengers travelling were killed. In later years the passenger traffic

from the liners calling at Plymouth was taken over by the Great Western Railway.

39 The Caledonian Railway coat of arms.

The Caledonian Railway was one of the great institutions of Scottish life in years before the grouping of 1923. A study of the coat of arms, carried on engines and carriages alike, would suggest that it was a nationally-owned concern, because this insignia consisted of nothing more nor less than the Royal arms of Scotland, with the Royal mottoes included. Heraldically this device was without any justification, and probably without authority too! But in assuming this magnificent device the Caledonian was perpetuating a crucial point in its history. It was not by any means the first railway in Scotland, and its origin was the subject of acute controversy. The conception of a trunk line from Carlisle to Glasgow came from the Grand Junction Railway, and Scottish sentiment resented a project that had its origin in England! Nevertheless, many far-seeing Scots backed it wholeheartedly, while others were equally strong in their opposition. But to conceal the English influences in its origin the name Caledonian was chosen. Once launched the ambitions of the promoters knew no bounds, and one feels that the accent in the title was intended to be on *the*, and not necessarily on 'Caledonian'. In other words, it was to be *the* railway of Scotland – hence the adoption of the Royal arms. Other Scottish interests took a very different view, and the entire history of the railway right down to the time of its inclusion in the L.M.S.R. was of fierce rivalry with the other Scottish lines – particularly the Glasgow and South Western.

40 The North British Railway coat of arms.

In the nineteenth century, and indeed for some years afterwards, it was quite usual to refer to Scotland as 'North Britain', and letters from England addressed to Scottish towns and villages had the letters 'N.B.' added, in addition to the normal address. The title 'North British Railway' could thus be construed as equally all-embracing as that of 'Caledonian'; and the two railways certainly had almost equal claims to be considered the premier line of Scotland. The North British, though of relatively limited extent, was of even older origin than the Caledonian, but had the distinction of being the first railway to cross the Anglo-Scottish border. Originally it extended only from Edinburgh to Berwick-upon-Tweed, and it is the arms of these two places that are embraced in its coat of arms, together with the thistle and the rose. But eventually the 'North British' came to include many other lines, including the much older Edinburgh and Glasgow Railway and the group of local lines around Edinburgh. Like the Caledonian the original name survived until the time of the grouping, though the country served by the 'N.B.R.' came to extend into the Western Highlands, and as far north as Fort Augustus. Yet its engines and carriages still carried the same coat of arms with the insignia only of Edinburgh and Berwick encircled within the garter.

41 **Highland Railway coat of arms.**
In every facet of its history and activities the Highland Railway was one of the most distinctive in the whole of Great Britain. The name itself dates from 1865, when the Inverness and Nairn, the Inverness and Aberdeen Junction, and the Inverness and Perth Junction Railways were amalgamated, and the line over the Grampian mountains was opened throughout. The company later came to include the various northern and western extensions from Inverness that eventually took the line to Wick and Thurso, and to the Kyle of Lochalsh. In the first place,

however, the over-riding purpose of the railway promoters in Inverness was to establish direct connection with Perth, and it is this union by the line over the crest of the Grampians that is symbolized in the coat of arms. The Highland eagle is displayed, embracing in its outstretched wings the arms of the city of Perth, and the arms of the burgh of Inverness. Both are remarkable devices in themselves: that of Perth consists of the Holy Lamb, carrying the banner of St. Andrew, a device frequently used for inns having the more prosaic name of 'The Lamb and Flag'. The arms of the burgh of Inverness depicts our Lord upon the Cross, and thus both shields in the Highland Railway coat of arms have a deeply religious flavour. It was, however, not until relatively late in the history of the company that the full coat of arms was carried on locomotives, and then it was only used on the largest express passenger engines.

42 **The Glasgow and South Western Railway coat of arms.**
This railway, like the North British, retained for its entire lifetime the emblem of one of its earliest constituents. In the case of the G.&S.W.R. the emblem takes things right back to the very origin of railways in south-west Scotland. It was the emblem of the Glasgow, Paisley, Kilmarnock and Ayr Railway, which was incorporated as early as 1837. It was no less the existence of this railway that led to the acute controversy over the route of the proposed line from Carlisle to Glasgow. Purely Scottish interests argued that with a line already in existence as far south as Kilmarnock the new railway should be made to connect with it; and this argument was given an added force when the first surveys from the south, by Joseph Locke, favoured going via Dumfries and Nithsdale. This would have been ideal if nothing more than a line between Carlisle and Glasgow had been

contemplated; but the Grand Junction Railway, which was the moving spirit behind the English end of the enterprise, had plans for a considerably wider field of activity, and a route up Annandale was chosen instead. This brought the Caledonian into conflict with the G.P.K. &A. people; an independent route to the south was projected, and from 1847 the name Glasgow and South Western Railway was taken. The emblem of the G.P.K.&A. was adopted, because it was equally appropriate to the enlarged company. The three devices banded together by the crown are the wand of Mercury, symbolizing the carrying of traffic; the distaff, associated with Minerva the goddess of handicrafts, symbolizing the industries of the country served by the railway; and the trident of Neptune, symbolizing the connection with various ports on the Ayrshire coast. The Glasgow and South Western Railway later became a very successful operator of steamship services in the Firth of Clyde.

43 Picnic Saloon; London and North Western Railway.

In these days of private motoring it is difficult at times to appreciate what travelling conditions were like in Victorian times, especially when it came to holidays and other pleasure outings. With large families travelling for a month's stay at the sea, or in Scotland, the transport arrangements were a major problem and for the convenience of such parties the majority of railways constructed saloon carriages that could be hired by private individuals, and conveyed from the home station to any destination. These saloons were mostly six-wheelers, and included separate accommodation for the family servants and ample room for luggage. In the summer holiday season many of these saloons would be in use, and there is a recorded occasion on the Highland Railway when the 7.50 a.m. train from Perth

included private saloons from the London and North Western, Midland, and Great Northern Railways, and no fewer than *thirteen* different horseboxes. Even before the end of the nineteenth century the demand for private saloons for night travel was on the decline, with the general introduction of comfortable sleeping-cars with private berths on the night expresses, and the North Western converted some of their saloons for purely day use, and renamed them 'Picnic Saloons'. Our picture shows one of these interesting little coaches – a period piece not only in railway carriage construction, but as a reminder of the changing trends of railway travel requirements.

44 Chariot-ended first-class carriage; Highland Railway.

The Highland Railway was for many years distinguished by the spartan character of its passenger carriages, and the four-wheeled third-class vehicles used on the Inverness–Wick trains were only 25 ft. long and barely 8 ft. wide. Into those carriages were crammed seats for 50 passengers. The local people took this kind of thing as the ordinary way of travelling by train. Anything more luxurious would have been regarded as degenerate, or 'going soft'. The first-class carriages were naturally more spacious, and our picture illustrates one of the so-called 'chariot-ended' vehicles. The end compartments had seats on one side only and glass end panels. They were slightly shorter than the five-compartment 'thirds', but due to the more lavish nature of the accommodation they seated only 20 passengers. Even with this concession the journey from Inverness to Wick must have been something of an ordeal in four-wheeled non-corridor carriages, with none of the amenities of modern travel. The through trains took about 8 hours to cover the 160 miles, with stops at most stations. For many years the refreshment room at Bonar Bridge used to do a brisk trade in soup and hard-boiled eggs, at whatever time of the day the trains saw fit to arrive. They were often very much behind schedule. The green livery was standard except for a period between 1897 and 1907, when the upper panels of the coaches were painted white.

45 Composite four-wheeled carriage; Somerset and Dorset Joint Railway.

The Somerset and Dorset began its existence through the amalgamation of two very small local lines, and much of its business remained quite local and tuned to the leisurely tempo of life in a wholly rural community. Before it became a joint concern with the Midland and the London and South Western as equal partners, the initials 'S.&D.' were often interpreted as 'Slow and Dirty'! While in later years the line never exactly blossomed forth as one of the high-speed routes of this country any stimga of dirtiness vanished, and the highly distinctive blue engines and carriages were beautifully maintained. The coach in our picture, a composite of late Victorian times, is unusually spacious in its accommodation, and in addition to the handsome lining out in black and gold the coach carries the company's coat of arms, embodying the arms of the city of Bath, and of the town of Dorchester. When to the original line, meandering through exceedingly rural farming country, from Wimborne, via Wincanton and Glastonbury to Highbridge, there was added the line over the Mendips to Bath, coaches like that in our picture were confined to the slow local trains, and some pleasant bogie stock – albeit non-corridor – was built for the new line (see reference 133). But the four-wheelers represented perfect little period pieces, representative of the days when railways provided virtually the only means of travel in the rural communities.

46 Family Saloon; London Chatham and Dover Railway.

This picturesque little carriage, which dates from 1881, is typical of the many types of family saloon built for hire to private family parties. At first sight it would seem strange to find doors labelled 'first' and 'second'; but the door marked 'second' led into a fairly narrow compartment of the ordinary type wherein travelled the family servants. There were seats for at least six of them, on nicely upholstered though rather narrow seats, and the windows were curtained. A door from the middle of this compartment led into the main saloon. Next to the servants compartment was the section reserved for luggage, while at the opposite end was a compartment almost as large as the servants 'second' in which there were to be found all the necessary toilet facilities. All that was lacking in this little self-contained saloon were the means of cooking, or even boiling water. On the London Chatham and Dover Railway itself, however, journeys were not expected to last very long, though these private saloons were apt to be hired for journeys extending far beyond the confines of the owning railway. Some saloons included cupboards for crockery, though the carrying of this was inclined to be a hazardous business when saloons were being shunted from one train to another. An old friend who used to travel to Scotland in one of these saloons once said to me: 'We did wish that the crockery was the railway company's, and not ours!'

47 'L' class 4-4-0 locomotive; South Eastern and Chatham Railway.

The fusion of the former South Eastern, and London Chatham and Dover Railways in 1898 under a single Managing Committee did not amalgamate the two companies in a financial sense, but it produced unification of traffic operation and all engineering matters, and the partnership of H. S. Wainwright as

Locomotive Superintendent with Robert Surtees as Chief Draughtsman resulted in a range of beautiful and successful locomotives. The design for a new express passenger type – a powerful superheater 4-4-0 – was completed just at the time of Wainwright's death, but orders for it had not then been placed. The new locomotive engineer was R. E. L. Maunsell, formerly of the Great Southern and Western Railway, in Ireland; but apart from some changes in the detail of the valve gear he accepted the design as prepared by Surtees. The year was 1914. The new engines were urgently needed, but neither the company's works at Ashford nor any British manufacturer could give the quick delivery required, and the order for the first batch was given to the German firm of A. Borsig of Berlin. The engines were shipped in parts and erected at Ashford, and there was a flavour of the dramatic about this work because Borsig's men were engaged upon it to within a few weeks before the outbreak of war with Germany in August 1914. Ironically enough, one of the first duties of the new engines was to work troop-trains in connection with the war. They proved excellent, hard-working and long-lived engines, and all of them survived to do good work through the *second* world war. They were the first S.E.&C.R. engines to have the less-ornate livery in which all the elaborate lining and ornamental brasswork was abandoned. Our picture shows the class as it ran originally in 1914. In later years the livery became even more sombre – one of plain dull grey.

48 A Continental boat train carriage; South Eastern and Chatham Railway.

The boat expresses of the S.E.&C.R. were most foreigners' first introduction to England, and great importance was attached to the provision of first-class rolling stock. In the early years of the twentieth century there was no comparison between the accommodation provided in England and France. Across the Channel, although the speeds run between Calais and Paris were much higher than on the S.E.&C.R., the journey was performed more often than not in dingy six-wheelers, and the riding was usually rough and uncomfortable. The S.E.& C.R. trains were made up of excellent bogie carriages, though at that time they were not vestibuled throughout. Some Pullman cars were included in the make-up, but most of the stock was non-corridor, though plentifully provided with lavatories. Our picture shows a tri-composite carriage, on which the roof board reads 'Continental Express London & Folkestone'. In this carriage, with two compartments for each of the three classes, there was seating for 10 first-class, 14 second-, and 16 third-class passengers. The boat train runs, whether to Folkestone or Dover, lasted only a few minutes over $1\frac{1}{2}$ hours, and in those far-off days there were no such things as Custom examinations at the ports. England was then a free-trade country and one stepped straight down from train to boat, and departure took place in a very short time.

49 Drummond's 'double-single' No. 720; London and South Western Railway.

The idea that the coupling of the driving wheels of a locomotive impaired its free qualities died very hard on the railways of Britain. On the Great Northern Railway that great Scottish engineer Patrick Stirling built none but single-driver locomotives for express work, but one would hardly have expected his brother Scot, Dugald Drummond, to have cherished any of the same ideas. He had built very successful four-coupled engines for both the North British and the Caledonian Railways, though at the same time it must be recalled that it was his one and only Caledonian single-wheeler,

No. 123 (reference 12), that had performed so well between Carlisle and Edinburgh in the Race to the North, in 1888. Be that as it may, his first express passenger engine for the London and South Western was a four-cylinder machine with the two sets of cylinders driving separate axles. Engine No. 720 was completed at Nine Elms works in 1897. The first boiler fitted to this engine was not large enough to supply steam to *four* cylinders, and not only were the cylinders lined up to reduce their diameter by no less than $2\frac{1}{2}$ in. – from $16\frac{1}{2}$ to 14 in. – but a much larger boiler was fitted, and in this guise No. 720 became the exceedingly handsome engine shown in our picture. She was a swift runner but, it must be admitted, no faster than Drummond's four-coupled and six-coupled passenger engines. She had a skilful regular driver, Geare by name, who knew all her little peculiarities, and took an immense pride in her turnout. But No. 720 was an odd engine – the only one of her kind. There were five other four-cylinder uncoupled eight-wheelers on the L.S.W.R.; but these five had smaller boilers, and could not compete in performance with No. 720.

50 **Main-line carriage;** London and South Western Railway.
One can appreciate the policy of the South Eastern and Chatham Railway in having none but non-corridor carriages on even the finest of its express train services; but it is remarkable to recall that the same practice prevailed over the greater part of the London and South Western system which, of course, had much longer journeys to perform. It is true that on the principal services to the far west – to Plymouth, North Devon and North Cornwall – some corridor trains were run with restaurant cars; but until after the end of World War I the popular express trains to Bournemouth and Weymouth were made up entirely of non-

corridor coaches. Of course there was a strong practical reason for using non-corridor coaches as much as possible. One could convey many more passengers for the same dead weight of carriage, and thus the loads hauled by the locomotives could be kept down, and the cost of running the trains not excessive. A single comparison will make this point clear. Before the war the load of the fast 2 p.m. express from Waterloo to Bournemouth was about 270 tons – entirely non-corridor. After the war, with a train vestibuled throughout the load was usually at least 320 tons. Non-corridor carriages remained in use on the Bournemouth trains for many years after the war, and in the early 1920s I made many journeys in vehicles of this kind – not very attractive for a run of $2\frac{1}{2}$ hours.

51–52 **Early semaphore signals and box;** Stewarts Lane Junction.
In the earliest days of railways pointsmen were employed, stationed at the actual junction, to pull the points over by hand as and when required. As the speed of trains increased it was necessary to give drivers some prior indication of whether it was safe to proceed, and on which route, and at a number of places a semaphore type of indicator was installed. It then became desirable to include some mechanism to prevent the wrong signal being lowered, and this led to the development of interlocking between the levers controlling the points and those controlling the signals. It was then a logical step to put the levers all together, and provide a shelter for the man working them, and in such a way the earliest signal boxes were developed. These boxes, like the famous one at Stewarts Lane Junction, Battersea, shown in our picture, had all the associated signals carried on masts extending above the roof of the box. These signals told a driver whether he must stop or proceed, and it was left to his experience and judgment

as to *where* he should stop, if the signals indicated so. For instance, if his line converged with another one he was expected to stop short of the other line, so that his locomotive would not foul the path of another train. It was soon found necessary, however, to erect the semaphore signal at the exact spot where he was required to stop. This necessitated wire connections from the signal box to the post and made things more complicated from the viewpoint of signal engineering. But this development greatly lessened the chance of any misjudgment of distance by the driver, and with increasing density and speed of traffic it was essential. Picturesque old signal boxes, like that at Stewarts Lane, lost the arrays of signals carried on their roofs, for all the semaphores became fixed at specific points in the layout. The signal box at Stewarts Lane was the trade-mark of the famous signalling firm of Saxby and Farmer Ltd., one of the pioneers of the art of interlocking, and thus of the safety features so essential to the working of railways.

53–54 **Brunel's disc and crossbar signal;** Great Western Railway.

In the pioneer days of railways each engineer seemed to have his own ideas as to the equipment needed for operating the traffic. There was little in the way of consultation towards standard practice, and one has only to look at these Great Western signals and to recall that they were in use at the same time as the Stewart's Lane signal box to realize how divergent the practices of different railways were. But in almost every respect the Great Western did things differently from everyone else. In the gauge of its track, in the form of its permanent way and in the design of its locomotives it stood apart. Its great Chief Engineer, I. K. Brunel, the great protagonist of the broad gauge, invented the very distinctive disc and crossbar type of signal, which in one respect was much in advance of some

contemporaries. In some forms of semaphore, when 'all clear' was indicated the arm dropped down into a slot inside the post and became invisible. Unfortunately the same indication could have been given if the connections had broken, or the arm had fallen off completely. It was not a positive indication. Brunel's was vastly better in principle, for by rotating the mechanism on a vertical axis the disc was displayed to the driver to indicate stop, while something quite different – the crossbar shown broadside on – indicated all clear. By modern ideas it was a crude, cumbersome arrangement; but the principles were sound enough. Life was strenuous for the maintenance men in those old days. Nothing so luxurious as a ladder was provided for them to climb to attend to the lamps, or oil the bearings. Small notches were cut in the post to provide a foothold, and with no more help than this the maintenance man had to climb to the top of a post which in some cases might be 40 ft. or 50 ft. high!

Alongside the disc and crossbar in our picture is shown one of the 'Fantails', or 'Ten Minute Signals', which were used on the Great Western Railway for more than 20 years. These boards, like the disc and crossbar, were rotated on a vertical axis, and were the forerunners of the modern semaphore 'distant' signal. The 'Fantails' had *three* positions. One side was painted red, and if this were displayed it meant 'stop'; the 'green', as shown in the picture, meant 'caution', and that a driver must travel slowly; but when no message was to be conveyed the board was turned to the third position, namely edge-on.

55 **West Coast Joint Stock coat of arms.**

The origin of the West Coast Joint Stock, operated by the London and North Western and Caledonian Railways, has been referred to under reference 28. Although the so-called West Coast route begins at Euston the 'joint stock' was used only on Anglo-Scottish expresses, and it included passenger vehicles, dining-cars and sleeping-cars, and all kinds of postal and passenger luggage-vans. The emblem – for one could hardly call it a 'coat of arms' – was in keeping with the style of the two companies concerned. The North Western took Britannia as its emblem, and the Caledonian, the Royal arms of Scotland. The West Coast Joint Stock had nothing more nor less than the lion of Scotland, set off with some pleasant ornamentation including the rose and the thistle. The name 'West Coast' was strictly speaking much of a misnomer, because it was only for a brief 2 miles north of Lancaster and again at the Solway Firth that the line came in sight of the sea. In Scotland, indeed, if the journey in a 'W.C.J.S.' vehicle was being continued to Aberdeen, the line crossed the country and for the last 16 miles was running close beside the *east* coast, in full view of the North Sea! But in so far as the route was the most westerly of the three trunk routes from London to Scotland the name 'West Coast' was justified.

56 East Coast Joint Stock coat of arms.

The East Coast route to Scotland, in which the Great Northern, North Eastern, and North British Railways were partners, first approached the actual coast at Alnmouth, Northumberland. But after that it became truly a coastal route, and there were not many stretches between that station and Montrose when the line was far from the sea. Oddly enough, however, the last 38 miles of the journey to Aberdeen from Kinnaber Junction were made by the exercising of running powers over the metals of the Caledonian, and thus over the *West* Coast route. The East Coast Joint Stock coat of arms is a pleasing example of a gartered emblem, including the three lions from the Royal arms of

England; the lion of Scotland, and in the two lower quarters the arms of the cities of Edinburgh (left) and London (right). Again the ornamentation includes the rose and the thistle. It is of interest to note that the two upper quarters of the shield later formed the centrepiece of the Great Northern coat of arms used from 1910 onwards. Although a purely English railway, the G.N.R. in this later design thus took the lions of both England and Scotland, and included also the thistle and the rose. The Great Northern may not have been the largest or the richest partner in the East Coast alliance; but it was always unquestionably the pace-maker, and in its coat of arms of later years it proclaimed, for all the world to see, that its interests lay as much in Scotland as in England.

57 The Royal Mail coat of arms; Travelling Post Offices.

All travelling post office vans carry the Royal arms of the United Kingdom of Great Britain and Northern Ireland, and in showing this beautiful device in our picture it is appropriate to refer back more than three centuries in history to find how the postal system of this country became the 'Royal Mail'. The times of the Tudor monarchs were troubled. England had only just emerged from the carnage and misery of the Wars of the Roses. Bitter feelings remained. Intrigue was rife, and many means of communication were surreptitiously practised. The threat of the Armada compelled a tightening up, and the posts were brought under the control of the Crown. But for some time many unofficial postal systems continued, offering conveyance at cheaper rates. These had to be suppressed by law, and eventually in the years 1635-51 a system of mail routes and post towns covered the whole of England, and one route across the Border, from Berwick via Dunbar to Edinburgh, was organized by one Thomas Witherings, with Government authority. But the postal service was to undergo many vicissitudes before the picturesque system of Royal Mail coaches and galloping postboys was firmly established, and in 1830 a start was made in transferring the conveyance of mails to the new railways. In 1838 the first travelling post office with the Royal arms on its central door went into service on the Grand Junction Railway. Since that time T.P.O. carriages have been operated on many routes, and there are now two exclusively postal trains – one from Euston to Glasgow and Aberdeen, and one from Paddington to Penzance.

58 The Great North of Scotland Railway coat of arms.

This little railway with the high-sounding title actually operated only in the north-eastern corner. It was promoted with the idea of making a railway from Aberdeen to Inverness; but owing to financial difficulties and a good deal of bad management it never got farther from Aberdeen than Elgin. Indeed it reached that northern burgh only after the Highland Railway had struck first, and secured the most direct route through the hilly country eastwards from Elgin to Keith. But from a bad start, and after passing through a long period of bad relations with its neighbour railways, the 'Great North', to which its name was frequently abbreviated, developed into a smart and efficient concern. Although most of its interests lay north of Aberdeen, in through connections to Inverness and farther north and in the fisheries of the north-east coast, it had the important Deeside branch to Ballater, under regular Royal patronage for the annual visit of the Queen, and later her son, and her grandson, to Balmoral. There may have been ambitions to reach Inverness and to extend beyond into the Western Highlands; but Aberdeen was the nodal point of the system and it is the city arms of Aberdeen, the three silver towers, that

figure in two out of the four quarters of its shield. The alternate quarters bear the lion rampant of Scotland. It is definitely known that this design was never registered at the College of Heralds, when submitted to Lord Lyon. Had it been submitted one feels that it would have stood a strong chance of rejection, through use of part of the Royal arms of Scotland. In this, however, it was no more unorthodox than the coats of arms of the Caledonian, of the London and North Western, and of the West Coast Joint Stock.

59 The '1020' class 4-4-0 locomotive; Great Central Railway.

The extension of the one-time Manchester, Sheffield and Lincolnshire Railway from Annesley, in north Nottinghamshire, through to London in 1899, and its assumption of the title of Great Central Railway, was followed by a period of intense activity in search of new traffics. The new line had to fight on all fronts, and its campaign was waged by the introduction of very fast and comfortable trains, lavishly equipped with restaurant and buffet cars. And although passengers were not many at first, the company needed to be ready for expansion. In June 1900 John G. Robinson was appointed Locomotive Engineer and he embarked upon a programme of building large and powerful new locomotives. Really they were too large for the traffic that then existed; but the policy was pursued of being ready for any development. The '1020' class, as it can conveniently be called, was introduced at the end of 1901. It was at once distinguished by its very graceful proportions. It seemed as though an almost loving care had been lavished upon every detail of the design, from the handsomely shaped chimney, to the sweeping curve of the driving-wheel splashers and to the canopied cab. The painting was tastefully done, with the basic rich dark green set off by the dark purple-red underframes and the use of the company's new coat of arms on both engine and tender. These engines were not merely good to look at; they were capable of hard work at high speed, and by 1905 they were running the 103 miles between Marylebone and Leicester in 105 minutes. These engines, good though they were, proved no more than a curtain-raiser to Mr. Robinson's programme of engine building; but as the locomotives that inaugurated the fast services on the London extension line they have a special place in railway history.

60 Vestibuled clerestory carriage; Great Central Railway.

There were no half-measures about the Great Central extension to London. The line was engineered so as to permit full-speed running throughout from Leicester to the point where it joined the Metropolitan Railway north of Aylesbury. Even the smallest country stations were laid out in the most spacious manner, and the train services were operated with sets of splendid new carriages. The Great Central adopted the slogan, so far as its London trains were concerned: 'every express train vestibuled throughout, with buffet or restaurant car'. This was, in modern parlance, 'quite something' in 1900. The old-established main lines from Kings Cross and Euston were introducing new corridor coaches in a big way at that time; but if extra coaches were required on a train those extras were more often than not non-corridor, and six-wheelers into the bargain. The Great Central also changed their liveries, both of engines and carriages. The Manchester, Sheffield and Lincolnshire, like its ally the Great Northern, had carriages finished in plain varnished teak; but the Great Central at first adopted the very smart two-tone scheme of grey and dark brown. These coaches were adorned with no fewer than *three* coats of arms on each side. The set trains used on the London

extension usually consisted of five of these handsome new carriages; but as one observer commented, the new trains were 'too smart to be recognized', and after a few years the G.C.R. reverted to varnished teak.

61 Ivatt 4-2-2 locomotives; Great Northern Railway.

Until the death of Patrick Stirling the G.N.R. had used single-driver express locomotives to the exclusion of all others on the principal expresses, but his successor, H. A. Ivatt, began immediately to build larger engines of the 4-4-0 and 4-4-2 types. Train loads were very much on the increase, and greater adhesion was required for rapid starting, and climbing of the long gradients en route. In view of this change of policy it was therefore something of a surprise when Ivatt himself built a bogie single-driver express locomotive in 1898 and continued during the years 1900–1 until there were 12 of them in service. The early 1900s were a period of intense competition between the various independent companies, and particularly in respect of the London services to and from Leeds and Bradford the G.N.R. was being hard pressed by the Midland. The Great Northern reply was to put on some lightly-loaded high-speed trains, and for these the new Ivatt single-wheelers were ideal. These engines were not only light-load machines. For many years the 5.30 p.m. dining-car express from Kings Cross to Newcastle was worked by an engine of this type between Grantham and York, with a load of 200 tons, and their timekeeping was always good. These engines also had the melancholy distinction of being scrapped *en bloc*. Usually engines are withdrawn one by one, as their useful work-life is finished, or when deterioration of the frames has gone beyond repair. But these Ivatt singles were deemed obsolete in 1918, lined up in a single long line at Doncaster, and the whole class scrapped at a single blow, as it were. They were excellent engines in their day.

62 Clerestory brake composite carriage; Great Northern Railway.

The G.N.R., like its great rival from Euston, was somewhat reluctant to employ large bogie coaches; but when the time came for changing old policies it was done in no half-hearted way. The new stock used on the mid-day Anglo-Scottish express from July 1897 was truly magnificent, both from its sheer size and for the splendour of its appointments. The traditional livery of varnished teak remained, but on these tremendously long coaches, with their six-wheeled bogies and high clerestory roofs, it looked superb. The coach chosen for illustration is a brake composite – a self-contained suite of compartments for use as a single through coach running to some destination not served by the main train, and containing accommodation for first- and third-class passengers, and space for their heavy luggage and a seat for a guard, or a travelling inspector. These fine carriages were used on the Leeds trains in addition to the Scottish expresses, and on the through Kings Cross–Manchester service, which the G.N.R. operated in partnership with the Great Central via Retford and Sheffield. Like many picturesque features of the British steam railways these clerestory carriages were expensive to construct, and after Mr. Gresley had become Carriage Superintendent – he who afterwards achieved such fame as a locomotive designer, and a knighthood in recognition of it – the design of Great Northern carriages was changed to have a much simpler design of roof (see reference 65).

63 12-Wheeled dining car; West Coast Joint Stock.

One of the earliest London and North Western essays into the design of dining cars has already been described and illustrated (reference 30). The clerestory type of roof was employed probably to give additional daylight and ventilation in the roof. But whether this was the true reason, or not, the clerestory type of roof remained standard for all L.N.W.R. dining cars until the introduction of the 'American Specials', for working between Euston and Liverpool Riverside. All dining cars on the Anglo-Scottish services were clerestory roofed, and beautiful vehicles they were. At the turn of the century, and for many years after, an express train on the L.N.W.R. usually had a most variegated appearance so far as coaches were concerned. Old flat-roofed corridor and non-corridor vehicles were interspersed with newer types with high elliptical roofs; and in the midst of a long cavalcade would come one or two dining cars with clerestory roofs. In 1908 there were built at Wolverton works the splendid new 12-wheeled coaches for the afternoon Scottish expresses, and on these – at long last – one could have seen a perfect uniformity in coach styles, but for one thing; the dining cars in these new sets were still of the clerestory-roofed type. They remained so well into the days of the L.M.S.R. when these beautiful Anglo-Scottish trains were painted in Midland red. The North Western, and W.C.J.S. 12-wheeled dining cars represented a peak of achievement in railway carriage building, in the craftsmanship put into their construction and the perfect smoothness of the riding. Even in these days I have never known anything better.

64 Third-class dining cars; Midland Railway.

The Midland Railway carriage works at Derby, like those of the North Western at Wolverton, were past-masters in the art of building beautiful carriages, though the policy of the company so far as dining cars were concerned varied considerably up to the early years of the present century. On the Scottish trains the cars were vestibuled and connected to the rest of the train, whereas on certain highly-favoured Manchester expresses the dining cars were separate. Passengers wishing to dine travelled throughout in the car, and could not pass to any other part of the train even if they wished. The car illustrated, which was one allocated to purely internal services on the Midland Railway, was one of a group introduced by David Bain in the early 1900s. The ends were of normal Midland profile, but throughout the length of the actual dining saloon the body was bellied out, and earned for these cars the name of 'clipper sided'. Some similar cars were allocated to the joint Scotch services worked with the Glasgow and South Western and North British Railways. The coaches on the St. Pancras–Glasgow trains were lettered 'M.&G.S.W.' and those on the Edinburgh trains 'M.&N.B.' As with the West Coast Joint Stock all this joint Scottish stock on the Midland route was of Midland design and built at Derby. In contrast to the West Coast trains the Scottish expresses by the Midland route were entirely uniform in appearance, all having the same profile of clerestory roof. There were differences between the Clayton and the Bain coaches in the shape of the windows, and ventilators above the doors; but these were points for the connoisseur rather than the casual observer. Another is that during this period in the early 1900s the Midland never used the term Dining Car; whether first or third class they were always 'Dining Carriages'.

65 Bow-ended elliptical-roofed dining car; Great Northern Railway.

Yet another contrast in dining-car styles is to be seen in this fine example of a 12-wheeler from the Great Northern works at Doncaster – in this case titled a 'Dining Saloon'. On long distance express trains on which many passengers would be taking meals, it was the practice on all the three Anglo-Scottish routes to run

dining cars in pairs. One coach would be devoted entirely to third-class passengers, as in the Midland example, reference 64, and the other, as in this Great Northern example, would include a smaller saloon and also the kitchen, which would serve both saloons. On the North Western dining cars in pairs were run on the Liverpool, Manchester and Holyhead trains. On the Anglo-Scottish trains single composite dining cars were run separately in the Glasgow and Edinburgh sections of the trains. This Great Northern example illustrated the carriage-building style introduced at Doncaster by Mr. H. N. Gresley, with its bow-ended elliptical roofs. This was a style that persisted throughout Gresley's tenure of office on both the Great Northern and the London and North Eastern Railways. The latest examples of the style were fully air-conditioned coaches built for the Flying Scotsman trains as recently as 1938, in which the characteristic, highly varnished, teak panelling persisted to the end. The Great Northern cars, of which one is illustrated, were distinguished in the first-class saloons by their curtained windows, green leather upholstery, and the pink lampshades on the tables.

66 Composite 70-ft. Dining Car; Great Western Railway.

G. J. Churchward, Locomotive Carriage and Wagon Superintendent of the G.W.R., and later Chief Mechanical Engineer, not only built exceedingly powerful and efficient locomotives but displayed equal skill in designing carriages in which the maximum number of passengers could be conveyed in comfort for a given dead weight. Under reference 138 is a description of one of the earliest 70-ft. coaches, in which accommodation for 80 passengers was provided for a dead weight of only 33 tons. The dining car shown in this picture was one of the vehicles included in the new stock of the year 1923, when the older clipper-sided bodies, with recessed doors, had given place to smooth, steel-panelled exteriors. The elaborate lining of old was nevertheless fully restored on these coaches, in which a return was made to the old chocolate and cream livery, after a period when G.W.R. coaching stock was finished in the lake livery shown in reference 138. On trains like the Cornish Riviera Express and the Torbay Limited only a single car was run, including both first- and third-class accommodation, and a kitchen between. On the sharply-timed Great Western services weight could not be spared for running a pair of dining cars, as on certain L.N.W.R. and Great Northern services, and on West of England expresses at busy times it was quite normal to serve three sittings of lunch.

67 The Hughes 4-6-4 tank engines; L.M.S.R.

After the grouping of the railways in 1923 George Hughes, formerly Chief Mechanical Engineer of the Lancashire and Yorkshire Railway, was appointed to the same post on the L.M.S.R. and in 1924 he built a tank engine version of his 4-cylinder 4-6-0 passenger engine – the 'Lanky Dreadnoughts' as they were known on former L.N.W.R. lines. In their machinery and boilers the 4-6-4 tanks were the same as the 4-6-0 main-line engines, but they were intended for heavy short-distance hauls in the hilly districts north-east of Manchester. They worked to Blackburn and Burnley, while one or two of them were tried on the heavily graded Buxton line of the former L.N.W.R. Unlike most passenger tank engines of the period, they never carried the L.M.S.R. standard livery of Midland red. They never had L.&Y.R. numbers, but were L.M.S. 11110–11119 from the outside. Most of them ran throughout their short lives in plain unlined black, and only three of them were at any time painted red. As will be appreciated from

our picture, they were massive-looking and handsome engines; but they were rather too massive, and too expensive to maintain for the duties they worked. Four cylinders, and their attendant valve gear was certainly a complication for a short-distance tank engine, and they were displaced from their special duties after the introduction of the '2300' class 2-6-4 tanks (reference 175).

68 Adams 0-6-2 radial tank engine; North Staffordshire Railway.

Among the local railways of Great Britain the North Staffordshire was at the same time one of the oldest and one of the busiest. It had the teeming industrial districts of the Potteries virtually to itself, while enjoying a very useful alliance with the London and North Western whereby certain of the through expresses between London and Manchester travelled via Stoke and Macclesfield, and were hauled between Stoke and Manchester by North Staffordshire engines. The appointment of Adams as Locomotive Superintendent in 1902 marked the beginning of the modern era in North Stafford motive power, and the engine which is the subject of our picture belongs to a class of powerful general-service tank engines first introduced in 1903. They were primarily designed for heavy goods traffic, and had coupled wheels of only 5 ft. 0 in. diameter. For their day they were powerful units, and proved extremely useful in all kinds of local traffic in the Potteries, goods and passenger alike. There is, however, an occasion on record when one of them, engine No. 158, was called upon for a much more arduous duty. The North Staffordshire Railway always worked the heavy and important 12.5 p.m. express from Manchester to Euston, as far as Stoke, and one of the large 0-6-4 tanks was assigned to this duty. But one day a defect developed in the regular engine, and the only substitute available in Manchester was one of the 0-6-2 'radials'. This small engine had to tackle a substantial corridor dining-car train of 310 tons, but was driven and fired with such skill that the loss of time between Stockport and Stoke-on-Trent was trifling. Speed reached a maximum of 53½ m.p.h. on level track – quite a remarkable feat for a small local tank engine with a heavy express train.

69 4-6-2 Express tank engine; London and North Western Railway.

The successful application of super-heating to the main-line express passenger engines of Crewe design led to the introduction of tank engines for fast passenger working in which the greatly reduced coal and water consumption, consequent upon superheating, would permit of a greater sphere of activity than that usually associated with tank engines, and would release tender engines for other duties. These fine 4-6-2 engines, first introduced at the end of 1910 were generally similar in the design of their machinery to the main-line passenger engines, but they had a variation in the layout of the Joy valve gear, using direct instead of indirect motion, which was later applied to the 'Prince of Wales' class express passenger 4-6-os. The 4-6-2 tank engines had coupled wheels 5 ft. 8½ in. diameter, and from the outset they did excellent work on the longer-distance residential trains from London and Manchester. They were particularly effective on the heavily-graded line up to Buxton. One of their most interesting early duties was on the Central Wales line from Shrewsbury through Llandrindod Wells to Swansea. In later years some of them were transferred to the Northern Division, where they worked local trains on the Windermere branch, and put in some hard work as bank engines between Tebay and Shap Summit. The huge initials on the side tanks of No. 2665 were not used for very long. Like the 4-4-2 non-superheated

'Precursor' tanks they always carried the initials of the Company, but in a rather more modest size. The coloured picture was prepared from an official photograph and is curious in that for this short period the normal policy of the L.N.W.R., in not displaying the Company's name at all, was so blatantly reversed.

70 0-4-4 Passenger tank engine; Midland Railway.

To those who knew the Midland Railway in its later days, and equally the Midland division of the L.M.S.R., the 0-4-4 passenger tank engines were such familiar objects and so regularly entrusted to hard and important local duties that it is difficult to recall that the design originated as long ago as 1875. Moreover, the majority of the engines retained their outward appearance practically unchanged for more than 60 years. Liveries changed, of course. Until 1884 the standard Midland colour was green, with black and white lining. Then came the famous Derby red. The tank engines were not finished in so ornate a style. Many of them did not carry the Company's initials and the number was displayed in raised brass figures in the middle of the side tanks. Then came the style shown in our picture, which was followed by the L.M.S.R. red. The inevitable black followed, and finally a few of them survived into national ownership. In their hey-day there were no fewer than 205 of them in service, with numbers running from 1226 to 1430, and they worked all over the Midland system except over the Settle and Carlisle line. They were familiar enough engines around Leeds and Bradford, and some of them worked westwards from Skipton to Lancaster and Morecambe. In 1949 there were still 53 of them at work, but by that time most of them had been rebuilt, with new boilers having Belpaire fireboxes and plain-topped domes. With the passing of the picturesque original domes with Salter type safety valves mounted on them, and the beautifully shaped brass safety valve column over the firebox, much of their distinctive character disappeared; but their longevity is a tribute to the excellence of their mechanical design and of the workmanship put into their construction.

71 Great Northern Railway coat of arms.

This was probably the most elaborate emblem adopted by any of the British Railways, though some overseas administrations that were at one time strongly under British influence even exceeded the Great Northern in their comprehensiveness and ornamentation. Our reproduction of the device of the G.N.R. gives no impression of its size. Actually it was about twice the extent of the more normal coat of arms, and in its rich colouring it looked magnificent on the varnished teak carriages. It was not displayed on locomotives. In writing of the East Coast Joint Stock (reference 56) I, mentioned how the Great Northern was the pacemaker of the alliance. The interest of the company in Scotland is shown prominently on its own emblem with the thistle as prominent as the rose near the top, coming immediately below the arms of the City of London. Though the main business of the Great Northern came from the industries of Nottinghamshire and Yorkshire, London was always the main spring-board of its business enterprise, and on this heraldic device it fittingly crowns everything else. Three quartered shields are displayed beneath the thistle and the rose. The upper one has in its top quarters the three lions of England, and the lion rampant of Scotland, and below the arms of Huntingdon (left) and Peterborough. The leftward shield below symbolizes the one-time keen Great Northern interests to the west of its own main line, in association with the Great Central Railway. The arms are those of Grantham, Nottingham, Sheffield and Manchester. The rightward shield includes the Yorkshire centres of activity – Doncaster, Leeds, York and Bradford. Finally, at the bottom, in the centre, is the single shield carrying the arms of Wakefield. Two countries, twelve towns: such was the heraldic representation on the emblem of the Great Northern Railway. Sad to say, this device was abandoned after 1910 in favour of the smaller and less pretentious device mentioned in reference 56.

72 Great Eastern Railway coat of arms.

The line was an amalgamation of several smaller concerns operating in East Anglia, and it was one of the very few railways in England that enjoyed a monopoly in most of the territory it served. It is true that the Great Northern and the North Western penetrated into East Anglia as far as Cambridge, and north of Peterborough and March the Great Northern and the Great Eastern had certain important joint interests. Also the Midland and Great Northern Joint line cut across the northern part of Norfolk from King's Lynn to Cromer and Yarmouth. But elsewhere in East Anglia the Great Eastern had the field to itself and splendid service it rendered to the community. Its coat of arms was an assembly of the shields of eight cities and towns that it served, circled round the arms of the City of London, which again formed the centrepiece both businesswise and heraldically of the enterprise. The places represented round the perimeter are in some cases districts rather than centres of population, including the counties of Middlesex, Hertford, Huntingdon, and Northampton – all of which it penetrated. The towns represented are Cambridge, Ipswich, Maldon and Norwich. This again was a heraldic device that stemmed from earlier activities; otherwise one could be sure the important

Great Eastern associations with Lincoln and Yorkshire would have been symbolized, particularly in regard to the coal traffic from Doncaster and Mansfield areas, to East Anglia, and to the important north-country connections made at York. The Great Eastern once ran an express passenger service between London and York in opposition to the Great Northern, advertising the attractions of the 'Cathedral Route', travelling via Ely and Lincoln.

73 Great Central Railway coat of arms.

One naturally considers the Great Northern, the Great Eastern, and the Great Central together, because in the early years of the twentieth century their working arrangements were becoming so close that complete amalgamation was at one time seriously considered. The Great Central, as I have already emphasized under references 59 and 60, was a line that had to fight hard for existence after its audacious extension to London in 1899. Its coat of arms, so proudly and liberally displayed on engines and carriages alike, symbolized the speed and dash of the new organization. Crowning all was a locomotive, flanked with wings. The shield itself was a clever device, having at the top the arms of the three cities primarily served by its progenitor, the Manchester, Sheffield and Lincolnshire. Below is an adaptation of the familiar arms of the City of London, this time with two daggers instead of one – as a warning presumably of a readiness to fight! In the centre, what a railwayman with other sympathies once described to me as the 'flying bowler hat' (!) is the winged cap of Mercury, all incorporated to intensify the impression of speed. Most prominent, however, was the motto at the bottom – 'Forward'. This the Great Central certainly emulated, and in later years it became the motto of the London and North Eastern Railway, to which the men and traditions of the Great Central had much to contribute.

74 North Eastern Railway coat of arms.

Except for the mild incursion of the Hull and Barnsley Railway on its southern flank the North Eastern had a monopoly of the country between the Humber and the Tweed. With a huge traffic in coal, in relatively short hauls to the numerous small ports exporting to the Scandinavian countries and the Baltic, its revenue was at one time princely, and it could afford to take a more leisurely view of the passenger traffic flowing through its districts. So far as the East Coast service was concerned the Great Northern had sometimes to do not a little 'prodding' in order to get acceleration of the principal through trains. The North Eastern had two distinct coats of arms; the circular one shown in our picture, which was used on carriages and on the splashers of certain express locomotives, and a larger and more ornate device embodying the same three shields, and surrounded by a lot of decoration, which was displayed on engine tenders between the words NORTH and EASTERN. The large express locomotives, like the 'V' class Atlantic reference 117, thus included both varieties, the circular one on the driving-wheel splasher and the large one on the tender. In both devices York had the uppermost shield to itself. The other shields were those of two important constituents, to left, that of the Leeds Northern, and to right that of the York, Newcastle and Berwick. The former includes the city arms of Leeds, symbolic of the wool industry; the ship, typifying the maritime activities of Tees-side, and the other quarters representing industry and agriculture, rather than any particular places. The York, Newcastle and Berwick shield includes the arms of York in the first and fourth quarters,

Newcastle in the second, and Berwick in the third.

75 Four-cylinder compound 4-4-0; London and North Western Railway.

During his long career as Chief Mechanical Engineer of the L.N.W.R., F. W. Webb built a large number of compound locomotives at Crewe. His earlier types all had three cylinders, with two high-pressure cylinders outside, and one very large low-pressure cylinder between the frames. All his passenger engines on this system, including the eight-wheeled *Greater Britain* (reference 27) and the *Queen Empress* (reference 29) had the two pairs of driving wheels uncoupled, and there were times when differential slipping occurred. In his later designs, which were of the 4-4-0 wheel arrangement, all four cylinders drove on to the leading pair of coupled wheels and by this proper synchronization between the high- and low-pressure systems was secured. The engine illustrated, No. 1955 *Hannibal*, was built at Crewe in 1902, and was one of 40 units in the *Alfred the Great* class. They were powerful engines, and could handle heavy loads; but through a rather complicated arrangement of the valve gear, and low-pressure cylinders that were small in relation to the size of the high-pressure cylinders, they were not capable of any sustained high speed. At the time of their introduction there was a general move to accelerate all express passenger train services, and the 'Alfreds' unfortunately did not rise to the occasion. Webb's successor, George Whale, who took office in 1903, greatly improved them by providing them with a separately controlled valve gear for each set of cylinders. Even so, they were never very speedy engines, and their life on first-class express work was relatively short. Nevertheless, they represent an important stage in the evolution of British locomotive design, which inevitably had its setbacks, no less than its great successes.

76 45-ft. Corridor 'brake-first'; West Coast Joint Stock.

It was in the Diamond Jubilee year, 1897, that the West Coast Companies put on the first all-corridor train running between England and Scotland – the famous 2 p.m. from Euston to Glasgow and Edinburgh, to which there were corresponding southbound departures from the Scottish cities. They were not the first all-corridor trains to run in this country; that distinction belongs to the Great Western Railway. But whereas the Birkenhead train from Paddington soon disappeared from prominence the West Coast trains became a perfect institution. To every railwayman up and down the line the 'two-o'clock' was always known as 'The Corridor', and the name lingered on well into L.M.S.R. days when the special stock built for it had been replaced by modern standard vehicles. The coach illustrated in our picture was of earlier build than the original stock of the corridor train of 1897, and dates from 1896. But it was similar in style and construction. The original 'Scotch' corridor trains had the following make-up:

For Glasgow:	Third brake
	Third corridor
	Third dining car
	First diner and kitchen
	First diner
	First corridor
For Edinburgh:	Composite
	Third brake
For Aberdeen:	Composite
	Third brake

All these coaches, although rather narrow by modern standards, were luxuriously appointed. The 'firsts' seated only two aside, and the 'thirds' three. It will also be seen from the make-up that a lavish amount of dining accommodation was provided.

77 'Duke of Cornwall' class engine; Great Western Railway.

Once the broad gauge had been abolished

in 1892 the Great Western management embarked upon a great plan of modernization and some fine new locomotives were built in large quantities at Swindon. In broad-gauge days the important junction of Newton Abbot had formed a divisional point between the fast-running sections of the West of England main line, and the very hilly and sharply curved line in South Devon and Cornwall. Engines were always changed at Newton Abbot, and at first the same practice was continued on the narrow gauge. Through expresses to the West came down from London behind the beautiful Dean 7 ft. 8 in. 4-2-2 singles and were taken forward by massive small-wheeled 4-4-0s of the 'Duke of Cornwall' class – usually known as the 'Dukes'. This class was first introduced in 1895, and 40 were built in the ensuing 2 years. Another 19 were added in 1899. They all had beautiful West Country names. Some were topographical, such as *St. Anthony, Tintagel, Eddystone, Mounts Bay*, others were of associations with the countryside such as *Cornubia, Tre, Pol, and Pen*, and *Cornishman*, while a few, including the one chosen for illustration, were of West Country characters in literature, such as *Amyas*, the very beautiful *Armorel, King Arthur* and *Sir Lancelot*. As motive power units the 'Dukes' were excellent engines, and after being displaced from regular passenger working in the West they still did much express work as bank engines assisting the newer machines whenever they needed help on the South Devon inclines. It was not unusual in the height of the summer to see one of the mighty 'King' class 4-6-0s piloted by a 'Duke'. After grouping, some of them were drafted to Central Wales and did good work on the former Cambrian line.

78 Narrow gauge clerestory coach; Great Western Railway.

At the turn of the century, when the new Dean 4-2-2 and 4-4-0 locomotives were setting up new standards of service on the narrow gauge Great Western lines, some excellent new carriages were also introduced, and our picture shows a 'composite' with the characteristic clerestory roof and the elaborate lining-out on the picturesque chocolate and cream basic livery. Great Western coaching-stock of that period was mounted on the Dean bogie, which was different from any other kind of bogie then in use. Reference has already been made (20) to the very good riding qualities of Midland bogie carriages. The suspension in these was adapted by T. G. Clayton from the American-built Pullman cars that were imported in 1874. The Great Western did not adopt this simple and successful design. Instead Dean brought out a design of his own, which had no centre at all, and the amount of sideplay was controlled by a peculiar method of suspension from the main frames. It proved very successful and was used on the Great Western for many years, until Churchward introduced his own design of bogie for the huge 70-ft. vehicles (reference 138). These Dean clerestory carriages had wooden centres to the wheels, built up in sections.

79 A 6-ft. 'Castle' class 4-6-0; Highland Railway.

In the year 1915 the Highland Railway had on order from Hawthorn Leslie and Co. Ltd., six 4-6-0 locomotives of a very powerful new design to be named after 'Rivers'. But by a combination of unfortunate circumstances they were not permitted to run on the Highland line, and they were sold to the Caledonian. To replace these engines orders were placed for further batches of well-tried existing designs: three of the 4-4-0 'Loch' class, for working on the Dingwall and Skye line which was carrying a very heavy wartime traffic, and three of the 4-6-0 'Castle' class, which had proved extremely reliable and hard working engines. The new engines, of which the *Brodie Castle* is shown in our picture, were not identical to earlier batches. The original design, first introduced in 1900 had 5 ft. 9 in., coupled wheels and the very small smoke-box then typical of many engines of that period; in fact the length of the smoke-box would seem to have been dictated by the size of the chimney – it was made just big enough to take the base of the chimney, and no more. A later batch of these engines had extended smokeboxes and certain changes in detail design. In the last three, ordered in 1916, the diameter of the coupled wheels was increased to 6 ft. 0 in., but there was one feature that the enginemen did not like at first, namely, the provision of a horizontal screw reversing gear in place of the steam reverser which had been traditional on the Highland Railway for many years. Because of the intense preoccupation of the North British Locomotive Company with war work, it was not until the year 1917 that the engines were delivered.

80 **Composite Corridor Carriage;** Highland Railway.

One naturally associates the Highland Railway with heavy tourist traffic in the summer holiday season, and with through carriage workings from England – so much so that some of the most important trains running between Perth and Inverness were composed almost entirely of 'foreign' stock, West Coast Joint, East Coast Joint, or Midland. Many of the purely Highland services were, even down to the time of grouping, worked with non-corridor trains, though bogie coaches had by then largely replaced the very spartan four-wheelers of the nineteenth century. But on the day trains of the Highland Railway the 'foreign' stock, from the North British and Caledonian Railways, did not provide all that was necessary and some fine corridor coaches were introduced just before the first world war, and built by Hurst, Nelson and

Co. Ltd., of Motherwell. These, as shown in our picture, were finished in a handsome style of plain olive green exactly matching the locomotive style of the period as depicted on the 4-6-0 *Brodie Castle*. An attractive point of detail about the finish of these coaches was the shading of the bold block lettering, which was in emerald green. These carriages also had the Highland Railway coat of arms, displayed twice on both sides. At that time, although engines and carriages were painted the same colour, it would be rare to see an entirely green train. Almost every express would have some carriages from further afield in its make-up: Caledonian and North British on the day trains; W.C.J.S. on trains to and from England.

81 **'Scott' class 4-4-0 locomotive;** North British Railway.

The rivalry between the Caledonian and North British Railways will be referred to later (reference 102), and between 1900 and 1910 both were indulging in much publicity in their several ways. Until the turn of the century the Highland was the only Scottish railway which had persisted in the practice of naming its locomotives. The North British had a short spell during the time of Dugald Drummond, but in the flood-tide of publicity that accompanied the 'war' with the Caledonian it was resumed, and applied to all the principal express locomotive types. The 4-4-0s of the 'Scott' class were introduced in 1909 specially to work express trains between Edinburgh and Perth in connection with the Highland Railway. They were designed to use saturated steam, and were powerful locomotives for their day. But in 1914 an improved version of the class followed, equipped with superheaters, and it is one of these that is illustrated. They were all named after characters in the Waverley Novels, except for the first of the series, which was, of course, *Sir Walter Scott*. The earlier, and less powerful members of the class inevitably had the better known names, such as *Rob Roy*, *Red Gauntlet*, *Jeannie Deans*, and *The Fair Maid*. When it came to the superheater engines of 1914 there were some names that would have puzzled all but the most ardent of Sir Walter's 'fans', such as *Caleb Balderstone*, *Cuddie Headrigg* and *Dumbiedikes*; though equally there were some generally familiar ones, like *Kenilworth*, *Quentin Durward*, *The Talisman*, and the subject of our picture, *Claverhouse*.

82 Non-corridor first-class carriage; North British Railway.

At the present time one thinks either of corridor carriages for long distance travel or of diesel or electric multiple-unit trains for local or branch working, and the entire trend in recent years has been to build coaching stock in which the passengers could move about, either by means of the corridor, or through the passageways in the open saloon type of vehicle. In consequence one is apt to pass over a very interesting period in railway development when quite luxurious non-corridor stock was built for relatively short distance traffic. To represent the practice of the North British Railway, at a time when the 'Scott' class 4-4-0 locomotives of the super-heated variety were introduced, a very fine non-corridor first-class bogie coach has been chosen for illustration. The North British, in addition to its fast inter-city services and its participation in the East Coast services, operated some well-patronized local trains, used by season ticket holders working in Edinburgh and Glasgow, who would appreciate the comforts provided by carriages like the one shown in our picture. In addition to providing very comfortable accommodation these coaches, which were built by Hurst, Nelson and Co. Ltd., of Motherwell, were beautifully finished outside, with full lining and the N.B.R. coat of arms carried twice on each side of the vehicle.

83 0-6-4 Passenger tank engines; Midland Railway.

First among a group of four distinctive designs of passenger tank engines is R. M. Deeley's 0-6-4 of 1907, designed particularly for heavy coal traffic. It was in some ways a tank-engine version of the standard main-line goods locomotive, but provided with side tanks with a capacity of 2,250 gallons and a coal capacity of $3\frac{1}{2}$ tons. This would enable engines of this class to run considerable mileages without refuelling, and in the operation of a heavy local service would cut to a minimum the time for shed duties needed between trips. Because of the unusual appearance of the side tanks these engines were nicknamed 'the flat-irons'. The large coal bunker in rear and the need to provide a trailing bogie instead of the more usual 0-6-2 type for local tank engines at that period made it necessary to give special attention to the suspension and bearings for all the wheels. The leading pair of wheels had the Cartazzi form of axle box, in order to permit of a degree of side play. Similarly, the joint in the coupling rods was equipped with spherical bearings to accommodate the side play in the leading coupled wheel axleboxes. Despite these special features the 'flat irons' were not very successful engines. They rode badly, and it was inadvisable to run them at any substantial speed, and they were eventually transferred to goods workings on which their tractive power could be utilized, but which needed no fast running.

84 W. Pickersgill's 4-6-2 tank engine; Caledonian Railway.

These handsome engines, of which 12 were built in 1917 by the North British Locomotive Co. Ltd., formed part of Pickersgill's general adoption of outside cylinders for large new locomotives, in contrast to the practice that had prevailed on the Caledonian since the days of Dugald Drummond. The fast trains from

Glasgow to the Clyde Coast stations of Gourock and Wemyss Bay had hitherto been worked by tender engines, some 4-4-0, some 4-6-0, and a number with large-wheeled 0-6-0s. But tank engines were ideal for these relatively short runs, and from their introduction the Pickersgill 4-6-2 tank engines had a virtual monopoly of the Gourock and Wemyss Bay services, until they were superseded, in L.M.S. days, by very efficient Fowler 2-6-4 tanks (reference 175). But the Pickersgill machines were strong, free-steaming engines, and a very useful task was found for them in banking duties at Beattock. The great majority of trains, passenger and goods alike, needed rear-end banking assistance over the very severe 10-mile bank between Beattock station and the summit, where the gradient is about 1 in 75 for most of the distance. On this duty some of the Pickersgill 4-6-2 tanks survived into the era of nationalization, and having borne the emblems and liveries of both the Caledonian and the L.M.S. they eventually carried the name BRITISH RAILWAYS on their side tanks.

85 Robinson's 4-6-2 passenger tank; Great Central Railway.

Reference has already been made (reference 59) to the work of J. G. Robinson on the Great Central Railway. The 4-6-2 tank engine illustrated is a very neat and handsome example of that engineer's designing skill applied to a powerful unit for fast suburban service. The first of the class, No. 165, was completed at Gorton Works at the end of 1910, and was, by a very short lead, the first of this wheel arrangement to be used in Britain. This Great Central example was followed very shortly by 4-6-2 tank engines on the London Brighton and South Coast Railway, and on the London and North Western (reference 69). The G.C.R. engines were designed for working from the London end of the line. One could hardly describe their work as suburban, because the first stations out of Marylebone were at Wembley Hill, on the Wycombe route, and at Harrow on the main line via Aylesbury. Their work thus consisted in a fast initial run through the immediate suburban area, with speeds of 60 m.p.h. or more, and then hard work in climbing the heavy gradients through the Chiltern hills. On some stopping trains, originally, they worked as far north as Leicester. On these duties, with an excellent boiler and relatively small coupled wheels, they proved a great success, and they worked on the residential services from Marylebone for nearly 40 years. After grouping, when engines of greater power were needed for the Tees-side services this Great Central design was chosen by the L.N.E.R. for further multiplication in preference to an existing North Eastern design.

86 Reid 4-4-2 tank engine; North British Railway.

The last of this group of passenger tank engines, the North British, dates from 1915, and was a superheated version of an earlier variety. The lines over which these engines were required to work were severely graded but, as in the case of express-passenger locomotives, W. P. Reid preferred four-coupled, to six-coupled wheels, and these 4-4-2 tank engines certainly did some good work. They were used on the longer distance residential trains from Edinburgh, working to Galashiels, both via Peebles and via the main line of the Waverley Route, over Falahill summit. Like all the North British designs they were massively built, and in consequence they were very low in maintenance charges, and had a long life. After larger and more modern engines had been put on to the fast suburban services around Edinburgh and Glasgow the Reid 4-4-2 tanks were usefully employed on lighter duties in Fife, on the Clyde Coast, and on certain workings that took them up the West Highland line as far as Ardlui. The entire stud of North British 4-4-2 tank locomotives – the original non-superheated batch of 30, introduced in 1911, and the 21 superheated engines put to work from 1915 onwards – all survived to enter national ownership, in 1948, and it was not until the dieselization programme got under way from 1955 onwards that they were withdrawn.

87–89 Dynamometer Cars; Great Western Railway; North Eastern Railway; London and North Western Railway.

The accurate measurement of the performance of locomotives is an essential part of the science of railway engineering; but on many railways in pre-grouping days the size of the locomotive stud and the nature of the work involved did not justify the expense of constructing a dynamometer car, or of maintaining the necessary technical staff to man it, and to assess results. In pre-grouping days four companies owned dynamometer cars, and three of these are illustrated in our coloured pictures. Before mentioning the cars of the G.W.R., of the N.E.R., and of the L.N.W.R. individually, some reference is needed to the function of these cars. The basic function in all cases is to measure the work done by the locomotive, and this is first of all registered by a powerful spring, in exactly the same way as an ordinary spring balance works. The dynamometer, however, not only registers the pull at any moment, but in combination with an instrument called an integrator it clocks up the total amount of work done on the journey. The performance of the locomotive is recorded on a continuous chart passing through the integrator, registering also the speed at any moment. Automatically there are records produced on the chart which show speed, drawbar pull, total work up to the particular moment, while observers in the dynamometer car note the time of passing each milepost, important stations and junctions, and other incidents of the journey. An engineer is always riding in the cab of the locomotive, and he communicates by telephone details of the engine working, such as the extent to which the regulator is open, steam pressure, position of reversing gear, and so on. All these are noted down at the appropriate moment on the chart passing through the integrator, so that on completion there is a continuous record of the performance of the locomotive.

The Great Western car (reference 87) was built in 1903, and was used in recording the performance of the new standard range of locomotives Churchward was designing. In heavy express passenger work it was desired to have engines capable of sustaining a drawbar pull of 2 tons at 70 m.p.h., and the dynamometer duly recorded that the 'Saint' and 'Star' engines could do that. In 1924 the same car was used for the trials of the 'Castle' class 4-6-0 No. 4074 *Caldicot Castle*, and when the results were published the performance of that engine was so efficient so far as fuel consumption was concerned that engineers of other railways just could not believe it. The car was used extensively in the Interchange Trials of 1948, after nationalization, when locomotives of the Southern, Eastern and London Midland Regions were tested between Paddington and Plymouth; but one of the mightiest exhibitions of power output that this car was ever called upon to record was in 1953, when the ex-G.W.R. 4-6-0 No. 6001 *King Edward VII* was set to haul a train of *twenty-five coaches*, at normal express train speed, and this tremendous load of 800 tons was run for long stretches of the line at 65 to 70 m.p.h.

The North Eastern car (reference 88), shown in L.N.E.R. livery, was in many ways a copy of the Great Western vehicle. Wilson Worsdell, when Chief Mechanical Engineer, had borrowed the latter car, and then proceeded to build one of his own. The car shown in our picture recorded some famous occasions in locomotive history, such as the trials in 1923 between Great Northern and North Eastern 'Pacifics', and the high-speed running of the early streamlined 'A4' engines. But the greatest occasion in its career came in July 1938 when it was coupled next to the engine on the test train when the Gresley 'A4' Pacific No. 4468 *Mallard* made the world's record speed with steam traction. The instruments in the dynamometer car recorded the very thrilling speed of 126 m.p.h.

The London and North Western car (reference 89) was built in 1908, to replace the curious little six-wheeled car used by F. W. Webb. The handsome car shown in our picture was commissioned in time to record the magnificent performance of Bowen-Cooke's first superheater express locomotive, the *George the Fifth*, in 1910, and in 1913 it was used in the trials of the 'Claughton' class 4-6-0 No. 1159 *Ralph Brocklebank*, when some maximum output trials were conducted first between Euston and Crewe, and then between Crewe and Carlisle. On that occasion the values of horsepower registered were the highest that had been noted up to that time with any class of British locomotive. The maximum effort was one of 2¾ tons at 69 m.p.h. with an indicated horsepower of 1669. Thus each of these pre-1914 dynamometer cars had their great moments. After grouping the L.M.S.R. used the Lancashire and Yorkshire car in preference to that of the North Western.

90 **Dynamometer Car No. 3;** London Midland and Scottish Railway.

The science of locomotive testing had notably advanced in the years between the two world wars, and just before nationalization of the railways in 1948, the L.M.S.R. had completed an entirely new dynamometer car embodying the latest practices, and arranged for a novel new form of electrical control in testing. One of the advantages claimed for a stationary testing plant is that the speed of a locomotive can be kept constant. To work in conjunction with the new dynamometer car two mobile test units were designed, which with electrical controls could keep the speed of a locomotive constant, whether it was running uphill or down. The loading was entirely electrical, so that with the dynamometer car and two mobile test units, the effect of any weight of train encountered in ordinary service could be simulated. It sometimes caused astonishment to onlookers to see a powerful locomotive working very hard, hauling no more than three coaches, and possibly not exceeding 40 m.p.h. When maximum output trials were made of certain British Railways locomotives, as a counterpart to the 25-coach trials made with the G.W.R. 'King' class engine, the running characteristics of 850 and even 900-ton passenger trains were simulated without having to haul an inordinate number of coaches. Over the Settle and Carlisle line a 'Britannia' class 4-6-2 successfully hauled an equivalent load of 850 tons up the 14 miles of 1 in 100 gradient between Settle Junction and Blea Moor, while the Stanier 'Pacific' engine No. 46225 *Duchess of Gloucester* made equally good time with an equivalent load of 900 tons. The latter was without much doubt the greatest task ever set to a British express-passenger locomotive, and it was duly recorded in the dynamometer car shown in our picture.

91 **London and South Western Railway coat of arms.**

The South Western device is unusual in that it included five quarterings. This may seem a contradiction in terms, since a thing divided into five could hardly be considered to consist of 'quarterings'. But in writing of heraldry one uses heraldic terms, and the South Western device had two quarterings on the left hand, or dexter side, and three quarterings on the right, or sinister side. Originally there were only four quarterings, covering the extent of the London and Southampton Railway as originally built: London and Southampton, on the dexter side, Winchester and Portsmouth on the sinister. Later, when the first westward extension was constructed in the form of the branch from Eastleigh to Salisbury, the arms of the City of Salisbury were added – a simple device consisting only of eight bars alternately gold and blue. In later years the London and South Western Railway extended far beyond the territory indicated by the five towns on its coat of arms. Bournemouth, Weymouth, Yeovil, Exeter, Barnstaple, Plymouth, and Padstow were all served by fast express trains from London; but the coat of arms was not changed again, after the first amendment that took in Salisbury. On the timetables right down to the years just before the grouping the oldest form of the coat of arms was used, omitting Salisbury. The one shown in our picture was used on the Drummond locomotives, carried on the driving-wheel splasher. In the last locomotive built for the L.S.W.R. just before grouping the splashers were so small that the coat of arms could not be used.

92 South Eastern Railway coat of arms.

This line and its great rival, the London Chatham and Dover, were very much intertwined in the county of Kent. Most towns were served by both companies, and there was a great deal of overlapping and uneconomic working, so that amalgamation, or a fusion of interests was the inevitable outcome. But both the South Eastern and the London Chatham and Dover were concerns of great individuality, and the former in its coat of arms had a most beautiful design. It was rare, in not following the pattern of so many railway heraldic devices, but was a wholly original design. The centre-piece is the White Horse of Kent displayed on a red cross. This might have been intended as the emblem of the City of London; but the familiar dagger has been omitted, and it could have signified the St. George's Cross, of England. Above the cross, and still within the shield, are to be seen a demi-lion and a demi-ship. These items were taken from the coat of arms of the Cinque Ports, all of which were served by the South Eastern Railway. The heraldic design is completed by the crest surmounting the shield, which is a pleasant allusion to Dover Castle – Dover being the first terminus of the line. As can be seen from our picture, the colouring was magnificent, and the ensemble, encircled by the familiar garter, included the motto of the Company – 'Onward'. There were times during the nineteenth century, when passengers by the railway must have felt that the motto had more than a slightly cynical ring; but there were no half measures about the enterprise displayed, during the years of fusion with the 'Chatham'.

93 London Chatham and Dover Railway coat of arms.

The 'Chatham', as it was popularly known had a very chequered career in its early days, and the audacity with which it entered London and opened a series of highly competitive services with the slenderest of financial backing is one of the most fascinating and exciting stories of mid-Victorian railway history. But however daring, unconventional and provocative its early policies may have been, in its heraldry it displayed great dignity and beauty of design. The garter encircles four shields, and in depicting the final version in our picture it is interesting to recall an earlier one, in which London was not so much as included. The railway had its origin in the country, and made its way to London later, and the shields first included within the garter were those of the county of Kent, and of Rochester, Canterbury and Faversham. The device illustrated has at the top the White Horse of Kent, and then from left to right, the City of London, the City of Rochester, and on the right, Dover. Although Chatham figured so prominently in the railway name the arms of the town were not displayed. Those responsible evidently thought that the ancient city of Rochester, so relatively near, was more appropriate than the dockyard town. The 'Chatham' also included a motto on their coat of arms 'Invicta' – always associated with Kent. The arms of the London Chatham and Dover Railway can still be seen, magnificently displayed on the piers at each end of the railway viaduct adjacent to Blackfriars Bridge, in London. The viaduct carries the busy line leading to St. Paul's and Holborn Viaduct stations.

94 London Brighton and South Coast Railway coat of arms.

This magnificent device was used rather sparingly on locomotives and coaching stock of the L.B. & S.C.R., and took two different forms. There was one in which the central shield was simply enclosed in a garter, and the more elaborate one shown in our picture, in which the shield had as supporters a griffin on each side, the wing of a griffin as the crest, and the Company's name on a ribbon below. This elaborate version was used on a few specially selected locomotives, and on certain saloon carriages. The towns included in the shield are top left, London; top right, Brighton; bottom left, and bottom right, Portsmouth. The town shields of Brighton and Hastings are in themselves of particular interest. Brighton itself is represented by the two dolphins on the shield within the shield, and the surrounding piece including the six martlet birds was added when Brighton was made a county borough, in 1897. The martlets formed the coat of

arms of one of the oldest Sussex families – that of Radynden – through whose land the railway passed. The arms of Hastings are rather complicated heraldically, and are connected with the position of Hastings as the Premier Port of the Cinque Ports Confederation. Many other towns of importance were served by the L.B.&S.C.R., but in addition to London and Brighton, those of Hastings and Portsmouth were obviously chosen as representing the most easterly and westerly points reached by the railway.

95 Travelling Post Office van; Highland Railway.

The inception of the travelling post-office service has been described under reference 57, and before the end of the nineteenth century all the major railways, and some of the minor ones were running special vans for postal traffic. The Highland services were operated both north and south of Inverness, and the apparatus for picking-up and setting-down mail bags without stopping was in use at nearly all intermediate stations along the line. A characteristic of all T.P.O. vans is the gangway connection at the ends set to one side, instead of centrally on the coach. The T.P.O. vans are not connected to the ordinary passenger-carrying part of the train, and the offset gangway is to clear the sorting bench that extends from end to end of the vehicle. If it were not for the off-set the bench would have to be cut short, or tapered off at the ends to allow men to pass freely from one vehicle to another. The Highland van illustrated is one of three that have a very interesting history. During the first World War, when the Grand Fleet was based at Scapa Flow in the Orkneys, a huge volume of letters for the men passed over the Highland Railway, and the relatively small T.P.O. vans that had sufficed for the normal peacetime mail were quite inadequate. So three new vans were built at Lochgorm Works, Inverness, embodying the characteristic narrow side-panelling, and the handsome, though very simple style of lettering and finish. These three vans had a long and strenuous life. They ran continuously on the Highland mail trains for 45 years, and were withdrawn at the end of 1961.

96 **Combined passenger coach, and travelling post office;** Great Western Railway.
In recent years the mail-train services on British Railways have come very prominently into the public eye through the dastardly attack and robbery that took place on the West Coast 'Up Special' some years ago; and in recent times generally attempts have been sustained to segregate mail from ordinary traffic on those trains that convey travelling post offices. It is all the more interesting therefore to study the picturesque Great Western clerestory roofed vehicle of Victorian times that includes a post office and passenger accommodation in the same coach body. The three third-class compartments at the left-hand end are non-corridor, and the gangway at the right-hand end in the picture is of the offset type for connecting to other postal vehicles that might be marshalled in the train. One can imagine that this hybrid form of construction was adopted for reasons of coach standardization. The Post Office would have specified the size of compartment they required for letter-sorting and other work, and this would not have required more than a six-wheeled coach, of similar length to the Great Northern T.P.O. van (reference 108). But rather than build a special length of frame and body the Great Western used their standard dimensions, and took advantage of the spare space that would have been available to put in these passenger-carrying compartments, and reduce the dead weight of the rest of the train by avoiding the use of extra carriages.

97 **Tri-composite corridor brake coach;** South Eastern and Chatham Railway.
For all its own services, including the most luxurious of the Continental boat trains, the South Eastern and Chatham used only non-corridor carriages. But in the early 1900s, the enterprising management concluded arrangements with both the London and North Western and with the Midland Railways to run through-carriages from the Kent Coast resorts to certain northern cities. These coaches were worked to Willesden Junction in the one case, and to Kentish Town in the other, and there attached to expresses from London to the Midlands and the North. These involved long journeys, such as to Leeds or Manchester; and so that passengers in the through S.E.&C.R. coaches could enjoy the amenities of long-distance travel, such as restaurant cars, special corridor carriages were constructed. They included first-, second- and third-class compartments, and a commodious luggage compartment. This had also the picturesque and characteristic S.E.&C.R. 'birdcage' roof, whereby the guard could look out over the roofs of the ordinary carriages. It made an interesting sight to see one of these vehicles, in the rich lake colour of the S.E.&C.R. marshalled next to the engine on a London and North Western express. Equally strange was it to see on the Midland Railway a vehicle providing second-class accommodation. The Midland was the first railway to dispense entirely with second class. This bold move took place as long previously as 1875. Ordinarily one could not buy a second-class ticket on the Midland; but obviously some special arrangement must have been made for the running of those S.E.&C.R. through-carriages, because second-class accommodation was available in them throughout from Leeds, or Manchester to Dover! On the L.N.W.R. there would be no difficulty, as that company was still

150

booking all three classes in the early 1900s.

98 Tri-composite lavatory carriage; Cambrian Railways.

The headquarters of this otherwise very Welsh railway was in England, at Oswestry, Salop. This was not only the administrative centre of the Cambrian, but also the site of the locomotive and carriage works. At the turn of the century the engineer in charge of these works as Locomotive, Carriage and Wagon Superintendent was Mr. Herbert E. Jones. All his training and early engineering experience had been on the Midland, and he had served under such outstanding railwaymen as Matthew Kirtley, S. W. Johnson, and that most distinguished of nineteenth-century carriage designers, T. G. Clayton. This goes some way towards explaining the remarkably comprehensive and enterprising work carried out in the shops at Oswestry. There, not only were locomotives maintained, and repaired, but new construction was undertaken from 1901 onwards; and some fine examples of contemporary coaching stock were also built in this relatively small works. In actual style the coaches of the Cambrian Railways may not have been very outstanding; but the livery was most distinctive, and their riding qualities excellent. The Cambrian participated in the working of many through-carriage services with the London and North Western Railway, and though such vehicles were not required to run fast on the parent system, they were taken along pretty smartly once they passed off Cambrian metals at Whitchurch. The roof boards on these through-carriages were evidently designed to have a keen advertising value, as for example when one saw a six-wheeler prominently labelled thus: CAMBRIAN RAILWAYS THROUGH CARRIAGE BETWEEN LIVERPOOL (Lime Street) AND ABERDOVEY TOWYN AND BAR-MOUTH VIA CREWE AND WHITCHURCH. There were no abbreviations to shorten the legend – not even an St. for Street, and no short cuts by use of the ampersand. In later years the Cambrian, like the Brighton, the Furness, and other users of two-tone colour schemes, abandoned the white upper panels, and painted its coaches green, though still handsomely lined out.

99 'Experiment' class 4-6-0; London and North Western Railway.

After George Whale had succeeded F. W. Webb as Chief Mechanical Engineer of the L.N.W.R. in 1903, a complete modernization of the motive power was undertaken, and following the great success of the 'Precursor' class 4-4-0s in the Southern Division an adaptation of the same general design to suit the Northern Division was prepared. To provide greater adhesion, for coping with the steeply graded line through the Westmorland fell country, six-coupled wheels were used, instead of four, and this involved an important change in the design of the firebox. At first the men found some difficulty in mastering the technique of firing this shallow grate, and the engines got an indifferent reputation. Some doubts were also spread in certain quarters by the choice of name for the class. The first engine took both name and number from the first Webb three-cylinder compound, which certainly *was* an experiment. Whale's 4-6-0 of 1905 was equally not one, and when the men had mastered the art of firing, the engines did good work. Eventually no fewer than 105 of them were built at Crewe works, and although the increasing loads of the Scotch expresses led to their early replacement on the mountain section they put in many years of useful service in general passenger work all over the L.N.W.R. system. They were very fast runners, and several instances of speeds in excess of 90 m.p.h. have been recorded with them.

100 57-ft. Corridor composite carriage; London and North Western Railway.

At the same time as modernization of the locomotive stock of the L.N.W.R. was in progress at Crewe, the carriage works at Wolverton was engaged in the production of some fine new rolling stock. The carriages of the North Western, and of the West Coast Joint Stock had always been renowned for their comfort and smooth riding; but with the exception of the beautiful twelve-wheeled dining cars the carriages had been rather narrow, and with relatively low ceilings inside. The production of the so-called '57-ft. stock' was a major advance, and it included spacious new carriages for the 'set' trains on the Liverpool and Manchester, and the Anglo-Scottish services, and the production of new self-contained composite carriages with luggage compartments, for use on services where a single through-carriage was run from destinations off the principal express routes. Until the grouping, in 1923, a single coach was all that was generally needed for the day service between Birmingham and the Scottish cities, and a 'brake-composite' labelled BIRMINGHAM NEW STREET AND GLASGOW CENTRAL was attached at Crewe to the front of the 10 a.m. express from Euston to Glasgow. When originally built the North Western was still booking second-class passengers on its internal services, and some of these composite carriages provided accommodation for all three classes.

101 A 'Barochan' class 4-6-0; Caledonian Railway.

Caledonian locomotive practice had some points of similarity to that of the L.N.W.R. in the use of medium-powered 4-6-0 locomotives on many passenger trains, although the Caledonian used a few very large engines on the Anglo-Scottish services, over Beattock summit. The engine illustrated was one of an important intermediate class, with coupled wheels, 5 ft. 9 in. diameter, against the 6 ft. 6 in. of the largest passenger engines. They were used on the north line from Glasgow Buchanan Street to Perth, where there are heavy gradients, and little chance of really fast running, and they were also used on some of the highly competitive services from Glasgow to Gourock, where the combination of train and boat used to involve all-out races from Glasgow across the Firth of Clyde to Dunoon. Again there were certain hindrances on the run down from Glasgow at junctions where speed had to be reduced. In consequence an engine with a capacity for rapid acceleration was essential in order to keep the sharp times required by the timetable. The *Barochan* was named after the residence of Sir Charles Renshaw, the Chairman of the Caledonian Railway, whereas the ever-famous main-line express engine *Cardean* was named after the estate of the deputy-Chairman. One might have imagined that the names would have been reversed, but the *Barochan* was used on Clyde Coast trains between Glasgow and Gourock, and daily passed near to Sir Charles Renshaw's home.

102 A 'Grampian' corridor carriage; Caledonian Railway.

In the early years of the present century the intense rivalry between the East and West Coast routes from London to Scotland which had reached a climax in the great Race to the North in 1895 had largely subsided south of the Border; but in Scotland the North British and the Caledonian were engaged in severe competition for the traffic from Glasgow and Edinburgh to Aberdeen. Not only were some very fast services introduced, but both companies built some luxurious new rolling stock for the principal trains. The Caledonian named its 10 a.m. express out of Glasgow the 'Grampian', although curiously enough its route to Perth and Aberdeen did not pass through the Grampians and gave its passengers no more than a distant sight of some of the eastern outliers of the range. Whether the name was strictly appropriate or not the rolling stock put on to that train was magnificent. All the coaches were mounted on twelve-wheeled bogies, and they rode superbly, although speeds were, by the very nature of the route, not exceptionally high. Some similar coaches, slightly shorter and on eight-wheeled bogies, were built for general service, and one of them was used on the through-carriage service between Glasgow and Bristol via the Severn Tunnel route. Two of these beautiful carriages have been preserved, and are restored to the original Caledonian livery as shown in our picture.

103–106 Semaphore Signals.

There was no more picturesque feature of the British steam railways than the semaphore signal. Through by far the greater part of the steam era signals of the lower quadrant type were used, and in general terms the indications displayed were widely known: Horizontal, with a red light at night, meant STOP, and an arm inclined downwards, with a green light at night, means ALL RIGHT, or PROCEED. What is not so generally appreciated however is the remarkable variation in detail that existed between the semaphore signals of the different railway companies. There were important differences in signalling practice – all, of course, within the code of safety working which was so cherished a tradition of all the individual railway companies – but in these first four examples I am concerned with differences in details of construction. To the casual

observer a 'semaphore signal' was just a signal, all looking very much alike; but a connoisseur, on coming upon a line of railway would be able to identify the owning company beyond any doubt from the form of the signals, before any train, or any other sign of ownership was sighted.

The Great Eastern semaphore (reference 103) As in the great majority of semaphore designs the arm itself was made of wood tapering in width from 11 in. at the top to 10 in. at the centre point of the pivot. Naturally a wooden blade of this kind, after years of service, tends to split, and one would often see metal bands put on to check this tendency. But the Great Eastern put these bands on when the signals were new. The arm pivot and spectacle was of an interesting design in cast iron, and the spectacle glasses were of a rather complicated shape that would have needed some careful cutting. The actual colour of the 'green' glass needs some further comment. Originally these glasses were of a very beautiful grass-green colour; but with an oil-lighted lamp behind them, and a flame having a strong yellowish colour, the result at night was a rather pale yellow-green. To counteract this, in later years the glasses were made of a strong blue-green colour – in fact some looked decidedly more blue than green. In combination with the yellow light from the oil lamp a much more distinctive green was displayed at night.

The Caledonian semaphore (reference 104) The signals of this railway were immediately distinctive in being carried on posts of open wrought-iron lattice work, instead of the more usual wood. The iron 'flats' forming the lattice were turned on edge, as seen from the front, and this earned for the particular form of construction the term 'inconspicuous lattice', as distinct from the 'conspicuous' lattice used on some posts on the Great Northern

Railway (see reference 191). Apart from the post itself, however, the Caledonian design of semaphore was distinctive in the method of attachment of the spectacle casting to the pivot plate. All the bolt holes were slotted, so that the position of the spectacle could be adjusted, within certain limits in respect to the centre of the post. So far as can be traced the Caledonian was the only railway to use this form of construction, which was adopted so as to facilitate the sighting of signals on curves where it might be necessary to set the line of the light beam slightly oblique to the line of the railway at the particular point where the signal itself was mounted. The Caledonian always retained the grass-green spectacle glasses, and until quite recent years one could see the pale yellow indication at night.

The North Eastern semaphore (reference 105)

As mentioned in describing the early primitive forms of semaphore (reference 51–52), the original method was to have the arm working in a slot in the post. The type of mounting was retained to the very end of lower quadrant semaphore signalling on the North Eastern Railway. The principle of working in a slot in the post was, indeed, used even when certain lattice post signals were installed; and to carry it out a somewhat complicated form of construction was necessary, in order to provide the necessary mounting in the middle of the lattice. On a wooden post, as shown in our picture, the cutting away of the centre of the mast to accommodate the arm and its bearings naturally weakened the post, and to compensate for this reinforcing strips were added on each side for the length of the slot. Another very characteristic feature of North Eastern signals was the pinnacle, which was no less than 4 ft. high! Actually this was a design used in many parts of the world by the famous

firm of signalling contractors McKenzie and Holland Ltd. of Worcester. The base and the ornamental fluted portion was of cast iron and the spire was made in sheet zinc, wrapped round, and secured to the topmost flange of the casting.

The Great Northern semaphore (reference 106)

This design, which originated after the disaster at Abbots Ripton in 1876, was intended to provide against the risk of an arm becoming weighted down by snow, and accordingly giving a false indication. It was pivoted at the centre of the arm, and was designed to assume a vertical position, when in the clear. In actual practice the arms rarely came off to the truly vertical position. It was more usual to see them as in the illustration of the Great Northern gantry (reference 191). This design was taken up by McKenzie and Holland Ltd. as one of their standard products, and it was adopted by the local railways in South Wales, and also on certain railways in Australia. It provided a splendidly distinctive day indication, and naturally made any line belonging to the Great Northern instantly distinguishable. Our picture shows one of these centre-balanced arms – sometimes referred to as 'somersault' signals – mounted on a wooden post, though in later years it was more normal to mount them on lattice-iron posts of the 'conspicuous' type.

One feature that will be noticed in comparing these four examples of lower quadrant signals, is that while the form of the arm – a red blade with a white band – is standard, the proportions of the red and white portions vary considerably. There was certainly no uniformity between the various railway companies in this respect.

107 Ocean Mail stowage van; Great Western Railway.
The conveyance of mail by railway has

led to the construction of many distinctive and extremely interesting vehicles, and two of these have already been noticed under references 95 and 96. For the Ocean Mail traffic from Plymouth to London the Great Western built some huge 68-ft. stowage vans, with sliding doors, and high elliptical roofs, in complete contrast to the clerestory-roofed vehicles that had been standard on the G.W.R. from quite early broad gauge days. These vans were completed in 1904 in time to be used on the very fast runs made in the spring of that year when competition with the London and South Western Railway was at its height. Some similar vans were included in the new all-Postal train to the West of England put into service in 1905, though this train included a number of older vehicles with clerestory roofs. This mixed formation on the West of England postal special persisted for more than 20 years. The record-breaking mail train of May 9, 1904, when the 4-4-0 locomotive *City of Truro* attained a maximum speed of 100 m.p.h. descending Wellington bank, consisted of four of the big 68-ft. stowage vans and one older vehicle. This latter was detached at Bristol, and the load with which the Dean 4-2-2 engine *Duke of Connaught* completed the 118 miles from Bristol to Paddington in the amazing time – for the year 1904 – of 99¾ minutes, was four of the stowage vans, a total of 120 tons.

108 **Six-wheeled Travelling Post Office;** Great Northern Railway.
The network of postal services conveyed by railway reached its maximum in the years just prior and after the first World War, before the rapid development of motor transport on the roads. There were three main postal routes for long-distance traffic, and many others were feeders or subsidiaries. Strange though it may seem, at first sight the principal route from London to the North East coast was from

Euston, and not from King's Cross, using the trains to be mentioned under references 109 and 110; but the Great Northern Railway had a number of post office contracts for both day and night services to districts lying short of the main arteries of North Country postal services, and for these some travelling post office vans were constructed. In the early years of the present century the apparatus for picking-up and dropping mail bags at speed was very extensively used, and there were postal nets at many stations along the routes. The local postmen used to clear these nets, and delivery of the mail was within quite a limited area. Nowadays the 'apparatus' as it is known in the postal service is used to no more than a limited extent, and loading and unloading of mails is largely confined to the stations at which the mail trains stop. The Great Northern T.P.O. van illustrated is typical of the six-wheeled era, though the coachwork and the finish, in varnished teak, was as fine as anything put into the most palatial corridor carriages or dining cars of a later time.

109 **T.P.O. van for the Postal Special';** West Coast Joint Stock.
In ordinary railway parlance a 'special' is an extra train: something outside the ordinary timetable. In the Post Office, however, the DOWN SPECIAL and the UP SPECIAL are the regular Anglo-Scottish postal trains which convey no passengers, except on the final section of the Aberdeen run, north of Perth in each direction. It was the UP SPECIAL that was concerned in the great mail robbery when the train was so audaciously held up near Leighton Buzzard. The DOWN SPECIAL in steam days usually left Euston with 12 vehicles. Some of these were stowage vans for through traffic, but a number of them contained the 'apparatus', and even today mails are exchanged at quite a number of places enroute. Mails for North-Eastern England

are conveyed by this train as far as Tamworth, where they are transferred to the Midland train (reference 110) and there is a general exchange of mails during the stop at Crewe. The mail-exchanging apparatus is fixed only on one side of the carriage and the sorting bench extends the full length of the carriage on the opposite side. The lineside nets are, of course, be mounted on the left-hand side of the line, looking in the direction of running, and because of this the train has to be turned end for end before commencing the return journey so as to have the apparatus on the correct side for the nets. At the London end the train is turned on the Mitre Bridge triangle at Willesden. Our picture shows one of the vans built specially for the service by the L.N.W.R. at Wolverton Works.

110 Six-wheeled Travelling Post Office van; Midland Railway.

The Midland and the North Eastern Railways combined to operate the second important trunk route of railway postal service in this country, operating between Bristol and Newcastle, and intersecting and connecting with the West Coast 'Specials' at Tamworth. The route of the 'Midland T.P.O.' as it is identified on postmarks of letters posted on it is via Gloucester, Birmingham, Derby, Sheffield, and York, and thus connects with many centres of population and industry. Subsidiary services feed into it at Bristol and Cheltenham, and it receives a heavy mail from the south at Tamworth, where special arrangements are in force for rapid transhipment of mailbags between the high-level Midland platforms, and the low-level North Western below. The Midland van illustrated is an early clerestory-roofed vehicle of Clayton's design, with the simple lettering 'M.R.'; but the bogie T.P.O. vans used on this service at a later period bore the initials 'M.&N.E.J.P.S. – Midland and North Eastern Joint Postal Service. Whether in

Midland or North Eastern territory, however, the postmark in recent years has always been 'Midland T.P.O. Going North' or 'Midland T.P.O. Going South' as the case might be. Our picture shows clearly the offset gangway, and the ventilators for the gas lamps that provided the internal illumination. In later years, with electric lighting, additional lights were mounted low down on the bodies outside for the benefit of men working the 'apparatus'.

111 Robinson's standard 0-6-0 goods engine; Great Central Railway.

Following the construction of the London Extension line, in 1899, and the tremendous drive for new traffic that followed J. G. Robinson embarked upon the building of a new standard range of locomotives that would anticipate the needs of the traffic; and at the same time as he introduced the 4-4-0 express-passenger class, reference 59, he built a generally similar 0-6-0 for general goods service, as illustrated in this picture. Rarely can there have been a neater, or more handsome 'common hack' freight engine. They were nicknamed the 'Pom-poms', and although superseded later by the much larger and heavier eight-coupled engines introduced by Mr. Robinson their general usefulness continued without any break. On four occasions the greatest possible tribute was paid by other railway authorities to the locomotive designs of J. G. Robinson. First, during World War I, his 2-8-0 was chosen by the Ministry of Munitions as a standard for working on the military railways behind the Western Front. Then, after grouping, two of Robinson's designs – the 4-6-2 passenger tank, and 4-4-0 'Director' class – were chosen for further construction by the L.N.E.R. Lastly, and perhaps most remarkable of all, in 1945, when Sir Nigel Gresley's successor, Edward Thompson, was drawing up a schedule of standard locomotives for the future requirements of the L.N.E.R. the 40-year-old Great Central 'Pom-pom' was chosen to be the future standard medium-powered goods and branch-line engine. Unfortunately for the memory of the Great Central Railway nationalization supervened, and no further engines of this class were constructed; but in 1945 there were 174 of them at work.

112 **Composite slip-brake carriage;** Great Central Railway.
Under reference 60 one of the early carriages built for the London Extension services was illustrated, in the very handsome colours then adopted. In later years a reversion was made to the varnished teak style of the old Manchester Sheffield and Lincolnshire Railway, and the accompanying picture shows a clerestory-roofed carriage of this later period. The Great Central made very extensive use of slip carriages, for giving fast services to intermediate points without stopping the main train. One of the most remarkable was that of the so-called 'Sheffield Special', which, in fierce competition with the Midland, ran non-stop from Marylebone to Sheffield, not calling even at Leicester or Nottingham. A slip-coach was detached at Leicester, covering the 103 miles from London in 105 minutes. The Great Central, like the great majority of railways using slip coaches, did not provide gangway connections to the rest of the train, so that the 'slip' itself had to be self-contained with first- and third-class compartments, lavatories, luggage space, and compartments for the slip guard at either end. An interesting example of multiple slip-coach working was to be seen on Great Central line right down to the year 1936, on the 6.20 p.m. express from Marylebone. The train ran non-stop to Leicester, but carried two slip coaches, the first detached at Finmere, whence it was conveyed forward to serve the intermediate stations of Brackley, Helmdon and Culworth, and the second at Woodford. In those later years, however, the slip coaches were of Mr. Robinson's massive elliptical-roofed later design, similar in general appearance to the coach reference 132; but the service remained the same.

113 **Bogie third-class carriage;** London Brighton and South Coast Railway.
The Brighton has sometimes been referred to as little more than a suburban railway, and now, with almost the entire mileage of the old L.B.&S.C.R. electrified on the third-rail system the vision of the management of some 60 years ago has come true. So far as train services are concerned, it is almost as convenient for a London business man to live at Brighton, as in an outer residential district of London. In these days of extreme road congestion he probably gets home quicker! Even back at the turn of the century the Brighton was a short distance main line and there was no thought of introducing corridor stock. The type of coach illustrated was in regular use up to the time of grouping, and thereafter until new stock was put on by the Southern Railway. It is true that on some later trains newer coaches with high elliptical roofs were put on. But these, too, were non-corridor. Our picture shows the two-tone colour scheme in use in the early 1900s. Memories of these coaches extends as much to the insides as to the exteriors. While most other railways decorated the interiors with attractive pictures of places served by the railway, and both the Great Western and the Midland used the beautiful photochrome prints of the period, the Brighton filled the space over the headrests with snappy advertisements. One that I always remember ran thus:

'When nights were bold
They all wore armour;
Nights hot or cold
Wear Swan's pyjamas!'

Not living anywhere on the Brighton line I never discovered what Swan's pyjamas were like; but such is the value of advertising, in that the amusing piece of doggerel so sticks in the memory.

114 Billinton's 2-6-0 express goods engine; London Brighton and South Coast Railway.

Although the Brighton Railway was above all a passenger line, there was a considerable freight traffic to and from the Continent via the Newhaven–Dieppe route. In Victorian times the celebrated superintendent William Stroudley had produced his famous small-wheeled 0-4-2 type of locomotive for the 'Grand Vitesse' continental goods service, and Billinton was following in the same tradition in 1913 when he built the first example of the 'K' class 2-6-0 for the continental traffic. At that time the 2-6-0 was coming rapidly into favour as a standard type for mixed traffic, and its success on the Great Northern and Great Western undoubtedly prompted this interesting Brighton development. Five of the 'K' class were built in 1913–14; but due to the heavy increase in traffic by the Newhaven route during the war, five further engines of the class were built in 1916. The Brighton Works had a long and cherished tradition of excellent workmanship and massive construction, and these 2-6-0s were ideal for the fast and heavy goods trains. After the war some further engines were built at Brighton, but the grouping of the railways in 1923 resulted in no further construction of them once that batch was completed. Nevertheless, they were long-lived engines, and 'saw steam out' on the continental freight workings.

115 Rebuilt non-superheater 4-4-0; Midland Railway.

In the early years of the present century R. M. Deeley, who succeeded S. W. Johnson as Locomotive Superintendent of the Midland Railway, commenced a large programme of locomotive modernization, part of which consisted of the rebuilding of many of the older 4-4-0 locomotives with large boilers. Johnson had made something of a point in having small boilers, as a means of ensuring that the engines were worked 'on a light rein' as it were, and thus with maximum economy. Deeley's reboilering, though still using saturated steam, increased the nominal capacity of the engines, though this programme of renewal was accompanied by a general re-organization of the locomotive department which fixed rigid limits for train loading. These rebuilt 4-4-0s, which were placed in No. 2 class, were limited to a maximum load of 180 tons, and a great deal of double-heading was required as a consequence. Nevertheless these rebuilt engines filled a useful gap between the passing of the Victorian era, of very small engines, on the Midland, and the era of superheater engines – albeit still of small proportions – as inaugurated by Sir Henry Fowler. The re-organization of the locomotive department was accompanied by a complete re-numbering of the stock. The small raised brass figures on the cab sides previously used were replaced by large transfer numerals on the tender, while at the same time the style of lining-out was made less ornate. But the turnout of individual engines remained as always on the Midland, immaculate.

116 David Bain's design of 'brake-first'; Midland Railway.

In 1902 there began a change in carriage design on the Midland that coincided roughly in time with the modernization of the locomotive stud. Bain, who succeeded T. G. Clayton in that year, came from the North Eastern Railway, and while he followed the handsome profile of Clayton's later clerestory carriages he came to abandon the rectangular panelling, and windows with top lights, in place of a more conventional appearance. Furthermore, the vogue of large numerals, evident on the engine tenders, also spread to the carriages, which had large figures '1' and '3' on the doors, instead of the full word 'first' and 'third'. The Bain carriages were magnificently finished both inside and out. The upholstery in both first- and third-class compartments were the finest of the day, and the exterior finish included no fewer than *seventeen* coats of paint. The ordinary carriages, as distinct from the dining and sleeping cars, were lit by compressed oil gas, and this was unfortunately the cause of two not very serious collisions becoming major disasters, through the igniting of the gas and many coaches being burnt out. Notwithstanding the tragedies of the Hawes Junction and Aisgill disasters, in 1910, and 1913 respectively, the Midland clerestory carriages both of Clayton and Bain are remembered with admiration by those who had to make long journeys in them. Our picture shows a purely Midland vehicle, as used on London–Leeds, London–Manchester and Bristol–Leeds expresses. Similar coaches were provided for the Scotch services worked jointly with the North British and with the Glasgow and South Western Railways. These carriages were lettered 'M.&N.B.' and 'M.&G.S.W.' respectively.

117 Worsdell's 'V' class Atlantic; North Eastern Railway.
The early years of the twentieth century, if not a time for any great competition in speed between the various British railways, was a time for competition in passenger amenities and in the building of very large and imposing locomotives. In retrospect one queries if such great machines were really necessary at that time; but whether necessary or not, the North Eastern Railway was certainly in the forefront of the movement, and the magnificent-looking 'Atlantic' engine shown in our picture could scarcely be bettered on the score of fine appearance. It was built at Gateshead in 1903 and was the forerunner of a class of hard-working, heavy weight-pulling machines, that had a life of more than 40 years. The inspiration for the adoption of the 'Atlantic' type was said to have come from a visit of North Eastern Railway officers to America, where they were able to witness the good work being done on the Philadelphia and Reading Railroad. But there is another story of their introduction that is amusing. When Wilson Worsdell returned from his visit to America his Chief Draughtsman, Mr. W. M. Smith, was ill. Now Smith was a most forceful personality, as well as a very sound engineer, and when he was restored to health, and returned to his office the story goes that he was extremely annoyed that the big new 'Atlantic' had been designed in his absence and orders given for its construction. Wilson Worsdell had a very difficult hour, listening to all the reasons why the engine should not be built. But events had progressed too far for any alteration to be made, and eventually the 'V' class engines proved to be good, hard-working machines, though somewhat heavy on coal.

118 Elliptical-roofed corridor carriage; North Eastern Railway.
In referring to the later Midland Railway coaching stock (reference 116) mention was made that David Bain had previously been Carriage Superintendent of the North Eastern Railway. In his time the coaching stock was mainly with clerestory roofs: a square type, as used on the Great Western, and in Clayton's earlier work on the Midland Railway, for non-corridor coaches, and an ornate bow-ended design on those coaches that were built by the North Eastern Railway for the East Coast Joint Stock. During the early years of the twentieth century Mr. H. N. Gresley, as he then was, developed an entirely new style of carriage roof on

the Great Northern Railway, using a high elliptical shape, and at the same time an elegantly curved bow-end. Carriages of this design were built for the London–Newcastle services operated jointly by the Great Northern and the North Eastern Railways, and lettered 'G.N.&N.E.'. The Gresley style influenced carriage design on the North Eastern itself, and the coach illustrated is one of a series built for the North Eastern Scotch services between Leeds and Glasgow. This provided a fast morning connection to Edinburgh and Glasgow, with connections at Edinburgh for Aberdeen and Inverness, and the fine stock run in these trains was always very much admired. Similar coaches were used on the Newcastle–Liverpool expresses run jointly with the Lancashire and Yorkshire Railway. In this case the stock was provided in equal numbers by both companies, each running complete trains.

119–124 Subsidiary Semaphore Signals.

The signals previously described and illustrated under references 103 to 106 are what are termed 'running' signals. They were used to control movements from one signal to the next, and if encountered in the danger (horizontal) position compelled a stop. In the vicinity of stations, however, many shunting and subsidiary movements are required, and where it was necessary to authorize a driver to proceed for a limited and clearly defined distance within the station or yard limits, or to back, small subsidiary semaphores were mounted on the same posts as the running signals, and below them, to authorize some restricted movement beyond a running signal that would be in the danger position. The form of such subsidiary signals was not governed by any national code of aspects. In most cases they were designed to suit the conditions existing on individual railways and as can be seen from the illustrations (references

119 to 124) they exhibited some striking differences, though not all these signals had the same function. In general the idea was to have some signals that would be not only much smaller than the standard semaphore, but quite unlike it in form, so that there would be no chance of confusion. In later years, also, some endeavour was made to avoid using red lights as the stop indication of these subsidiaries, so that when a running movement was signalled and the main arm was cleared the driver did not have to pass a red light, albeit a very small one.

Great Western Railway (reference 119)
This little arm certainly passed the test for distinctiveness from the main-line running signal. The striping was horizontal instead of vertical, and it authorized a shunt ahead, for a limited distance beyond the running signal which would be mounted on the same post. In certain localities notice boards were erected at the side of the line displaying the words LIMIT OF SHUNT.

London and South Western Railway (reference 120)
This semaphore performed the same function as that of the Great Western Railway (reference 119), and the diamond-shaped plate made it instantly distinguishable from the ordinary running signals. The London and South Western Railway also used the form of subsidiary arm shown in reference 121, for what is referred to as a 'calling on' movement, and in this respect the usage was similar on the Great Eastern Railway, which is the actual design illustrated, and also on the Highland Railway.

Great Eastern Railway (reference 121)
The function of a 'calling on' signal may best be explained by an actual instance of operation. As its name suggests, it was used to 'call on' a train, at very slow

speed, into a section that was already occupied. One could imagine a long platform being no more than partly occupied by a train, while another one was waiting at the entrance. Under strict working rules the signal at the entrance to the platform would be kept at danger, because the line between that signal, and the next one at the exit from the platform was occupied. But having stopped the second train at the entrance, time would be saved by 'calling it on', at dead slow speed into the platform, up to the limit that the line was unoccupied, so that loading, and unloading could proceed. The 'calling on' signal had in its turn to be distinctive in shape from a 'shunt' signal, because the former gave authority to proceed as far as the line was unoccupied – often until the engine of the second train almost touched buffers with the last coach of the first one – whereas the shunt signal only authorized a movement up to a certain place on the line.

Midland Railway (reference 122)
This shunt signal was, except for one detail, a miniature edition of the ordinary running signal, even to the distinctive Midland shape of the spectacle plate, and the form of the stop, that prevented the arm rising to any extent above the horizontal position. The only distinctive feature was the 'T' portion on the end, which certainly showed well on these little arms in the day time.

London Brighton and South Coast Railway (reference 123)
The use of ringed arms varied considerably on different railways, but it was certainly an excellent way of providing a distinguishable mark for a subsidiary signal. A very interesting feature of this Brighton signal is that no indication at all was provided at night when the arm was in the 'on' position. The red light of the main signal was evidently considered sufficient, without there being a sub-

sidiary red light. When the arm was lowered the white light of the oil lamp became visible, and thus there was no possible chance of any confusion with the red and green lights of the main signal.

Great Western Railway (reference 124)
This company used quite a variety of subsidiary arms, and the one illustrated in this picture was termed a 'backing' arm. It was often to be seen at the *entering* end of a station platform, facing the opposite way to the main direction of traffic. At many stations it was necessary to attach or detach vans, or small coaches, and the backing arm would be used to signal away a station pilot engine that had been used for marshalling work, or to signal the driver of a train to set his whole train back from the platform into a siding for traffic purposes.

The six examples of subsidiary signals selected for illustration are only a very few out of a great variety of types that were used on railways in the pre-grouping era. They are nevertheless sufficient to indicate the ingenuity and care taken in the steam era to safeguard and expedite the working of the traffic.

125 **The Taff Vale Railway coat of arms.**
This amazing little railway, which had such a traffic in coal that it took some 270 locomotives to work 112 miles of line (!!) originally had a coat of arms enclosing the feathers and motto of the Prince of Wales in a circlet; but this was later abandoned in favour of the remarkable affair illustrated in our picture. A humorous description of it written in 1921 by the great locomotive historian E. L. Ahrons cannot be bettered: 'There are some large railway companies in this country whose coats-of-arms are too involved to attract attention, and, on the other hand, there are other designs which one notices at once. Amongst the latter is the familiar London & North

Western's Britannia. But the Taff Vale picture puts even Britannia completely in the shade, and is evidently emblematic of the whole of Wales, though the Taff Vale occupies only a very small corner of that country. It must be the goat that does it. He is perched on the top, evidently monarch of all he surveys, and you cannot miss him, even if you try. I like that goat. I have seen him marching at the head of a famous Welsh regiment with the same air of proud defiance that he shows on the Taff Vale carriages. But the animal which accompanies the goat, placed within an oval scroll beneath him, is by no means so majestic. At first glance he looks like a screaming eagle of the American pattern, but a closer examination shows him to be intended for something else. Some years after my first acquaintance with him, I learnt that, in addition to the goat, Wales claims a heraldic dragon, and I suppose, though I am open to correction, that the Taff Vale coat of arms endeavours to depict that animal, though I hope that the real Welsh dragon is of more respectable appearance. The Taff Vale variety – genus *Draco Tonypandiensis* – is a dancing, shrieking, riotous beast, engaged in putting out his tongue at the goat and doing his utmost to disturb the stately serenity of the latter. He would even shake up a Chinaman who is popularly supposed to know something of the habits of his kind.' The whole thing is tremendous, and is fitly concluded by the unpronounceable motto beneath: *Cymru a fu Cymru a fydd*, which means 'Wales hath been and Wales shall be'.

126 Rhymney Railway coat of arms.
The Rhymney was the near neighbour and close rival of the Taff Vale in conveying coal from the mountain valleys to the Cardiff Docks for shipment, literally to all parts of the world. The pronunciation, by the way, is 'Rumney'. Great foreign railways like the Paris, Lyons and Mediterranean sent their own colliers to Cardiff to fetch the choice Welsh coals, and the Rhymney Railway on its coat of arms symbolized the great business activities of the region rather than the flamboyant national sentiments emblazoned on that of the Taff Vale. But that was typical of the intense rivalries of the railways in the valleys. It was not so much a rivalry for traffic in the boom years, for there was so much coal produced that the extreme congestion nearly brought both railways to a standstill, and the coal owners promoted yet another line to tap both the Rhondda and the Rhymney valleys, and take a proportion of the coal to a new port at Barry. The Rhymney Railway coat of arms embodied a curiosity in that it included, bottom right, the arms of Newport, which it never served. The other shield is that of the City of Cardiff. Above is a picturesque drawing of an Egyptian furnace, as introduced at Rhymney Iron Works in 1828, while the inclusion of a ship emphasizes the great importance of the export trade in coal. Altogether this was a very interesting and colourful coat of arms.

127 Cambrian Railways coat of arms.
The name of the interesting system was always used in the plural, so much so that on wagons which were not large enough for the full name, it was abbreviated to CAM.RLYS. The Cambrian, in geographical extent was much the largest independent railway in Wales, though, of course, its traffic was not to be compared with the prodigious carriers of coal in the mining valleys. The Cambrian was rather a line of mid-Wales, though curiously enough its headquarters, and locomotive and carriage works were in England, at Oswestry, Shropshire. The Cambrian was a main line, and it had several important through connections with both the Great Western and with the London and North Western. With the latter

company its principal connection was at Whitechurch, on the Shrewsbury-Crewe line, and over this route through-express services were run between Aberystwyth and Manchester. There were two different colour schemes in its coat of arms. The one included in our picture was that used on locomotives, with the central shield divided between the dragon of Wales and the rose of England. On the handsome green carriages, one of which is shown in reference 98, the background to the shield was black and the dragon and rose were on a background of orange and deep purple respectively. The surrounding garter had orange letters and cords, and above, left and right on the black ground to the shield were the letters 'C', 'R' and 'Co'.

128 Festiniog Railway coat of arms.
It is no exaggeration to write that this little narrow gauge line in North Wales has a history not only without parallel in its vicissitudes and fascinating interest; but it is a history with a significance out of all proportion to the size and traffic of the railway itself. The coat of arms now carried on locomotives and carriages includes the insignia and motto of the Prince of Wales, just as the locomotives of the Cambrian Railways carried that same insignia on their tenders. Nevertheless, while the Festiniog Railway continues to be a living symbol of Welsh enterprise and is a first-class tourist attraction today, its original purpose was the conveyance of slates, and out of the problems arising from the phenomenal growth of that traffic came the development of the articulated Fairlie double-engine, two examples of which are still at work on the line. It was on the Festiniog that the potentialities of the articulated principle were so vividly demonstrated, and although subsequent development took ways other than the original Fairlie design, the seeds were sown on the

Festiniog, and the development many years later, in the form of the Beyer-Garratt, proved to be one of the finest products of the great British export trade in steam locomotives. If ever the Festiniog Railway Company should consider adopting a different or a more elaborate coat of arms, I would suggest that slates and the articulated locomotive should find a part in it.

129 Ocean special saloon; Great Western Railway.
In years between the two world wars the attention of the Great Western Railway upon the ocean traffic at Plymouth took a new form. Whereas in the early 1900s it was a case of making record times with the mails, and beating the London and South Western, at the later period, when Southampton had become the terminus station of Cunard and White Star liners, the Great Western was strongly advocating the calling of eastbound liners at Plymouth to save English passengers the time spent in what was otherwise the normal procedure, namely of making the first European call at Cherbourg, and then crossing to Southampton. By calling at Plymouth a full day was saved on the journey from New York to London. Everything possible was done to make things attractive on the railway journey. The Ocean Specials were given preferential treatment on the line, and the coaching stock provided was of the very finest. In addition to ordinary vehicles a small number of special saloons were built with particularly luxurious accommodation, and each named after a member of the Royal Family. These coaches were built out to the maximum width permitted by the generous Great Western loading gauge – no less than 9 ft. 7 in. in overall width. They were, without much doubt, the finest vehicles available to ordinary passengers that have run on the railways of this country.

163

130 David Bain's Royal Saloon;
Midland Railway.

Unlike the railways over which frequent Royal journeys were made, such as the London and North Western, and the Great Western, the Midland did not maintain a full Royal train; but the very fine vehicle illustrated in our picture was built in 1912 for inclusion with other vehicles if a special should at times be required. It was purely for day use, and internally contained a main saloon with a smoking-room and a ladies retiring-room at either end. Presumably one did not smoke in the main saloon! Although not built until 1912 its interior decoration contained all the rich ornamentation and upholstery characteristics of the Edwardian era. Royal journeys on the Midland Railway may not have been very frequent but, as can well be imagined, when the opportunity came the Company did things in style. The saloon would be marshalled in a train of David Bain's finest clerestory carriages, finished as only Derby could finish coaches in those spacious days when even the ordinary 'thirds' had seventeen coats of paint. The engine used also had special treatment. It was not enough to select a specially good one and burnish it to the last degree. For the occasion it became completely anonymous. The large number on the tender was painted out, and instead of the beautiful Midland coat of arms on the cab sides (see reference 24) the Royal Cipher and crown was substituted.

131 Saloon Carriage No. 1; Furness Railway.

Although it was no more than a local line, the Furness Railway had a reputation of doing things in good style, and the handsome saloon shown in our picture is a good example. In its early days the railway had its rather primitive coaching stock finished in a nondescript style of varnished wood, without any lining, as illustrated in Sir James Ramsden's inspection car

(reference 10). But as the railway got into its stride and began to develop that high sense of publicity and purpose that came hand in hand with the vast development of the traffic centred upon Barrow, the old style of coach painting was changed for the distinctive two-tone royal blue and white shown in the picture. This harmonized remarkably well with the engines in iron-ore red. In the ordinary way Furness carriages did not work far beyond the confines of their own system. The through services to other parts were usually worked by 'foreign' carriages, London and North Western for Euston, and Midland to Leeds and St. Pancras. But the Furness carriages, quite apart from the vehicles like special saloons, were very good and would have been an excellent advertisement for the company wherever they went. In World War I the two-tone colour scheme was abandoned, and the coaches painted royal blue over-all, though retaining their gold lining, and the Company's beautiful coat of arms, see reference 175.

132 Open Saloon 'third'; Great Central Railway.

In its period of development, following the completion of the London Extension in 1899, the Great Central was using every known device to attract more traffic, and much was being done to advertise the attractions of what was then still a new route, by the running of attractive and extraordinarily cheap excursions. One of the most remarkable was an Easter excursion from Manchester to Plymouth, worked throughout by a Great Central engine. In 1910 under the direction of Mr. J. G. Robinson some fine new saloon carriages were built specially for the excursion traffic, at Dukinfield Works. These had doors only at the ends, and a characteristic feature, not at all usual then in British practice, was the use of large, deep windows each covering one section of the car. The interior was divided equally into smoking and non-smoking sections, and each had seats for 32 passengers, with 8 tables for four at each side of the centre gangway. The idea of providing tables opposite every seat was an extension of the rather exclusive dining car idea of the Midland and of the Great Northern in which dining passengers were a race apart, as it were. But on the Great Central here was the same principle applied to very cheap fare excursion travel. Externally the coaches were attractively finished with narrow vertical panelling in varnished teak, and the coach bodies built out to the maximum permitted by the loading gauge.

133 Corridor third-class carriages; Great Eastern Railway.

The enterprise of the Great Eastern Railway in the early years of the twentieth century knew no bounds. Before the end of the Victorian era, although the lengths of run were short compared with those of the great trunk lines to the north and west of England, the Great Eastern had introduced restaurant cars on the Cromer expresses, though at first unconnected with the rest of the train. But full corridor trains soon followed and the Company reached the height of its holiday traffic prestige in the working of the celebrated Norfolk Coast Express which ran non-stop over the $130\frac{1}{4}$ miles from Liverpool Street to North Walsham. This was a train solely for the Norfolk Coast. Large centres like Colchester, Ipswich and even Norwich were passed without stopping. The minimum load of the train was one of 12 coaches, of which 8 went to Cromer, 2 to Sheringham, and 2 to Mundesley. The coach illustrated formed part of the very fine and uniformly styled trains of 1907, and was used in the summer service each year from July to September. During the winter months there was not so great a demand for bulk travel from London to the Norfolk coast. There were times,

of course, when extra vehicles had to be added to the regular set, sometimes at the last minute, and then it was not always possible to preserve the fine uniformity of the train. Older coaches, sometimes even six-wheelers were used for 'reinforcing' – as the railway operating term goes. But uniformity or not, the Norfolk Coast Express was an outstanding railway operating achievement.

134 Twelve-wheeled dining car; Midland joint Scotch stock.

The Midland Railway, unlike its rivals on the East Coast and West Coast routes to Scotland, had to feed two entirely different routes north of Carlisle, in providing through-trains to Edinburgh and to Glasgow. It is true that both East Coast and West Coast routes served both Scottish cities as well; but their operating arrangements were simpler. Trains for both Edinburgh and Glasgow, by West Coast took the Caledonian route out of Carlisle, and the bifurcation did not take place till Carstairs. On the East Coast route, one travelled through Edinburgh to reach Glasgow. On the Midland route, for many of the services, separate trains for Edinburgh and Glasgow were run throughout from London, each having their own restaurant car, or sleeping cars in the case of night journeys. In the early days of Clayton's very fine bogie coaches it was difficult, at a first glance, to distinguish the dining cars from ordinary vehicles, as both had the small windows traditional from the earliest days. But on the great majority of Midland trains, Anglo-Scottish or otherwise, the dining cars were the only vehicles in the trains to carry roof-boards. Our picture shows a typical dining car of the period before 1890, when Clayton had temporarily abandoned the clerestory roof. The car is one allocated to the joint service with the Glasgow and South Western Railway, and is labelled 'London St. Pancras and Glasgow St. Enoch'.

135 Non-corridor bogie composite carriage; Somerset and Dorset Joint Railway.

The picture to which this note refers has been chosen not so much to represent the Somerset and Dorset Joint Railway, as to be typical of the ordinary English railway carriage of the early Edwardian era. It is relatively simple and unpretentious in appearance, yet designed to provide comfort and space, if not the height of luxury in both first- and third-class compartments. It made tolerable the jog-trot of the ordinary through-trains between Bath and Bournemouth, and being non-corridor it provided more seating per unit of dead weight than would have been possible in a corridor vehicle and any reduction in dead weight was worth having on a line so severely graded as the Somerset and Dorset. In exterior design, if not in its livery, the coach bears a strong resemblance to the standard non-corridor coaches of the London and South Western Railway. This was no coincidence; for while the Midland Railway, as one of the two joint owners provided the locomotives, the South Western was responsible for the coaches, other than the corridor coaches of the Midland line which worked through to Bournemouth from the north. Though they were no more than local train stock these Somerset and Dorset non-corridors were beautifully finished externally with full lining-out, and the Company's coat of arms twice on each side.

136 Open 'brake-third' corridor carriage; Lancashire and Yorkshire Railway.

Much of the intense passenger business of the Lancashire and Yorkshire Railway was of a short distance nature. The policy of the Company was to run relatively short trains, and many of them. The express trains were sharply timed between the many intermediate stops, and on the purely Lancashire and Yorkshire service

between Liverpool, Manchester, Bradford and Leeds, the 'set' trains consisted of only 3 coaches. But the L.&Y.R. combined with the North Eastern to run an excellent dining train between Liverpool and Newcastle, for which the two companies provided a six-coach corridor train on alternate days. I may add that the North Eastern operated a similar service with the rival of the L.&Y.R. – also serving Manchester and Liverpool, with a through dining-car train from Newcastle. This, of course, was over the London and North Western route and served Leeds and Huddersfield intermediately, while the L.&Y.R. served Wakefield. Our picture shows one of the fine carriages built for the L.&Y.R. Liverpool – Newcastle service. The complete train, which included separate dining cars for first- and third-class passengers, accommodated 51 first and 226 third class. It was a very popular service, and frequently loaded almost to full capacity. In Lancashire particularly there was a great affection for the 'Lanky', as the line was popularly called. The local people felt it was their own railway, managed by local men, and they preferred it to the London and North Western, which some people felt was too big and widespread a concern to give proper attention to the particular needs of Lancashire. The status of the L.&Y.R. was nevertheless a national rather than a local one, and when the two companies amalgamated in 1921, it is significant that some of the most important posts in the new combine went to 'Lanky' men.

137 Churchward's 'County' class 4-4-0; Great Western Railway.

It was in 1901 that G. J. Churchward drew up his celebrated plan for the complete standardization of the locomotive stock of the G.W.R. The main-line engines were to consist of no more than six classes, all with two outside cylinders, and inside Stephenson link motion. The 'County' class 4-4-0 of 1904 was one of these standard designs. It was built to work over those sections of the line where 4-6-os were precluded from running because of weight restrictions; but these 4-4-0 engines were also on main routes for which 4-6-os could not be spared, on account of more arduous duties elsewhere. In consequence the 'Counties' were to be seen on the West to North route from Bristol to Shrewsbury via the Severn Tunnel; on the Bristol and Birmingham route via Cheltenham and Stratford-on-Avon, and on the main line to Worcester via Oxford. They were fast and efficient engines, though somewhat rough riding; and although they had relatively small boilers they steamed well, and did excellent work on the heavy gradients of the line through the Welsh border country. Their names covered all the counties served by the Great Western Railway in England and Wales, and also many counties in the south and west of Ireland which were reached by the Great Southern and Western Railway working in connection with Irish boat service via Fishguard and Rosslare.

138 **70-ft. Corridor carriage;** Great Western Railway.
In his great programme of rolling-stock modernization Churchward not only aimed to build more powerful and more efficient locomotives but designed carriages that should have a minimum of dead weight for the number of passengers carried. The Dean clerestory carriages were excellent examples of design for their day, and the all-third coaches weighed 24 tons, while providing seating for 54 passengers. In his new 70-ft. coaches of the early 1900s, Churchward provided seating for 80 passengers, in coaches having a tare weight of only 33 tons. The ratio of dead weight to number of passengers seated was reduced even though the new carriages were consider-

ably more spacious and generally more modern in their design. The first examples were painted in the traditional G.W.R. chocolate and cream livery; but as a measure of economy this was soon changed to all brown, and then to the handsome lake colour shown in our picture, which remained the Great Western standard until 1923. One drawback to the use of such lengthy carriages was that they could not be used on certain routes where the structural clearances were below those of lines at one time laid on the broad gauge. They could not be used on the West to North expresses, either by the Severn Tunnel route or on that via Stratford-on-Avon. A minor restriction in the West of England also prevented their being used on the Ilfracombe branch.

139 **Hawksworth's 'County' class 4-6-0 of 1945;** Great Western Railway.
The 'County' class engine of 1945 was the final development of the classic Churchward two-cylinder locomotive, with inside Stephenson link motion. It included a number of features pointing towards the future development of Swindon locomotive practice, particularly in its use of the very high boiler pressure, with a copper firebox, of 280 lb. per sq. in. This second 'County' class on the G.W.R. was, like the first one, built against restrictions in weight. It was originally hoped to use the same boiler as that on the 'Castle' class, but the weight came out too heavy, and the boiler used was to a new design. The locomotives were built just at the end of World War II when materials were in short supply, and it was difficult to get new tooling done. Because of this it was found convenient to use the flanging blocks that had been made during the war when Swindon Works were building, by Government order, Stanier 2-8-0 goods engines of the L.M.S. type. The 'Counties' were fast and powerful

engines, but their development was not fully completed by the time the railways were nationalized. Then other policies were adopted on a national scale. The 'Counties' did well on the heavy gradients of the Cornish main line, and especially so on the steeply graded route of the north main line between Wolverhampton and Chester. In all 30 were built and their names were taken from English and Welsh counties. There were no Irish names in the Hawksworth series.

140 Bow-ended corridor carriage of 1947; Great Western Railway.
When F. W. Hawksworth succeeded C. B. Collett as Chief Mechanical Engineer of the G.W.R. in 1941, it was soon clear that while many old Swindon traditions would continue in others changes could be expected. After the end of the war an entirely new style in main-line carriage stock was evolved. The Churchward practice of using 70-ft. coaches for heavy main-line working wherever possible had largely disappeared before the war, and after the special 'Centenary Riviera' coaches of 1935 (reference 158) a style very similar to that currently in vogue on the L.M.S.R. was adopted, with steel panelling, and large deep windows. After the war Hawksworth developed this style, but introduced the bow-ended roofs that had been so marked a characteristic of Great Northern and L.N.E.R. practice. The new coaches, which were not restricted by length in their sphere of operation, were thus a blend of L.M.S.R. and L.N.E.R. practice, while retaining the beautiful chocolate and cream livery of the Great Western. Their introduction was to a large extent piecemeal and there were no new dining cars to match. Luxuries had to give way to necessities in those years of austerity. Trains like the Cornish Riviera Express continued to be a mixture of old and new stock, and it was not until the Bristolian express was restored to its full pre-war

speed in 1954 that a complete seven-coach train of the Hawksworth carriages was seen in regular operation.

141–144 Distant Signal Arms.
The function of a 'distant' signal in semaphore days was to provide drivers with ample warning that they were approaching a signal at which a dead stop might be required. As the stopping distance from a speed of 60 to 70 m.p.h. might be more than half-a-mile these 'distant' signals had to be located some distance before the 'stop' signals and some method of distinguishing them from signals at which a stop was compulsory was desirable. Until the 1920–30 decade the danger position of both distant and stop arms was indicated by a red light at night, though the arms themselves were distinguished by a fish-tailed end. Later, an amber light became the standard night indication of a distant signal in the caution position. Prior to that, one of the few attempts to distinguish home and distant signals at night was the Coligny-Welch illuminated indicator placed alongside the lamp as shown in our picture of a London-Brighton and South Coast distant signal arm (reference 141). At that time the painting of the arm was the same as for a stop signal, namely red and white, though the white band took the form of a chevron, in conformity with the shape of the end of the arm. In localities where track alignment, or other local conditions made it undesirable to indicate the existence of a clear road through the station ahead by exhibiting a distant arm in the clear position, 'fixed' distant signals were used, and an example of this, on the London and North Western Railway is shown in our picture (reference 143). This signified a permanent state of caution over the line ahead. This illustration also shows the distinctive L.N.W.R. type of semaphore arm which unlike most of its contemporaries was a steel pressing, with longitudinal corrugations to give stiffness.

These arms were made in the locomotive works at Crewe. Reference 142 shows the earlier form of distant arm used on the Midland Railway, when the front face of the blade was painted red, with a white disc, and the back was white with a black horizontal stripe from end to end. The back of the blade was divided equally into three sections painted white, black and white respectively. Of these different versions of the distant signal arm the last (reference 144) shows the final design used on the Great Western Railway, when amber had been standardized as the night indication of the 'caution' aspect. At the same time, distinction in the day-time indication was made, not only in the use of the fishtail end to the arm but by painting the blade yellow, with a black chevron. The latest Great Western semaphore arms were made from steel pressings, but of a considerably simpler design than that of the London and North Western Railway. Stiffness was achieved by means of a simple flanging of the edges, keeping the face of the blade completely flat.

145 **Tall Semaphore Signals;** Great Western Railway.
This illustration provides an interesting case where two pairs of semaphore arms are used on the same post co-acting with one another. A description of the actual location will make it clear why this form of construction was adopted. The line is on a slight left-hand curve, and the speed of express trains was high. To give long-sighting over the top of the station buildings the main arms had to be fixed high; but as such they would have been almost impossible to see from the guard's stance when giving the 'right-away' to a stopping train from the rear end of the platform. Co-acting arms were therefore necessary; but owing to local conditions and considerations of the sighting from the footplate the signal post had to be

placed as close as possible to the track. A special design of arm was used, in which nothing projected beyond the right-hand side of the post. This design of co-acting arm, in a main running signal, is a greatly enlarged version of the mechanism used in the shunt arm (reference 119), though in this case with standard painting. This form of arm, which was used in a number of localities where clearances were limited, enabled the post to be located a good 12 in. nearer to the running lines than would otherwise have been the case. The co-acting arm was identical in size and painting to the standard 4-ft. running arm, while in the assembly shown in reference 145, the arms at the top of the post were the standard 5-ft. arms.

146 **Tall Semaphore Signals;** London and North Western Railway.
The need to provide the earliest 'advanced information' of the state of the line ahead was well recognized on all railways where the schedules demanded fast running, and the London and North Western Railway more perhaps than any other administration carried this principle to an extreme extent in providing signals of exceptional height, that could be seen from long distances away against a 'sky' background. Posts of 50 ft. and 60 ft. were common, and there were a few as high as 70 ft. In certain cases co-acting arms were used lower down the post, but the example shown in our picture is representative of standard practice on quadruple tracked sections of line. First of all, the signals relating to the fast and slow lines were distinguished by those of the latter being fitted with a ring. Some companies used ringed arms only for subsidiary purposes, and others, like the Great Western, used them only in sidings. But the North Western used them for running movements on the main line, where there were fast and slow lines alongside. Another characteristic of the

L.N.W.R. was to place all these tall signals at the left-hand side of the line. Thus between Roade and the approaches to London, a distance of nearly 60 miles, the signals for the up-fast line would have to be read across two intervening tracks, as the sequence of running lines on this section, from left to right seen from the engine was: 'Up Slow'; 'Down Slow'; 'Up Fast'; 'Down Fast'.

147 Large-boilered 'Claughton' class locomotive; London Midland and Scottish Railway.

When C. J. Bowen-Cooke was planning a 'super' express passenger engine for the London and North Western Railway, in 1910, by using four cylinders all driving on to one axle he hoped, by the elimination of all hammer-blow effect on the track, to be able to use a considerably heavier load per axle that had hitherto been permitted by the civil engineer. But Bowen-Cooke was in advance of his time, and it was dead weight and the effect of unbalancing that governed the civil engineer's judgment, and as originally built the 'Claughton' class engines had to have smaller boilers than were originally planned. In 1924, however, after Bowen-Cooke had died, and the L.N.W.R. had become part of the huge L.M.S.R. system, the work of the Bridge Stress Committee showed that the original contention had been correct. Locomotives that were scientifically balanced were allowed to have considerably greater axle loads than previously permitted, and a number of the 'Claughtons' were rebuilt with much larger boilers. The engines had then been displaced from the heaviest express duties by the new 'Royal Scot' class; but the rebuilt engines were used to great advantage on the Irish Mails, on the Manchester expresses working over the North Staffordshire line, and on the Liverpool and Manchester Scotch expresses between Preston and Carlisle. Engine No. 5986

shown in our picture was one of those stationed at Preston for the last-mentioned duty.

148 Open-third saloon carriage; London Midland and Scottish Railway.

In the last years of the Midland Railway, when David Bain had been succeeded by R. W. Reid, as Carriage and Wagon Superintendent, the long tradition of clerestory-roofed carriages was ended, and coaches generally similar to the final Bain design, but with high elliptical roofs were introduced on the principal express services. At the time of grouping R. W. Reid became Carriage and Wagon Superintendent of the L.M.S.R. and the Midland influence was naturally strongest in formulating the designs of new carriages. Except for dining cars, the Midland had previously used none save compartment stock – unlike the Great Northern and the Great Central which had included a number of open saloons in the make-up of many trains. But in the new era the L.M.S.R., while continuing to build compartment corridor stock, very similar in outward appearance – as well as in colour – to the final Midland designs, also introduced the open saloon type of carriage, with tables for four on each side of the gangway. These had the advantage that they could be used simply as saloons, but also as third-class dining cars. In some of the new trains used soon after the grouping an entirely separate eight-wheeled kitchen car was run, marshalled between the first- and the third-class dining car. On large and important trains, such as 'The Royal Scot' and 'The Merseyside Express', additional open-third saloons were included, apart from those reserved particularly for dining.

149 Rebuilt 'Lord Nelson' class 4-6-0; Southern Railway.

When O. V. S. Bulleid succeeded Maunsell as Chief Mechanical Engineer of the Southern Railway he made a number of striking changes, both to the design and to the appearance of some of the existing locomotives. The 'Lord Nelson' class in its original form had been no more than partly successful. The boiler was not over-free in steaming, and the cylinder and valve design although permitting of very fast running on occasions, did not develop a very high output of power. Although no external change was apparent, the cylinders were completely redesigned; but the most striking external change was made to the chimney. Instead of the previous single blast-pipe of conventional design, Bulleid substituted the five-nozzle multiple blast-pipe designed by the French engineer Lemaitre, and this needed a chimney of much greater diameter. This change, combined with the redesign of the cylinders, put the 'Lord Nelson' class in the very front rank of British locomotive practice. Perhaps even more startling to the eye was the change in style of painting. In the place of the quiet, almost sombre, olive green of Maunsell's day Bulleid painted the Southern express locomotives in a vivid malachite green, which made them as spectacular to see as their performance became under his changes in technical detail.

150   Standard corridor coach, Bulleid era; Southern Railway.

Bulleid applied himself no less energetically to the matter of main-line carriage design on the Southern Railway. With the object of eliminating the cost of painting he made some experiments with plastic-sided luggage vans, and in an attempt to convey more passengers in the suburban rush hours he built for experiment some double-decker trains. Neither of these experiments was successful; but in the development of standard main-line corridor stock he built some fine new train sets for the Bournemouth service in 1947. These trains were built in six-coach sets, and it is the 'brake-third' of one of these sets that is illustrated in our picture.

These trains were also finished in malachite green to match the locomotives; but quite apart from painting some interesting details of their construction may be noted. In the compartment stock in particular the slenderness of the side walls was evident, arising from the all-welded body framing, eliminating the need for heavy uprights, and the laying of plates, and so on, one above the other in building up. Externally the finish was completely smooth, and while lovers of the historic may perhaps regret the passing of the traditional form of carriage construction with stout timber bodies and elaborately lined panelling, as an expression of modern techniques the Bulleid carriages were very fine.

151-4   Auto-trains.

The problem of securing economic operation of country branch lines was receiving the attention of many railway managements in the early 1920s. Until that time the general practice had been to use small locomotives that had been displaced from more important duties, and to make up the branch trains from equally obsolescent rolling stock. The passengers had to put up with cramped and out-of-date carriages, and the locomotive working in many cases was neither smart nor efficient. Then there developed the idea of the self-contained auto-train, or steam rail motor cars, as they were sometimes called. Our pictures show some variations of this principle, which was to have a small steam locomotive of modern design and a coach mounted on the same frame, to work one unit. In some cases the engine was designed powerful enough to haul a trailer, if necessary. But in all cases a commodious carriage of modern design was provided, and the smart turnout make an attractive ensemble. The Furness Railway rail motor (reference 151) was typical of the type using a vertical boiler and a roomy driving cab at the front of the unit. It was designed to haul a smart four-wheeled trailer, and curiously enough both motor coach and trailer were unusual in Furness Railway coaching stock practice in having clerestory roofs. It was used at various times on the short branches running from the main line into the heart of Lakeland, and was very popular in connection with the numerous circular tours by rail, coach and steamer organized by the Furness Railway. One of these branches ran from Ulverston to Lakeside station, at the foot of Windermere, and the second ran from Foxfield, up steep gradients to Coniston. These auto-trains looked very smart in the white and royal blue livery, though for reasons to be [mentioned later they had a relatively short life. On the Great Northern Railway rail motors of a different type were constructed for light branch working. Our illustration shows a combined unit designed for the Edgware branch. Here again the locomotive and carriage were mounted on a single frame, but the locomotive had a boiler of the orthodox type, and the driver and fireman worked from a normal locomotive footplate, albeit rather a small and cramped one. The carriage was a large affair, built to main-line standards, and by painting the locomotive green and finishing the coach in varnished teak, another very attractive-looking unit was produced, see reference 152. The Lancashire and Yorkshire Railway became quite an extensive user of rail motor cars and at one time no fewer than 18 of them were at work. They were introduced at various times between 1906 and 1911, and some of the engines lasted until 1948. These L.&Y.R. rail motors were more successful, and more long-lived than most of their contemporaries because the engines and carriages were readily detachable from the others, although coupled into a single unit for operating. The coach unit was mounted on an ordinary coach bogie at the rear

end, and at the forward end it was secured to the engine by an extension girder. Engines and coach units could be interchanged and this eliminated the disadvantages of the single-unit type, like the Great Northern, in that an engine needing repair did not necessarily put the auto-train out of commission, as another engine unit was available to couple to the coach. For serving intermediate places, with the least possible expenditure on new equipment, a number of 'halts', without platforms were established, and to enable passengers to descend in comfort, retractable steps were fitted on the coaches. As our picture (reference 153) shows, engines and coaches were painted in the standard Lancashire and Yorkshire style. Some rail motor cars introduced at about the same time had the engine units painted in the carriage colours. This was the case on the South Eastern and Chatham, and on the Glasgow and South Western Railways. The Great Western, as might be expected from its multitude of country branch lines, was a very large user of steam rail motor cars, and by the year 1908 no fewer than 99 motor coaches, and many trailers, were at work. The standard types developed after early experiments were built externally in style of the latest main-line corridor stock, in two lengths, 70 ft. and 59 ft. 6 in. Our picture shows a 70 ft. motor coach, to haul a 59 ft. 6 in. trailer. Internally, like all the rail motor cars illustrated under references 151–154, the coaches were of the open saloon type, one class only, but extremely comfortable. I have the most vivid recollection of these cars in their hey-day, because I frequently travelled on one working on the branch from Reading to Basingstoke as a very junior schoolboy returning from Reading West station to Mortimer. They worked all over the G.W.R. system, frequently being used to provide stopping trains, or feeder services, on the main lines, between the running of fast expresses. An interesting example was to be seen in the Chippenham and Bath districts in the 1920s. Rail motor cars were used on the Chippenham–Calne branch, and their workings were also dovetailed in with the main-line trains. For example the 4.15 p.m. Plymouth express from Paddington slipped a coach at Chippenham. This was then attached as trailer to a rail motor car, and the coach that had been hauled down from London at express speed was then taken forward to Bath behind a rail motor stopping at all stations, and providing an excellent fast service from London to roadside stations like Corsham, Box, and Bathampton. The over-riding disadvantage of the self-contained rail motor car like those used on the Great Western was that the slightest defect would put both an engine and a coach out of service, and for this reason the integrally mounted loco-motives were removed, and small tank engines of standard design used to haul the trailer cars.

155 The 'Maid of Morven' observation car; Caledonian Railway.

It was not until comparatively recent years that the scenic beauties of some sections of the British railways were exploited for tourist traffic. The London and North Western and Cambrian Railways built observation cars for working on certain routes in North Wales, and the North British put saloon carriages with large windows on to the West Highland line. But one of the finest cars ever built specially for a scenic route was the Pull-man observation car worked over the Caledonian line between Glasgow and Oban. The Pullman cars running in Scotland were used as restaurant cars on ordinary trains, rather than working in the English style as vehicles in which passengers travelled for the entire journey on payment of a small supple-

ment. In Scotland they were operated on a number of Caledonian routes, and there was one over the Highland line between Perth and Aviemore. All these cars were named after ladies famous in Scottish history, such as Mary Seton and Flora Macdonald. The beautiful observation car working on the Oban line was named *Maid of Morven*, and as our picture shows it was remarkable for the huge curved windows at the rear, extending almost from floor to ceiling. It was a wonderful experience to traverse the full length of the Oban line in this car, and to watch the gradual passage of magnificent mountain scenery. Once the Highland proper was entered, at Callander, there was no fast running and the journey could be enjoyed at leisure.

156 'Waverley route' sleeping car; M.&N.B. Joint Scotch Stock.

The operation of the through-express service between London St. Pancras and Edinburgh Waverley dates from 1876, the year in which the famous Settle and Carlisle route was opened. At first the sleeping accommodation on the night trains was provided in American type Pullman cars, but in later years the 'Mid-land and North British' joint stock, lettered 'M.&N.B.' was of standard Mid-land design and built at Derby carriage works. These cars had the standard low clerestory roofs, and were uniform in profile with the beautiful carriages form-ing the rest of the trains. Prior to World War I there were two night trains in each direction between St. Pancras and Edinburgh, and for a short time after the war this lavish facility was restored. But after the formation of the L.M.S.R., the night service over the Waverley route, via Hawick and Galashiels, was reduced to one sleeping-car express in each direction. After grouping, when new sleeping cars were required for this service they were built at Wolverton, to the latest London and North Western design as provided for the West Coast Joint Stock, and it is one of these cars that is shown in our picture. They were magnificently equipped and the external finish was, of course, in the standard L.M.S. style. It was nevertheless unusual to see a vehicle of L.N.W.R. design lettered 'M.&N.B.'.

157 The Coronation Observation Car; London and North Eastern Railway.

To mark the coronation of King George VI the L.N.E.R. put on a very fast after-noon service making the journey between London and Edinburgh in the unpre-cedented time of 6 hours, for the run of 392¾ miles. The streamlined 'A4' Pacific engines were used, as on the very success-ful Silver Jubilee service (references 159, 160), but Sir Nigel Gresley added to the Coronation trains the very distinctive 'beaver-tail' streamlined observation cars. The shape of these cars was not just a publicity 'stunt'; the form provided for a very smooth effect at the tail end, elimin-ating all the eddies and turbulence that exists in the immediate rear of a fast train. And the Coronation, like the Silver Jubilee did at times travel very fast indeed! On my first journey with the Coronation we attained a speed of 106 m.p.h. During the winter months the observation cars were not run, as almost the entire journey was made in darkness; but during the summer it was a delightful experience to ride in these cars, and to see all the incidentals of a busy railway journey receding rapidly from one's view. The coaches of the Coronation train were finished in two very pleasing shades of blue: Cambridge blue for the upper panels, and Garter blue for the bodies. The five locomotives originally allocated to the working of this train were also painted Garter blue, and this later became the standard colour for all the streamlined 'A4' Pacifics.

158 'The Centenary Riviera' stock; Great Western Railway.

In 1935 the Great Western Railway celebrated the hundredth anniversary of its incorporation. Because of the grouping of the railways in 1923, and of national-ization in 1948, no other railway in Great Britain will ever achieve the distinction of operating, under the same name, for 100 years or more. Naturally the event was made the occasion of many special celebrations. It was a time of steady evolution and a time when some old traditions were being discarded, and this trend was seen particularly in the new trains built at Swindon Works for the 'Cornish Riviera Express' service. The Great Western called itself 'The Holiday Line', and at that time there was a sub-stantial all-the-year-round traffic to Devon and Cornwall. The 'Cornish Riviera Express' was unquestionably the 'flagship' of the passenger services of the Company, and the new carriages were of special design, built to the maximum width permitted by the loading gauge. On routes which had been 'broad gauge' in earlier days the loading gauge was more generous than elsewhere, and advantage was taken of this to provide carriages of exceptional width and com-fort. Their use had to be restricted to routes where the loading gauge was wide, and on the sole bar there was a notice: NOT TO RUN OVER THE EASTERN OR WESTERN VALLEYS NORTH OF WOLVERHAMPTON OR BE-TWEEN LITTLE MILL JCT. AND MAINDEE JCT.

159–160 Britain's first streamlined engine and train; London and North Eastern Railway.

The introduction of the high-speed streamlined service between London and Newcastle in the autumn of 1935 was one of the truly outstanding events in British railway history. Sir Nigel Gresley was much interested in the working of the two-car high-speed railcar service introduced in Germany between Berlin and Hamburg, and some consideration was given to a similar service between London and Newcastle. But it was found that a far better train, with the usual lavish passenger accommodation could be provided with ordinary steam locomotives than with diesel-electric railcars of German design. Some high-speed trial runs were made with standard Gresley 'Pacific' engines, and the decision was made to introduce a high-speed train of limited coach formation to provide a four-hour service between London and Newcastle. A study of L.N.E.R. 'Pacific' performance in relation to more recent practice both in Great Britain and abroad suggested that improvements in design could be made with advantage, particularly in view of the continuous running at speeds of 75 to 90 m.p.h. needed with the new train. Furthermore, having regard to the special nature of the service, and the publicity that would undoubtedly be attached to it, it was decided that the locomotives should be streamlined externally. It was the year of the Silver Jubilee of King George Vs reign, and the train itself was named 'The Silver Jubilee'. Also Sir Nigel Gresley decided that instead of finishing engine and train in the standard L.N.E.R. colours – attractive and traditional though they were – the whole train, engines and coaches alike would be 'silver', with the coaches having stainless steel lettering on the sides. The combined effect of the streamlined exterior and the unusual painting was startling and from its first appearance the class 'A4' Pacific caught popular fancy to an extent unparalleled by any other new locomotive. It provided the silver streamlined link between London and Newcastle, and so 'Silver Link' the first engine was named. Four engines of the class were built, and the others were *Quicksilver, Silver King* and *Silver Fox*. If the appearance of the engine was startling,

even more so was its performance. On its trial run it attained a maximum speed of $112\frac{1}{2}$ m.p.h., and showed it could climb the long gradients on the route at a steady speed of 80 m.p.h. This was perhaps more important than the very high maximum, because it meant that a steady, uniformly-high speed could be maintained throughout. The original train consisted of 7 coaches, all of which included the principle of articulation, which Sir Nigel Gresley had very successfully used in his standard main-line corridor stock and dining cars. For example the dining cars of 'The Silver Jubilee', like those of 'The Flying Scotsman' and other trains, were assembled in a triple articulated set, with only four bogies under the three bodies, of first-class saloon, third-class saloon, and kitchen. This not only reduced the weight considerably, but with the jointing of the bodies over one bogie produced very smooth riding. 'The Silver Jubilee' had two 2-car twin coaches, and a triple articulated dining-car set. Our picture shows one of the 2-car sets, with the name of the train on the end corridor connection.

161 **Stanier streamlined Pacific;** London Midland and Scottish Railway. In the coronation year of King George VI, 1937, the L.M.S.R., like the L.N.E.R. built special trains for the Anglo-Scottish service, and while the L.N.E.R. named their train simply 'The Coronation', and decked it in two shades of blue, Cambridge and Garter, the L.M.S.R. in recognition of the names of their existing Scottish services – Royal Scot, Midday Scot, and Night Scot – named their train the Coronation Scot. When first introduced the engines and coaches of the Coronation Scot were painted in a dark blue like that of the Caledonian Railway locomotives in days before the more familiar bright blue was adopted. In 1939, however, when more locomotives of

the so-called 'Princess-Coronation' class were authorized, five were built in the original streamlined style and five non-streamlined. All were named after Duchesses, but the new streamlined engines were finished in standard L.M.S.R. 'red', with gold stripes, instead of the dark blue. One of the new engines, No. 6229 *Duchess of Hamilton* was selected to represent the L.M.S.R. at Chicago World Fair, which was to be held in the summer of 1939, and in view of the special nature of the visit to the U.S.A. the number and name of this new engine were exchanged with that of the original streamliner, No. 6220 *Coronation*. The latter engine, still in blue livery, ran for some considerable time as 6229 *Duchess of Hamilton*. Further engines of the 'Duchess' class were built from 1939 onwards and named after cities. These were streamlined, and our picture shows the first of the new batch, the *City of Birmingham*.

162 'Coronation Scot' stock for New York World's Fair.

The visit of the L.M.S.R. locomotive and train to the U.S.A. in 1939 was made the occasion of quite an extensive tour of the eastern railways, with the train travelling under its own steam, and coaches included in the formation were not representative of the 'Coronation Scot' service as normally operated between Euston and Glasgow, but representative of the different types of rolling stock worked on both day and night trains at that time. It included a sleeping car, and a special buffet lounge. Hauled by the red streamlined engine named *Coronation* specially for the tour, the train from landing at Baltimore visited Washington, Philadelphia, Pittsburgh, Cincinnati, St. Louis, Chicago, Detroit, Cleveland, Buffalo, Albany, Boston and, finally, to New York, for exhibition at the World's Fair. In the course of this tour the train travelled over nine different

American railways. But the Fair lasted until October 1, and by that time Britain was at war with Germany. Engine and train were thus marooned in the U.S.A. Arrangements were made to get the engine back to this country, where it was urgently needed for the wartime traffic. But the coaches remained in America for the whole of the war. In the U.S.A. railwaymen and railway enthusiasts came to calling the marooned train 'The Refugee Scot'!

163 Great Western Railway coat of arms.

The Great Western Railway, as incorporated in 1835, was no more than a line connecting Bristol with London. I have purposely put the two cities in that order, because the origin of the project lay at the western end, and it was, appropriately, in Bristol that some of the major functions in connection with the centenary celebrations in 1935 took place. The Great Western 'coat of arms' thus consisted of nothing more than the arms of London and Bristol. There was perhaps an even greater significance in this very simple device, in that originally very little consideration was given to any intermediate business, and many towns that might have been served were by-passed in the interests of having a straight, direct route suitable for making fast time from end to end. Even when the Great Western came to incorporate such important concerns as the 'Bristol and Exeter', the 'South Devon', the 'Cornwall Railway' and others in Wales and the West Midlands, the insignia was not changed. When it was applied to engine and carriage decoration, the first form that was used for about twenty-five years had the arms of the two cities encircled within a garter, after the fashion of so many of the railways in pre-grouping days. But from the nineteen-thirties the garter was not used, and the two arms were displayed alone, on engine tenders and carriages alike.

164 Coat of Arms; London Midland and Scottish Railway.

The constituent companies of the L.M.S.R. had between them a wonderful collection of heraldic devices. Some, undoubtedly, had no heraldic justification it is true, but in looking through the coloured illustrations in this book and studying the coats of arms of the London and North Western Railway, the Midland, the Caledonian, the Highland, the Furness, the Lancashire and Yorkshire, to say nothing of the North London, and the North Staffordshire, it could be well imagined a little difficult to devise something that would contain heraldic significance of the great amalgamation that had taken place. One could not, for example, take the devices of the constituents and group them in one, as the South Eastern and the London Chatham and Dover did, within the encircling garter of the Managing Committee. Instead, the L.M.S.R. adopted a very simple device including only the arms of London, the rose of England, and the thistle of Scotland. When the locomotive livery had been decided upon, and the style of the former Midland Railway adopted, the coat of arms of the L.M.S.R. was put on the cabs of express passenger locomotives, as the Midland one had been done, but in later years when the engine numbers were put on the engines, rather than in huge transfer figures on the tenders, the coat of arms had to be dispensed with, and it was then used only on main-line carriages.

165 Coat of Arms; London and North Eastern Railway.

After grouping, the L.N.E.R. – an amalgamation of the Great Northern, Great Central, Great Eastern, North Eastern, North British and Great North of Scotland Railways, together with some smaller lines – adopted what was without a doubt the most beautiful and appropriate heraldic device ever associated with a British railway company. The full heraldic description is:

'Argent on a Cross Gules between the first and fourth quarters a Griffin seqreant Sable in the second a Rose of the second leaved and slipped proper and in third quarter a Thistle also leaved and slipped proper the Castle of Edinburgh proper between four Lions passant guardant Or And for the Crest On a Wreath of the Colours Issuant from Clouds of Steam the figure of Mercury proper'.

The motto 'Forward' was, of course, that of the Great Central Railway. When this coat of arms appeared as a colour plate in *The Railway Magazine* early in 1924 enthusiasts naturally expected that this beautiful device would soon be displayed on locomotive and carriages, as the previous insignia of the North Eastern, Great Central and other constituents had so lavishly been done in the past. Alas no! It was painted by hand on the *Flying Scotsman* engine when decked in all its glory for exhibition at Wembley in 1924 and 1925; but no transfer was ever made, and the only other use of the coat of arms was on a small inspection engine, specially painted for hauling the directors' saloon after World War II.

166 Coat of Arms; Pullman Car Company.

Ever since their first introduction on day services in the South of England, in 1876, Pullmans have been synonymous with an extra luxury in travel. Large bogie carriages, with high clerestory roofs, stood apart from the ordinary run of British passenger carriages, and it was their influence that could be seen in the luxurious carriage developments on the Great Northern Railway, and in the London and North London dining car around the turn of the century. But it was, above all, the inception, in November 1908, of the Brighton Company's

Southern Belle that set the final seal upon the popularity of the Pullman car for luxurious day travel, with buffet facilities. From that time onwards the Pullman cars running in this country, with the exception of those on the South Eastern and Chatham Railway, were painted in a dignified livery of chocolate and cream, using a rather darker brown than that of the two-tone Great Western carriages. The first-class cars were mostly given female Christian names, but the third class only numbers; but all were alike in bearing the handsome Pullman coat of arms. This was displayed also inside the cars. Its rich colouring, on the background of the dark brown coach bodies, stood out very well. With the passing of the steam age, and the introduction of different kinds of Pullman trains, a different version of the device has been adopted. It is considerably less attractive than the old one, though no doubt more suited to the new conditions.

167 Thompson Class 'A2' Pacific; London and North Eastern Railway.

During the war years difficulty was experienced in maintaining the conjugated valve gear of the Gresley three-cylinder 'Pacific'. And although the design was, in ordinary circumstances, one of the most successful ever to be produced in Great Britain, Sir Nigel's successor, Edward Thompson decided for his future designs to use three sets of valve gear, and so to dispose the cylinders in relation to the driving axles that all three connecting rods were of equal length. This led to a spacing of the wheels that looked a little odd. The arrangement was tried out during the war on some Pacifics that were rebuilt from the Gresley 'Cock o' the North' class 2-8-2s; but our picture shows one of the post-war 'A2' class built new at Doncaster, and mostly named, like previous L.N.E.R. 'Pacifics' after racehorses. The new 'A2' engines proved fast and powerful machines, and

although their coupled wheels were only 6 ft. 2 in. diameter against the 6 ft. 8 in. of the Gresley 'Pacifics' they were very successfully used on the main line between King's Cross and Newcastle. Nevertheless, when A. H. Peppercorn in turn succeeded Edward Thompson as Chief Mechanical Engineer of the L.N.E.R., he did not perpetuate the 'odd' wheel spacing, but reverted to the Gresley spacing while retaining the three sets of valve gear, instead of the Gresley conjugated motion. Even so, neither the Thompson nor the Peppercorn 'Pacifics' came to supersede the Gresleys on the fastest and the most important duties.

168 Bulleid's 'Austerity' 0-6-0 goods engine; Southern Railway.

During World War II additional goods engines were required on the Southern Railway, but of a weight that would permit of their being used over almost the entire system. A good general purpose 0-6-0 existed in the Maunsell 'Q' class, which met requirements so far as weight was concerned. But Bulleid considered that greater boiler capacity would be an advantage for the wartime traffic, so he reconsidered the design using the largest boiler that could be produced for such a chassis from existing tools. The flanging blocks for the 'Lord Nelson' 4-6-0 were found suitable, and a design worked out for a much larger boiler than that used on the Maunsell 'Q' class 0-6-0. If the engine had been finished in conventional style the weight would have exceeded the limits imposed, and so every item that was not absolutely necessary was discarded. As will be seen in our picture there were no running plates, no wheel-splashers, and the outer plates containing the boiler lagging were finished in a most unorthodox manner. 'Austerity' was certainly the word for these queer-looking engines, which looked as though they were not finished. All the essentials were there however, and they proved excellent if somewhat inelegant tools for the wartime traffic.

169 'Schools' class 4-4-0 in wartime livery; Southern Railway.

The conditions of wartime imposed many difficult circumstances upon the locomotive departments of the British railways. Some of the workshops were engaged in direct production of munitions, others had their labour forces greatly reduced, and all the time difficulty was experienced in obtaining the choice materials specified in pre-war days for some of the important working parts of locomotives. Even so it was vitally necessary to keep the locomotive stocks in good working order. The tasks of express passenger engines like the 'Schools' were not so onerous in themselves as those demanded of them in pre-war days; but the wheels had to be kept turning with reliability, and when the time came for overhaul no effort could be spared to impart to repaired engines the spanking finish of peacetime. They were given the minimum necessary to preserve the metal, and that minimum meant nothing more than a coat of plain black without any lining. Little, if any, time could be spared at the sheds for real cleaning, and plain black was the most logical and serviceable 'colour'. Nevertheless, shorn of their pre-war finery, the handsome proportions of the 'Schools' class engine were still amply evident. Our picture, showing engine No. 930 *Radley*, is of one of those fitted by Mr. Bulleid with the five-nozzled multiple jet blastpipe, and having an unusually large chimney in consequence.

170 London Midland Class '5' 4-6-0 with Caprotti valve gear; British Railways.

After the end of World War II, in the few years that elapsed before the nationalization of the railways the L.M.S.R. made a number of experiments with accessories aiming at improved availability, more efficient performance, and a lessening of maintenance work. Taking the Stanier Class '5' 4-6-0 as a basis, a number of engines were built with experimental variations, so arranged that comparison could readily be made one with another. There was, for example, a straight trial of driving axles with plain against roller bearings, and other engines were fitted with different forms of valve gear as alternatives to the long-established Walschaerts radial gear. The engine shown in our picture was one of a batch fitted with the British-Caprotti form of poppet valve gear, and also fitted with roller bearings, while a single engine of the Class '5' group was equipped with Stephenson's link motion, outside. In these comparative tests, also, some engines were equipped with twin blastpipes and double chimneys. It cannot be said that anything positive came out of the valve gear trials, because Walschaerts was generally adopted as standard for the new British Railways locomotives. But for high-powered and medium-powered machines the advantage of roller bearings was clearly established. Our picture shows one of the ex-L.M.S.R. 4-6-0s in the first British Railways style of painting with the original number surmounted by the letter M to indicate London Midland Region.

171-2 Upper Quadrant Signals.

The lower quadrant signal had become one of the great institutions of the British steam railways. It was so simple and reliable, and so well understood by railwaymen and the travelling public alike! Those who travelled abroad could well be mystified by the curious array of signs and signals displayed on some foreign railways: semaphores that moved in odd and unexpected directions; boards and diamond signs in different colours that would suddenly startle the onlooker by moving round with a great clatter. The lower quadrant semaphore was such an institution in Great Britain that the mere suggestion of changing it was enough to arouse the most acute controversy. Yet in the years just before the outbreak of World War I there were pioneer spirits who felt that our code of signalling was growing inadequate. There had been one or two bad collisions through drivers disregarding signals, and with the development of three-position signalling in the United States some serious consideration was given to make similar changes here. It was essential that a three-position semaphore should work through the upper quadrant: horizontal for 'stop', inclined upwards for 'caution', and vertically upwards for 'clear'. An electrically-worked signal of this type was installed at Paddington, and towards the end of the war a contract was let for a complete installation of them at Victoria on the S.E.&C.R. side of the station. After the war the development of the colour light signal made this a much simpler way of providing three indications from one signal, with the now-familiar red, amber and green lights, that three-position semaphore signals made no further headway in Great Britain, though British contractors installed them in considerable numbers overseas. But an important sequel to the three-position controversy was the decision, by three out of the four big companies operated by the grouping of 1923, to standardize in future upon the upper quadrant type of semaphore for all ordinary mechanical working. This was done because in the first place the mechanism could be made much lighter. The arm returned to the danger position by gravity, and it was no longer necessary to build into the spectacle a heavy counterweight to ensure that the arm returned to the horizontal position if there was any mishap to the mechanism, or if the operating wire broke. Upper quadrant semaphores could readily be applied to existing posts, and

our pictures show groups of signals on both wood and lattice posts. The latter (reference 172), was a location on the former Great Northern Railway, where the upper quadrant arms had replaced the 'somersault' type. Of the grouped railways only the Great Western stood apart, and continued to use lower quadrant semaphores, many of which are still in service today.

173–4 **Groups of semaphore signals;** South Eastern and Chatham Railway.

The traditional lower quadrant signal was a picturesque thing in itself – always kept smartly painted, and having for the keen observer many features of individual interest as between the practice of the various railway companies. But on many railways the picturesque aspect of semaphore signals as such was greatly enhanced by the way they were multiplied and grouped in the approaches to large stations and junctions. There was at least one semaphore for each route a train could take, and if one added shunting and 'calling-on' arms, and the frequent mounting of distant arms on the same post as the stop signals associated with the same route one could have a truly extraordinary array. Two very large assemblies are illustrated under references 191 and 192, but the present pictures relate more particularly to the structures on which some of these arrays were mounted. It goes without saying that the more signals to be displayed the more complicated would be the track layout. Space on the ground would be at a premium, and in many cases quite large gantries and cantilevers had to be built in order to permit of the semaphore being mounted reasonably near to the tracks to which they applied. Of course this could not always be done to the ideal extent; but the configurations had to be designed so that the indications displayed could not be mistaken by the driver of a train.

Nevertheless, the driver had to 'learn the road', and sign a book expressing his familiarity with it; and that in many cases meant memorizing the signal configurations at large centres. The assembly (reference 173) is a most interesting one, and relates to the starting point from a main-line platform in a terminal station from which a train could proceed to any one of four routes. The semaphores by their positioning indicate the geographical direction – that is the arm farthest to the left signifies the route farthest to the left, and so on. The design of the supporting posts is interesting. It was necessary to have the arms as near as possible above the roofs of the carriages, and so the mechanism for working them was placed above. The second illustration (reference 174) includes a group with a different significance. All the arms in reference 173 related to one departure line and all routes were of equal importance. In No. 174, the subsidiary posts rising from the main cross-girder indicate that two separate running lines are involved, one on each side of the central post, and the arrangement of the semaphore above indicates a bifurcation, in each case with the left-hand route of greater importance than the right-hand one. Associated with each of these running lines is a shunt signal, with a ringed arm. The pictures 173 and 174 show two different styles of arm painting: that in 173 was the later one adopted on the Southern Railway generally after grouping, while the semaphores of the constituent companies remained in service. That in 174 was the standard South Eastern and Chatham style, with a white disc, instead of the more usual white band on the red blade.

175 **Fowler 2-6-4 fast passenger tank engine;** London Midland and Scottish Railway.
In 1927 the former Midland Railway drawing office was engaged on the design of a new express tank engine that would

be used at all large centres where fast and heavy residential passenger services were operated: around London, Manchester, Birmingham and Glasgow in particular. The design was conceived on traditional Midland lines, but at the last minute, fortunately, some changes were made in the design of the valve gear which resulted in an extraordinarily efficient and free-running engine. On the Euston–Watford services speeds of 80 m.p.h. were common on the trains running non-stop over this $17\frac{1}{2}$ miles. Although having coupled wheels no larger than 5 ft. 9 in. which gave them the capacity for quick acceleration, they ran with the freedom of an express-passenger engine, with wheels one foot larger in diameter. As originally built the first examples were painted in Midland red, as shown in our picture; but later ones were painted black. A total of 95 was built to the original design, followed in 1933 by a further 30 which differed in having side-window cabs. They fulfilled every expectation, doing splendid work on the local trains from Euston and St. Pancras, and on the fast trains between the Glasgow termini of Central and St. Enoch and the Clyde coast resorts. After Sir William Stanier had succeeded to the post of Chief Mechanical Engineer of the L.M.S.R. many more 2-6-4 tank engines were built, though these later ones had the Stanier type of taper boiler. Eventually there were 645 engines of this wheel arrangement on the L.M.S.R.

176 **Thompson 2-6-4 mixed-traffic tank engine, Class 'Ll';** London and North Eastern Railway.
In his programme for the standardization of the steam locomotive stock of the L.N.E.R., Edward Thompson made a particular feature of the use of existing standard parts and manufacturing equipment. A powerful suburban tank engine was needed, to take over duties on which relatively old engines had previously

been employed, and this new design was derived from the 5 ft. 2 in. 2-6-0 class 'K1', which in turn originally was produced by rebuilding one of Sir Nigel Gresley's three cylinder 2-6-0s of Class 'K4' with two cylinders and outside Walschaerts valve gear, in place of the previous conjugated gear. The same boiler, firebox, and frame design was used, and the new cylinders were also an existing standard. The 2-6-4 tank of 1945 was thus a tank-engine version of the 'K1', and a very solid and robust job it was, having a tractive effort of 32,080 lb against the 23,125 lb of the L.M.S.R. engine (reference 175). The difference between the two was that the L.N.E.R. was essentially a mixed-traffic engine, suitable for goods as well as passenger, and for use on services where heavy haulage capacity, rather than fast running was needed. Our picture shows one of these engines in the early style of painting used on British Railways, in lined black but before the totem had been introduced. More than 100 of these locomotives were built.

177 **Heavy mineral 2-8-2 tank engine;** '72XX' class, Great Western Railway.
In the year 1910 a useful addition was made to the standard locomotive types in use on the Great Western Railway. Churchward's original plan of complete standardization in 1901 included two tank-engine types, the 4-4-2 and the 2-6-2; but later the need was felt for a heavy mineral engine in South Wales that could handle loads equal to those worked by the main-line 2-8-0s, but were suited to short distance hauls. Thus the '42XX' 2-8-0 tank was put on the road. At a later period, between the two world wars, the increasing length of run on some of the coal train workings showed the need for a tank engine with greater coal capacity than the '42XX' class 2-8-0,

and so a number of these powerful engines were rebuilt with larger coal bunkers, and altered to the 2-8-2 wheel arrangement. Our picture shows one of these handsome engines. Among other duties they work the coal trains from Severn Tunnel Junction to the Southern line, travelling via the outskirts of Bristol, Bath, Westbury and Warminster, to hand over to the Southern at Salisbury. Their coupled wheels are smaller even than those of the L.N.E.R. 'L1' class, only 4 ft. 7½ in., and in consequence they have the still higher tractive effort of 33,170 lb. This is the same as that of Churchward's 2-8-0 tanks of 1910, as the engine and boiler are identical. The only difference between the '42XX' and the '72XX' classes lies in the size of the coal bunker and in the wheel arrangement.

178 **'BR4' Standard 2-6-4 tank engine;** British Railways.
The six-coupled passenger tank engines on three out of the four British main-line railways of pre-nationalization days, the Great Western, the L.M.S.R. and the L.N.E.R., had proved so useful in fast short-distance service that a design of this general type seemed almost a certainty in the new range of standard classes that were in course of preparation for British Railways soon after nationalization. There were 2-6-2s on the Great Western and the L.N.E.R., and 2-6-4s on both the L.N.E.R. and L.M.S.R. Of these the Stanier type on the L.M.S.R. was best suited to general use in all parts of the country where steam-operated short distance services were operated; but while the familiar Stanier taper boiler and trapezoidal-shaped firebox was adopted with very little alteration the cylinders were made with a smaller diameter and longer stroke; 18 in. by 28 in., against 19 in. by 26 in. on the L.M.S.R. engines. The coupled wheels were slightly smaller, and this produced an engine with slightly

higher tractive effort. The new engines, which were first introduced in 1951, were numbered from 80000 upwards, and they were styled in accordance with uniform 'look' persisting through all the new medium-powered classes in the British Railways standard range. They proved excellent engines in service, rapid in acceleration, very fast, and light on coal. They were certainly an admirable climax to the chain of development of the express-tank service for residential and medium-distance service.

179 Furness Railway coat of arms.

This was one of the most beautiful of all railway coats of arms, and unlike some devices – which though picturesque had a rather doubtful heraldic justification – it was most appropriate to the district served, and to some of the personal associations involved. The Furness Railway had nevertheless, a twofold function: to serve the rapidly expanding industries of Barrow and to provide transport for the iron ore in which the Furness and West Cumberland districts were at one time very rich; and secondly, to develop tourist traffic to the English Lake District. The intense industrialism of Barrow, and of many smaller towns along the coast of the Irish Sea finds no place on the Furness Railway coat of arms; instead it is the historic associations of the district that are depicted. The Madonna and Child, which forms the centre-piece, is part of the arms of the Abbot of Furness. The ruins of the once-great Cistercian abbey of Furness lie close to the railway by Furness Abbey station, in the oddly named Vale of Deadly Nightshade! The motto *Cavendo Tutus* – advance with caution – is that of the Cavendish family whose head, the Duke of Devonshire, always took a very active interest in Furness Railway affairs. The coat of arms, in its delicate detail, looked equally fine on the panels of the royal blue carriages, and on the locomotives in their distinctive 'iron ore' red livery.

180 Somerset and Dorset Joint Railway coat of arms.

The garter of this attractive device encircles the arms of the City of Bath, on the left, and of the ancient borough of Dorchester. But although these two places are truly representative of the counties of Somerset and Dorset the railway itself never extended to anywhere near Dorchester, and it was many years after its first incorporation that the line reached Bath. The railway was originally an amalgamation of two still-smaller concerns: the Somerset Central, and the Dorset Central, and this amalgamated company had a line that extended from Highbridge on the Bristol Channel to Wimborne. It crossed the London and South Western main line at Temple-combe, and eventually linked-up with the same company at Poole, and gained access to Bournemouth West. The amalgamation took place in 1862, and it was the result of a proposal to extend northwards from Evercreech to Bath that interested the Midland Railway, because it opened up the possibility of through services between the Midlands and Bournemouth. The line to Bath was completed in 1874, but so depleted were the funds of the company as a result of the heavy cost of building this line through difficult country, that for some time it hovered on the brink of bankruptcy. Eventually an agreement was concluded in which the Midland and the London and South Western took a joint lease of the line, in 1876. The joint ownership continued, indeed, through the grouping period, between the London Midland and Scottish, and the Southern. After nationalization it continued for eighteen years as part of British Railways, but it was finally closed in March 1966.

181 Hull and Barnsley Railway coat of arms.

This very enterprising local railway was born out of a desire to break the monopoly of the rich and powerful North Eastern Railway, which had the country between the Humber and the Tweed to itself. In Victorian times there was a very large export trade in coal from England to the Baltic and Scandinavian countries, and the coal-owners of Yorkshire, shipping through Hull, were very dissatisfied with the treatment they were receiving from the North Eastern. The coat of arms of the Hull and Barnsley Railway is a piece of history in itself, for it not only includes the arms of Hull and Barnsley, but it combined also the winged wheel of the railway with the dolphins of the Hull docks. The date, 1880, was the year in which the Act of Parliament authorizing the line received the Royal assent. Actually the railway was not opened until five years later. In Hull the line had three terminal stations – two at the docksides, and a central passenger station in Cannon Street. At the western end it did not reach Barnsley on its own metals; the last two miles were run over the tracks of the Midland. But it made connection with many of the South Yorkshire collieries, and it was from these that its principal traffic came. A fast passenger service was run between Sheffield and Hull, and the distinctive black engines of the Hull and Barnsley Railway were to be seen in the Midland station at Sheffield. In the coat of arms, the shield of Hull with its three crowns is a reminder of the full title of that city – Kingston-upon-Hull.

182 North Staffordshire Railway coat of arms.

The North Staffordshire Railway was the outcome of one of the earliest railway projects in Great Britain. Birmingham was the focal point of much earlier railway promoting in the Midlands, and at the time that the London and Birming-ham Railway was being discussed and the great trunk line to connect Birmingham with the Liverpool and Manchester Railway was also under active discussion, plans were also being prepared for a line between Manchester and Birmingham. Railway politics north of Birmingham became complicated and difficult in earlier days and eventually the Manchester and Birmingham project, instead of being an independent concern, running through the Potteries and serving the growing industrial districts that, even then, were beginning to cluster round Stoke-on-Trent, became watered down into nothing more than a relatively short-cut of a line from Manchester to join the Grand Junction main line at Crewe. Nevertheless, the original project of a line through the Potteries was still actively canvassed and it formed the nucleus of the North Staffordshire Railway system, which eventually formed part of a most important alternative through-route from Manchester to London via Stoke-on-Trent. The promoters were anxious to have a fast direct route, and consequently a number of towns in the Potteries were by-passed and had later to be served by branch lines which, of course, became something of an embarrassment with increasing traffic and the need to provide numerous feeder services to the main line. Although the North Staffordshire Railway maintained its independence to the very end of pre-grouping days, and it played a very considerable part in providing through-train workings to destinations far beyond its own territory, its activities were above all centred upon Stoke; and it is the arms of the City of Stoke-on-Trent, together with the traditional 'knot' of Staffordshire that forms the pervading *motif* of the handsome coat of arms adopted by this railway. It was carried on all the passenger and local tank engines and in earlier days some of them carried the 'Staffordshire Knot' as well.

183 *The Princess Elizabeth* **engine in black;** London Midland Region, British Railways.

Immediately after nationalization, in 1948, British Railways had to give consideration to the liveries to be adopted as a future standard, and a number of experimental styles were tried. In the pictures (references 183–6) are shown four styles three of which did not survive very long. There was a demonstration, at which express-passenger engines in various colours were slowly steamed past members of the Railway Executive; but one of those that created the biggest impression was the *Princess Elizabeth*, one of Sir William Stanier's famous 'Princess Royal' class 'Pacifics', which had been painted in the colours of the former London and North Western Railway; a magnificent glossy black, lined-out in red, cream and grey, to the tradition of the Crewe Works of twenty-five years earlier. Of course there is no doubt that a black locomotive, like a well-groomed black motor-car, can look superb, and on that day the *Princess Elizabeth* created a deep impression. But it was felt that to paint all British Railways locomotives in black would be to create a bad public image, and so the use of 'blackberry black', as it used to be called in L.N.W.R. days was confined to second-line express passenger, and mixed-traffic engines, and blue was selected, as a first choice, for the largest express-passenger classes.

184 **'Merchant Navy' class 4-6-2 in standard blue;** Southern Region, British Railways.

The shade of blue finally adopted for the large express-passenger engines was not finally determined after that first demonstration at Addison Road, and a number of engines were decked in the dark blue shown in the reference No. 185. The light blue, which was standardized in 1949 and used for a few years afterwards, was closely similar in its tone to the blue of the Caledonian Railway, but with black underframes and black wheels it did not have the same beautiful effect as the Scottish colour scheme of old, in which the wheels were blue, and the valances, and tender frames purple lake. Even so, the British Railways engines mostly looked very well in the blue. In addition to the 'Merchant Navy' class illustrated, the blue was applied to all the Stanier Pacifics of the former L.M.S.R., to all the Gresley 'Pacifics', to the new Peppercorn Pacifics of the Eastern and North Eastern Region, and to the ex-G.W.R. 'King' class 4-6-os. It must be admitted however that blue did not suit these latter engines. Their lavish array of brass and copper work was admirably set-off by the traditional Brunswick green of the Great Western Railway; but it did not go at all well with the blue, and I think everyone concerned with those engines was glad when the blue was abandoned by British Railways.

185 **A Gresley 'A3' Pacific in experimental dark blue;** Eastern and North Eastern Region.

The dark blue style of painting was no more than an experimental phase, when an attempt was made to secure the reaction of the public to some of the proposed liveries. It was endeavoured to keep the repainted engines available to work trains of coaching stock in the new colours, when complete rakes of repainted coaches, some in chocolate and cream, and some in the oft-derided 'plum and spilt-milk', were run on certain named express passenger trains. The dark-blue engines, like the L.M.S.R. *Coronation* of 1937, were reminiscent of the Caledonian in the late-Victorian era, though lacking the distinction of the purple underframes. But the British Railways experimental dark blue also included the old L.N.W.R. style of lining-out with red edging to the boiler bands, and red, cream and grey lining around the tenders and the cab sides. The repainting was done before the British Railways totem device had been designed, and the majority of the engines to be treated had the name BRITISH RAILWAYS painted in full on the tenders. In my opinion the dark blue would have looked better with a plain black and white lining-out. It was not applied to all engines of the Class '8' power classification; but 'Kings', 'Merchant Navy' 4-6-2s, 'Duchesses and Gresley Pacifics of both 'A3' and 'A4' classes were so bedecked for a few months.

186 A 'Castle' class 4-6-0 in the 'experimental' light green; Western Region, British Railways.

While trials were being made of dark blue as a livery for the largest express-passenger engines, during 1948 and 1949 certain selected express-passenger engines of lesser tractive capacity were painted in a livery of pale green. Included in this group were some ex-G.W.R. 'Castle' class 4-6-0s; ex-Southern 'Lord Nelson' and some ex-L.M.S.R. rebuilt 'Royal Scots'. Whether by accident or design the basic colour, which was a beautiful shade of green, was closely similar to that used at one time on the Adams express engines of the London and South Western Railway, and it was perhaps no more than a coincidence that of the three types chosen to display this experimental style the 'Lord Nelson's' looked incomparably the best. But incorporated with this pale green was once again the old Crewe type of lining-out, in red, grey and cream. One presumes the idea was to have the same style of lining-out, whether the basic colour of the engine was black, blue or green. But what looked superb on a black engine, was less effective on a dark-blue one, and perfectly horrible on light green! Fortunately this particular experiment did not last long. At a distance the light-green engines, particularly the 'Lord Nelsons', looked pleasant at the head of a train of

coaches in the experimental 'plum and spilt milk'; but closer acquaintance did not confirm that good impression, so far as the engine was concerned.

187 Double-chimneyed 'King' class 4-6-0; Western Region, British Railways.

In the last years of steam various measures were taken to improve the performance of existing locomotives, some definitely advanced in years, to enable them to carry on until steam would be superseded by one of the newer forms of motive power. The 'King' class 4-6-0s were introduced on the Great Western Railway in 1927, and for more than twenty years they had remained completely unchanged in their design. After World War II some modifications were made to the draughting to enable them to use more effectively the poorer grades of coal that were then coming into increasing use for British Railways; and then after a life of nearly thirty years, spent entirely in the heaviest express passenger service, the whole class of 30 engines was subjected to an important, yet simply made, modification by the fitting of twin blastpipes and double chimneys. This certainly made a definite improvement to the performance of the engines and, in conjunction with some structural renewal of the frames at the front end, gave the class a useful additional lease of life, enabling them to continue in heavy passenger traffic to the end of the steam era. Our picture shows one of these modified engines in the standard dark-green livery adopted for all major express-passenger classes in the last years of steam. It was almost exactly the same as the old Great Western standard, except for certain minor differences in lining.

188 Standard main-line coaching stock; British Railways.

After the various experimental liveries for locomotives and carriages tried out soon after nationalization, including the previously mentioned chocolate and cream, and the 'plum and spilt milk' the decision was taken to adopt a two-tone colour scheme that was entirely new, having cream upper panels, and bodies in a bright cherry red. This was certainly a very distinguished style, but one cannot say more than that about it. Coaches so repainted stood out vividly whether in the drab surroundings of an industrial area or out in the fairest countryside. But it was a synthetic colour scheme. It did not blend with the natural surroundings like the chocolate and cream of the Great Western, like the various varnished teak styles of pre-grouping days, or like the beautiful crimson lake of the Midland, which always seemed so particularly appropriate to the moorland landscapes of Derbyshire and the Northern Pennines. The earliest British Railways standard coaches were built at a time when austerity still had the railway economy in its grasp, and in comparison with some coaches of pre-war days the new stock was spartan in its appointments, and simple in its engineering detail. They were 'economy class' vehicles rather than a synthesis of all that was best in previous practice; but they served their day, and have now been largely displaced from the more important trains by later designs.

189 **Rebuilt 'Royal Scot' class 4-6-0 in standard green livery;** British Railways.

In discussing the experimental colours tried after nationalization, under references 183 to 186, I referred to the distinction originally made between the largest express passenger engines, and a selected group of lesser types. The former were originally painted blue, while after trial liveries the lesser group was finished in a dark Brunswick green, with lining closely similar to that of the former Great Western Railway. Eventually the blue was abandoned, and Brunswick green

adopted for all express classes. The 'Royal Scot' class engine shown in our picture is typical of the engines, having the number in transfer figures on the cab sides. The dark green was applied to all 'Pacifics'; to the 'Sandringhams' class 4-6-0s; to the 'Lord Nelsons' and 'King Arthurs' – though not, to the disappointment of many enthusiasts, to the 'Schools'. On the London Midland Region, in addition to the 'Royal Scots' it was applied to the Stanier 'Jubilee' class three-cylinder 4-6-0s, and to the 'Patriots', while on the Western Region it was used on 'Castles', 'Stars', 'Counties' and 'Halls'. In still later years some of the ex-L.M.S.R. 'Pacifics' were painted in red once again – the wheel having come full circle, through red, wartime black, two shades of blue, B.R. green, and finally back to red. But the greatest diversity of painting that was applied to any British locomotives was that on the Gresley 'A4' streamlined 'Pacifics'. In pre-war years the first four were silver, and later changed to Garter blue. A further batch was originally finished in standard L.N.E.R. apple-green like the non-streamlined 'Pacifics' and other express passenger engines. These were all changed to Garter blue in the last pre-war years. Then came the wartime unlined black when economy was carried to the extent of contracting the initials on the tender from L.N.E.R. to N.E.! Immediately after the war Garter blue was restored, to be followed by the experimental B.R. blues. Finally, these engines ended their careers in the dark Brunswick green: seven different styles in all, though not every individual engine had all seven!

190 **Standard main-line coaching stock with Commonwealth bogies.**

One of the problems faced by the engineers of British Railways was to provide good modern rolling stock that would give long service and a satisfactory ride with the minimum of attention. In the early days of nationalization, when express-train schedules were being speeded-up, adverse comment was frequently made upon the poor riding of the stock, and it was compared unfavourably to this or that design of pre-war coach, all of which were usually smooth at the highest speeds. What was not generally realized was that those earlier coaches had much closer and continuous maintenance, whereas in post-war years neither the finance nor the staff were forthcoming to provide such attention. A great deal of research in coach suspension and bogie design was undertaken in post-nationalization days to produce vehicles that would maintain their initial standards of riding over long periods with the minimum of attention, and one outcome was the fitting – largely as an interim measure – of many new coaches with the 'Commonwealth' design of bogie, while new designs were being worked out for future standards. The coach illustrated is typical of the second phase of British standard coach design, when 'Midland red' had once again been adopted as the standard livery for all except the Southern Region. This coach is representative of the very last days of steam, and it is a sign of the changing times that it is a 'dual heated', with provision either for steam or electric heating, while the prefix to the number on the body side 'SC', indicates that it is attached to Scottish Region. The distinctive yellow covers to the axle-boxes indicate the use of roller bearings. Since the introduction of these vehicles yet another change has been made in British standard coach livery to a pale grey and blue: but this takes us beyond the era of steam railways.

191 **Large signal gantry, with somersault arms;** Great Northern Railway.
In describing the interesting configurations of semaphore signals used on the South Eastern and Chatham Railway

(references 173 and 174), mention was made of still larger assemblies, and the present picture shows a typical gantry on the Great Northern Railway. It was one located at Red Bank, Doncaster, and shows an interesting grouping of the arms appropriate to the tracks below. The southbound main line, used by all passenger trains ran beneath the overhanging cantilever portion at the right-hand end. The tall 'doll' post at the extreme end related to the main line, with a 'distant' arm below the stop arm for the direct line to London. The two 'distant' arms immediately to the left indicated divergencies at the next signal box ahead to other routes. The other four tracks, two under each span of the gantry, were entirely goods lines, and the signals were used to regulate the movements of departing goods trains for the south. Beyond the gantry the goods trains left the extensive marshalling yards that lie on the south side of Doncaster station, and entered upon the main lines either towards London, towards the Eastern Counties, or westwards to the Yorkshire coalfields. In Great Northern days the distant as well as the stop signals had the blades painted red and the distant arms did not have the distinction of a chevron, instead of a plain white band. In later L.N.E.R. days the 'distant' arms on this gantry were painted yellow, with a black chevron, though retaining their somersault action. The main-line signals on the extreme right show the more usual angle to which these arms cleared.

192 **The great signal gantry at Rugby;** London and North Western Railway.
It would perhaps be an overstatement to suggest that this was the most famous signal gantry that ever existed; but certainly it was one of the best known, because of its great height and for the number of semaphore arms it carried, a

grand total of 44. There are actually two gantries, with the lower group of signals precisely duplicating the upper set. The reasons for this duplication will be explained later. Taking the grouping of the doll posts, these it will be seen, fall into three groups, corresponding to the three running lines approaching Rugby from the south – main line, Northampton line, and Peterborough line. Trains approaching on the main line could be routed to any one of three ways: into the goods lines, over the through-main line, or into the down-main platform, indicated by the three doll posts on the left-hand end of the gantry. Trains from the Northampton and Peterborough lines, as well as being routed to any one of the three just-mentioned lines could also be terminated in either of the two-bay platforms, so that additional semaphores are provided for these, to the right of the three through-running signals. Originally there was only the lower gantry, with 22 arms; but when the Great Central Railway constructed its London Extension line in 1899 its route crossed the tracks of the London and North Western Railway just to the south of Rugby station, and its massive girder bridge was built immediately behind the great 22 arms gantry. The existence of the elaborate criss-cross lattice work immediately behind the semaphore would have made sighting of them difficult, and so a duplicate gantry was built on which the semaphores mounted at a much higher level could be sighted against a sky background, well above the Great Central viaduct. As a condition for granting permission for the G.C.R. to cross their line at Rugby the North Western required the Great Central not only to bear the expense of duplicating all the semaphores, but to pay for the cost of maintaining them.

193 Class 'BR6' Pacific 'Clan' class; British Railways.
In the range of standard locomotives

introduced by the nationalized British Railways a need was felt for a locomotive of less power, and lighter axle loading than the well-known 'Britannia' class, that would undertake duties previously worked by such engines as the ex-L.M.S.R. 'Jubilee' and 'Patriot' class 4-6-0s, but which would be better suited to burning an inferior grade of coal. The new engines were therefore built of the 'Pacific' type, with large, wide fireboxes, and all the modern appliances for lessening shed duties and maintenance work, in the form of self-cleaning smokeboxes, rocking firegrates, hopper ashpans, and roller bearings on all axles. As the duties for which these engines were originally to be drafted were based upon Glasgow, in working the through-expresses between that city and Manchester and Liverpool they were given the names of Highland 'Clans', thus perpetuating some of the most famous names from the railways of pre-grouping days in Scotland. The 'BR6' engines worked regularly through between Glasgow and Manchester, and did much good work. They were also extensively used on express duties in Scotland itself between Carlisle, Glasgow and Perth.

194 'BR9' 2-10-0 with Franco-Crosti boiler; British Railways.
The very last steam locomotive to be built was of the 'BR9' class 2-10-0, the *Evening Star*, and the class as a whole proved one of the most successful ever to run in this country, because of its extreme versatility. It was a simple, straightforward design, embodying those features which by long usage had been found to give that reliability in service that is so essential in railway working. Nevertheless, at a late stage in the history of the steam locomotive a trial was made on ten of these 'BR9' 2-10-0s of the Crosti type of boiler, which had been used with success on a considerable number of Italian locomotives. This aimed at securing increased thermal

efficiency by pre-heating the water passing into the boiler. The exhaust steam from the cylinders instead of passing direct to the blastpipe as in a normal locomotive passed through long pipes to a blast chamber and thence to an exhaust outlet on the side of the boiler. These 'BR9' locomotives that were so fitted had a more orthodox look than their Italian counterparts, which had no chimney at all. In the British 2-10-0s the chimney on the front smokebox was used only when lighting-up. The exhaust normally from the pipe was on the side of the boiler. On British Railways experience with these ten locomotives was not sufficient to justify proceeding further with the experiment. Shortly after their construction the decision was taken to abandon steam altogether.

INDEX

Figures in heavy type are colour plates.
Figures in Roman, are descriptive notes.

The Pocket Encyclopaedia of

BRITISH
STEAM LOCOMOTIVES
IN COLOUR

by
O.S. NOCK
B.Sc., M.I.C.E., M.I. Mech E., M.I. Loco E.

With 192 locomotives illustrated by
CLIFFORD and WENDY MEADWAY

Bounty
Books

First published in Great Britain in 1964
by Blandford Press
Poole, Dorset

Reprinted 1966, 1968, 1973 and 2009

An Hachette UK Company
www.hachette.co.uk

A CIP catalogue record for this book is available from the British Library

Printed in China

CONTENTS

MAPS

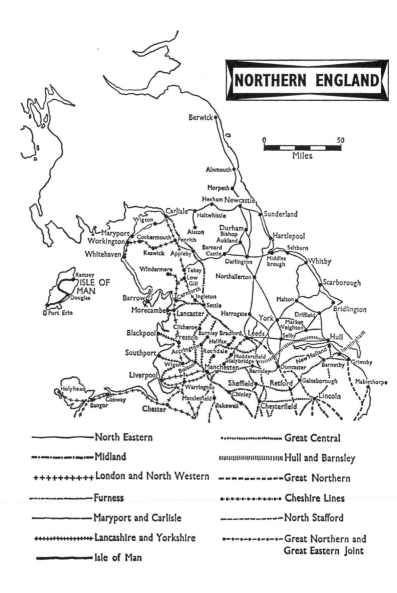

NORTHERN ENGLAND

0   50
Miles

Berwick

Alnmouth

Morpeth

Hexham Newcastle
Carlisle Haltwhistle   Sunderland
Wigton   Alston   Durham
Maryport   Cockermouth Penrith   Bishop   Hartlepool
Workington   Barnard   Aukland   Saltburn
Whitehaven   Keswick Appleby   Castle   Darlington   Middles   Whitby
      Windermere Tebay   Northallerton   brough
Ramsey   Low   Scarborough
ISLE OF   Gill   Malton   Bridlington
MAN   Barrow   Carnforth Ingleton
Douglas   Settle
Port Erin   Morecambe   Lancaster   Harrogate   York   Driffield
       Clitheroe   Market
      Burnley Bradford   Weighton   Hull
Blackpool   Preston   Leeds   Selby
         Halifax
Southport   Accrington Rochdale   New Holland   Grimsby
    Wigan   Huddersfield   Barnetby
      Bolton Stalybridge   Doncaster
Liverpool   Manchester Barnsley   Mablethorpe
Holyhead   Warrington   Sheffield   Retford   Gainsborough
Conway   Chinley
Bangor   Macclesfield   Lincoln
Chester   Bakewell   Chesterfield

——————— North Eastern

—·—·—·—·— Midland

+++++++++ London and North Western

—·········—· Furness

—··············— Maryport and Carlisle

++++++++++++++ Lancashire and Yorkshire

————— Isle of Man

············· Great Central

llllllllllllllllllllll Hull and Barnsley

—————— Great Northern

•·•·•·•·•·•·• Cheshire Lines

—————— North Stafford

•—·—·—·—·— Great Northern and
           Great Eastern Joint

PREFACE

When the idea of a book illustrating, in full colour, some 200 different locomotives was first put to me I must admit I was incredulous. The prospect seemed too near the railway enthusiast's conception of Valhalla to be true! But my friends of the Blandford Press showed me some beautiful volumes they had already produced in the same series, at a price within the pocket of the humblest of enthusiasts, and I listened to the production programme outlined to me with a quickened interest. Still there remained the question of the pictures. As the book was intended to cover the entire history of the British steam locomotive photographs were out of the question. One hundred and ninety-two pictures had got to be *painted*! It was then that I was introduced to Charles Rickitt and his Portman Artists. Still incredulous I chose a subject for a trial picture, but when I saw the result my doubts vanished, and the only problem that remained was that of getting the remaining 191 finished in time to meet the production schedule.

The only problem! There were many facets to it. The mere job of choosing the subjects – only 192 from the thousands of different locomotives that have run in Great Britain since the opening of the Stockton and Darlington Railway – was baffling at times, and embarrassing. Some claimants among the earlier subjects had to be discarded; information about their colour and finish was non-existent. But from the very outset I enjoyed the happiest of collaborations with Charles Rickitt, and with his artists Cliff and Wendy Meadway. From the first day, when we picnicked amid photographs, files, reference books and goodness knows what else in my home, locomotives have been painted with a speed and accuracy that could be likened to the production line of a modern factory. What might have been a nerve-racking race against time has been a great pleasure: sending the Meadways subject after subject in rapid succession, and seeing the results so swiftly and beautifully rendered.

In preparing the plates, we have made frequent reference to the well-established sources of historical railway information: to the Science Museum, London; to the Transport Museum at Clapham; and the railway museums at York and Swindon; to the files of 'The Locomotive Magazine'. For information upon certain specific liveries I am indebted to Mr John S. McLean, Mr Harold Chase, and to Mr Ivo Peters.

In points of detail, there may be readers who will feel that some locomotives might well have been left out, to make room for others of their own fancy. Partisanship for one or other of the pre-grouping companies certainly runs to fever heat at times, though not quite to the extent jocularly suggested by one of my closest railway friends. On telling him how carefully I had striven to try and give the fairest distribution among the companies he said: 'Oh well, if you've given 70 per cent to the Great Western and 30 per cent to the rest if would be about right'!

Our aim has been to provide the broadest possible picture of steam locomotive history. For that reason it has been impossible to include certain isolated 'specials', as when the London and North Western Railway painted one large express locomotive in pillar-box red and another in *white*, to celebrate the Diamond Jubilee of Queen Victoria's reign; or when the engines set aside for hauling the Queen's Messenger trains between Aberdeen and Ballater were painted in Royal Stewart tartan. Another livery that is missing is the short-lived 'silver' of the first L.N.E.R. streamlined 'A4' Pacific engines. No more than one picture could be allocated to each engine design, and as it was in the Garter Blue that the 'A4s' achieved their greatest fame, so it is in this style that the immortal *Mallard* is depicted.

As always, I have had invaluable help from Olivia, my wife. She too has her tastes in locomotive design, and in her view all single-wheelers not having slotted splashers should have been excluded! To her, as typist, art-critic and hostess to my collaborators, my best thanks are due.

Silver Cedars
High Bannerdown
Bath

Brock

March 1964

HISTORICAL INTRODUCTION

RAILWAYS in a number of crude forms had existed for many years before the birth of George Stephenson. By putting the primitive wagons of the day on to rails instead of trundling them along rough and badly maintained roads it was found that horses could pull far heavier loads, and the Stockton and Darlington Railway, which is generally considered to be the springboard from which the railway system of this country – and the world – originated, was laid out for horse traction. The geography of County Durham aided this general design. The country falls from the coalfields of Bishop Auckland to the sea, and horses could comfortably manage long trains of heavily loaded cauldron wagons, and equally well haul the empties back to the colliery districts. At the opening of the line, however, in 1825, the Company had one steam locomotive, the famous engine that now stands on a pedestal of honour in Darlington station, and in the great vision of development held by George Stephenson she was to be the forerunner of many more.

The *Locomotion*, for such she was named, was far from successful, however, and for many years George Stephenson and his strongest supporters had to fight an uphill battle against those who still favoured horse traction. And while the matter of motive power remained unresolved the rapid development of railways hung fire. The issue was settled beyond doubt by the trials at Rainhill on the line of the Liverpool and Manchester Railway in 1829, when the engine built by George Stephenson's son, Robert, won the prize offered by the directors for the best locomotive that could fulfil certain speed and haulage conditions. This locomotive was the *Rocket*, which more truly than the *Locomotion* of 1825 was the true progenitor of the machine that was to revolutionize inland transport in Great Britain. In the success of steam-worked railways men had both hopes and fears for the future. It was a time of great social unrest and evolution, and while facilitating the flow of commerce, railways would, it was feared, also make easier the movement of radical elements of the population, to spread discontent and trouble for the establishment. This, of course, was to take the narrowest possible view of a movement which, once started, proved to be irresistible.

Railways would have spread in any case, for transport of minerals, and the products of the new industries that were growing up in the country. But it was the steam locomotive that provided the factor that changed the entire life of the country – SPEED.

With speed also developed the capacity for the haulage of heavy loads. The steam locomotive not only provided means for enabling people to travel faster, but it made travel cheap. Simple souls who had never ventured beyond the confines of their own village could now travel at a penny a mile, or even cheaper on special excursion trips. Railways made easier the flow of commerce; merchants could travel easier and faster to see their clients; the day of the 'commercial traveller' was at hand. But perhaps of greater benefit to the country as a whole was the way in which railways, through the haulage capacity of the steam locomotive, brought down the price of consumer goods. An early railway manager was once horrified at the idea of carrying coal; but the opening of the Great Northern Railway, from Doncaster to London, in 1850, showed what could be done. This railway realized that far more revenue was likely to be gained from carrying minerals than passengers and the result of its enterprize and the effectiveness of the powerful locomotives used was so to revolutionize transport that the price of household coal in London was reduced from 30s. a ton to 17s.

The success of steam locomotives in both goods and passenger services led inevitably to greater demands being made upon them. Whereas today some of the greatest engineering brains are concentrated upon the development of nuclear power, electronics and so on, in mid-Victorian times the needs of railways and particularly the steam locomotive were second to none. These needs fostered the development of new engineering processes, in the iron and brass foundries, in heavy forging, and in the manufacture of iron itself. Railway needs led to improvements in technique that came to benefit the trade of the country as a whole. In no field was the development of the use of steel more striking than on railways. The need of something harder and stronger than wrought iron, for wheels, rails, and other moving parts subject to hard wear, fostered the rapid development of steel, and it is remarkable that the very first plant *anywhere in the world* for manufacture of steel on a commercial scale was put into operation at the Crewe locomotive works of the London and North Western Railway, in 1864. It was extensively used, not only for the production of locomotive parts, but to roll the rails they ran upon. By the year 1913 the output of the Crewe steel works had reached 50,000 tons per annum.

The influence of the steam locomotive was something infinitely greater than that of mere speed. Steam traction made travel cheap, easy, and relatively comfortable. While the rich travelled first class, in closed carriages that first resembled the old stage coaches, humbler folk experienced the pleasure of seeing something of the country from the open, third-class 'carriages'. Harrowing pictures have been painted of the miseries of travelling 'third' in those days, and spartan the conditions certainly could be in wet or wintry weather; but early excursion trains, however slow and draughty, were very popular, and undoubtedly contributed to the gradual spread of the broader education of the nineteenth century.

One is entitled to look with some awe and reverence to the unique, self-contained piece of machinery that was indeed the phenomenon of the nineteenth century. From the dawn of history the fastest mode of transport known to man was that of a galloping horse, and yet, within twenty years of the opening of the Stockton and Darlington Railway, there were steam locomotives capable of travelling at 60 m.p.h. By the seventies of last century speeds of 80 m.p.h. were occasionally being touched, and by 1904 a speed of 100 m.p.h. had been attained, on the Great Western Railway.

Inevitably the locomotive became the centrepiece of the entire railway scene. The passengers might be carried in open trucks, and later in roofed affairs that strongly suggested a cavalcade of dog-boxes, but the locomotives were arrayed in a splendour of polished metal and gleaming paint, and their drivers and firemen delighted in keeping them spotless. As the railway network of the country developed, and many of the earlier companies amalgamated to form the great trunk lines the names of which were household words prior to 1923, a series of very famous and beautiful engine liveries became established as standard, and in the colour plates of this book arranged largely, though not strictly, in chronological order one can follow this process of development. Among the larger railways the heights of magnificence were reached in the last years of the nineteenth century, and on such lines as the Great Western, the Midland, the Brighton, the North Eastern, and the Highland the dazzling array could not have been more ornate, yet withal in excellent taste.

In looking at the colour plates in this book one can trace how the quaint machines of the eighteen-thirties gave way to more solid, reliable locomotives. The overall efficiency was not very great, but in mid-Victorian times coal was cheap, and the main thing was to have machines that were inherently reliable. It was around the year 1880 that the sunny climate surrounding railway operation began to change. It is true that there had been lean times in the years following the railway investment mania, and the mid-sixties were a time of severe trade depression. But from 1880 onwards engineers began to seek means of securing greater efficiency in operation, and of reducing the coal bill. In marine engineering double- and triple-expansion engines were by that time commonplace, and many experiments were made with steam locomotives having compound or two-stage expansion of the steam. None of the nineteenth-century experiments in Great Britain had any lasting success – save one, chiefly because compounding brought with it certain gadgets, the ineffectiveness of which far outweighed any increase in thermal efficiency that might have been secured by compound rather than single-stage expansion.

There are pictures of the Webb compounds, built in such large numbers for the London and North Western Railway, at Crewe; there is one of the graceful and gaily adorned Worsdell von Borries compounds built at Gateshead, for the North Eastern Railway. But it was in purchase of a French-built de Glehn compound, the *La France* in 1903, that the Great Western virtually dealt the death-blow to the compound principle in Great Britain. For at Swindon, G. J. Churchward, one of the greatest masters of steam locomotive design, built single-expansion machines that were the superior of the French compounds, and *La France* was a very good compound too. The foundations of the modern engine were laid in those first momentous years of the twentieth century at Swindon, and in time all the railways of Britain were to adopt the principles established in the big Churchward 4-6-0s of the 'Saint' and 'Star' classes.

While these pages record the more spectacular developments in locomotive design they also reflect social history in depicting small tank engines that worked the breadwinners' trains around London. Richly adorned locomotives were not confined to main line expresses, and the tank engines of the North London, the London, Chatham and Dover, and of the Metropolitan, were little masterpieces of the decorative art. Goods engines were not excluded either, and the Stephenson long-boilered goods, used for hauling the coal trains on the Stockton and Darlington section of the North Eastern Railway, must surely rank as one of the most exquisitely painted pieces of machinery of all time.

When it comes to the conveyance of coal the local railways in South Wales have a place of their own. Each of the mining valleys came to have its own railway. Some of these lines were branches of the great trunk concerns like the London and North Western, and the Great Western; but in other of the valleys were to be found stoutly independent local companies like the Taff Vale, the Rhymney, and the Brecon and Merthyr. The faster they carried the coal down to the ports at Cardiff and Newport the faster it was mined at the pits, and eventually the trains of the various companies were virtually queueing up to get alongside the wharves in Cardiff. The coal-owners grew restive; congestion grew rather than lessened, and so a group of enterprising businessmen floated yet another new railway company, the Barry, and soon that line was also carrying coal almost to the limit of its capacity. The engines of the coal-carrying lines were not the least attractive in the zenith of the steam age.

As industry spread, fostered by the facility of rail transport, so the population grew and houses were in great demand. With that demand came a tremendous boom in the slate industry of North Wales. At Blaenau Festiniog the quarries were high in the mountains, and no locomotive power was needed at first to carry the slates down to sea-going ships at Portmadoc. The trains descended by gravity, and horses pulled the empties back to the quarries. But as the trade increased the loads became too much for the horses, and some of the most fascinating little narrow gauge locomotives ever devised – Robert Fairlie's 'double-engines' – were put to work. With the Festiniog came other narrow gauge railways in North Wales, while a classic example of one of these tiny concerns still remains in operation, the Talyllyn.

Railways, as required by British law, were expensive things to build and run where the traffic was light, and in many districts, long before the days of motor cars and lorries, something less pretentious was felt to be necessary. The necessary legislation, providing for numerous relaxations from main line standards, was given by the Light Railway Act of 1896, and a most picturesque line built under these provisions was to be seen in the Leek and Manifold Railway in the Derbyshire hills. Because of the strict limitation of maximum speed a light railway was not required to be fenced, and in consequence one saw, for the only time in England, locomotives with large headlamps to pick out animals or any other obstruction that might be on the rails at night. These narrow gauge lines, like the Lynton and Barnstaple, provided many attractions for the railway connoisseur, but few of them made any money for their owners.

In the twentieth century, on the main lines, the form and styling of locomotives is in some instances a reflection of national affairs. One by one the gay liveries of old began to disappear. Goods engines in ever-increasing numbers began to be painted black, and the onset of the First World War soon witnessed the painting over of much of the polished brass and copper work. The South-Eastern and Chatham, once re-nowned for a positively gorgeous turnout of its express locomotives, changed to a dark greenish grey, without any relief except a bold sans-serif rendering of the engine number in white paint. The Great Northern painted its goods engines in battleship grey, and the Great Eastern abandoned its rich royal blue for a dull slate grey. These were signs of the times, and some of the old liveries were gone never to re-appear. Then came the grouping of all the old independent railways of Great Britain into four large companies. Only a few of the joint lines and most of the narrow gauge lay outside this tremendous series of mergers.

From 1923 onwards the kaleidoscope of locomotive liveries that had so distinguished the railways of this country was suddenly contracted to four styles, of which three were green – those of the Great Western, of the Southern, and of the London and North Eastern. The London Midland and Scottish Railway retained 'Derby-red', but very soon all, except the top-line passenger types, were painted black. The Somerset and Dorset Joint and the Midland and Great Northern Joint retained their distinctive colours, and there were some gay interludes, as when Sir Nigel Gresley built the Silver Jubilee train in silver throughout, engine and coaches alike – and when the Coronation trains of 1937 were finished in blue. Otherwise it was a case of the traditional Great Western green; Derby-red; and L.N.E.R. apple green. O. V. S. Bulleid, in search for distinction, changed the Southern dark green to a startling synthetic hue known as 'Malachite Green', which is still to be seen on Southern Region passenger coaching stock today.

The nineteen-thirties were a time of great financial anxiety for the railways of Great Britain, and with traffic dwindling many devices of the showman's art were tried to win business. The streamlining of loco-motives had a value far greater to the publicists than to the engineers. At the same time speeds were soaring. For the first time a British train had made a considerably long run at an average speed of more than 80 m.p.h. from start to stop. The maximum speed record went up from 100 m.p.h., or slightly over, made by the Great Western *City of Truro* in 1904, to 108 m.p.h. by the Gresley non-streamlined Pacific *Papyrus* in 1935; to 112½ m.p.h. by the first L.N.E.R. streamliner *Silver Link* later that same year, and then to 114 m.p.h. by the Stanier Pacific

Coronation in 1937. Finally, in 1938, there came the record that is likely to stand for all time – the British and World record for steam, of 126 m.p.h. by the Gresley streamliner *Mallard*.

The Second World War brought an immediate end to all this activity, and the coloured section of this book records the locomotives built for war service, like the austerity 2-8-0, the L.N.E.R. 'B1', and the L.M.S. '8F' 2-8-0, which was ordered to be built for general service by a number of the once-independent railway works. The war was hardly over when nationalization of the railways took place, and the experience of the four main line companies was pooled in the work of a newly formed Railway Executive. From the plethora of strongly individual practices a single set of locomotive designs for the whole country was evolved and, although naturally there were some compromises and mistakes, the British Railways standard locomotives formed a worthy climax to the story. The last design of all, the big '9F' 2-10-0 freight engine, was in every way a remarkable machine.

This picture gallery, extending from the *Locomotion* of 1825 to the *Evening Star* of 1960, forms a deeply impressive record of a great national achievement. The book concerns only locomotives built for service on the home railways. There has been no space to illustrate any of the thousands of locomotives built in Great Britain for service in nearly every corner of the world, which, by opening up the countries, acted as influences for development of trade, industry and education, as well as being incomparable ambassadors of the skill of British engineering workmanship. The era of steam traction on British Railways is now nearly finished. It will go down in history as a period of the greatest social and industrial evolution the world has yet known.

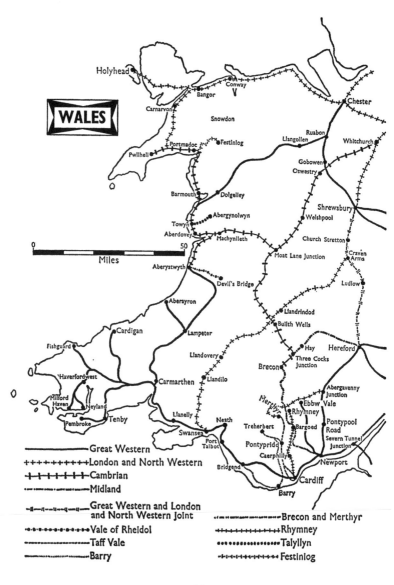

Holyhead

Conway

Bangor

Carnarvon

WALES

Snowdon

Chester

Portmadoc

Festiniog

Ruabon

Llangollen

Whitchurch

Pwllheli

Gobowen

Oswestry

Barmouth

Dolgelley

Shrewsbury

Abergynolwyn

Welshpool

Towyn

Aberdovey

Machynlleth

Church Stretton

Moat Lane Junction

Craven Arms

0   50

Miles

Aberystwyth

Devil's Bridge

Ludlow

Aberayron

Llandrindod

Builth Wells

Cardigan

Lampeter

Fishguard

Hay

Hereford

Llandovery

Three Cocks Junction

Brecon

Haverfordwest

Carmarthen

Llandilo

Abergavenny Junction

Milford Haven

Neyland

Llanelly

Neath

Merthyr

Ebbw Vale

Rhymney

Pembroke

Tenby

Treherbert

Bargoed

Pontypool Road

Swansea

Port Talbot

Pontypridd

Caerphilly

Severn Tunnel Junction

Bridgend

Newport

Cardiff

Barry

——————— Great Western
++++++++++London and North Western
+|+|+|+|+|+Cambrian
·—··—··—··—·Midland
—||—||—||—||—||— Great Western and London and North Western Joint
·•·•·•·•·•·•·•·•·•Vale of Rheidol
————————————Taff Vale
————————————Barry

·——··——··——··——·Brecon and Merthyr
++++++++++++++Rhymney
••••••••••••••••Talyllyn
·+·+·+·+·+·+·+·+Festiniog

14

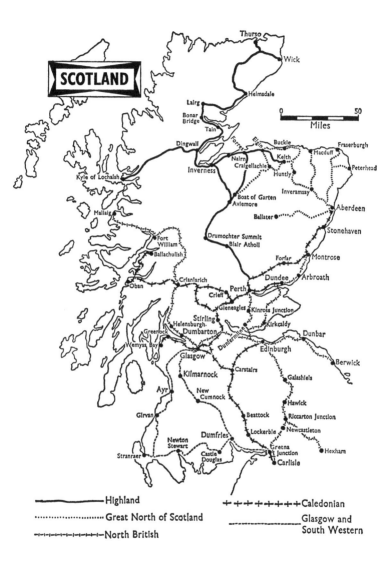

SCOTLAND

Thurso
Wick
Helmsdale
Lairg
Bonar
Bridge
Tain
Dingwall
Elgin
Buckie
Fraserburgh
Macduff
Nairn
Craigellachie
Keith
Peterhead
Inverness
Huntly
Inveramsay
Boat of Garten
Aviemore
Aberdeen
Ballater
Drumochter Summit
Stonehaven
Kyle of Lochalsh
Mallaig
Fort
William
Ballachulish
Blair Atholl
Forfar
Montrose
Oban
Crianlarich
Dundee
Arbroath
Crieff
Perth
Gleneagles
Kinross Junction
Stirling
Helensburgh
Dumbarton
Kirkcaldy
Greenock
Dunfermline
Dunbar
Wemyss Bay
Edinburgh
Glasgow
Berwick
Carstairs
Kilmarnock
Galashiels
Ayr
New
Cumnock
Hawick
Girvan
Beattock
Riccarton Junction
Newcastleton
Newton
Stewart
Dumfries
Lockerbie
Castle
Douglas
Gretna
Junction
Hexham
Stranraer
Carlisle

0   50
Miles

———————— Highland
·················· Great North of Scotland
-ı-ı-ı-ı-ı-ı-ı- North British
+++++++ Caledonian
————— Glasgow and
        South Western

15

THE COLOUR ILLUSTRATIONS

A full description of each
locomotive appears between
pages 113 – 186

1 **"Locomotion"**; engine No. 1 of the Stockton and Darlington Railway, built 1825 by George Stephenson.

2 **The "Rocket"**, built by Robert Stephenson 1829, and winner of the Rainhill trials. Liverpool and Manchester Railway.

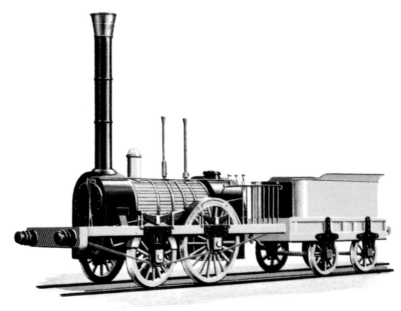

3 **Planet Type 2–2–0** engine of 1830, inside cylinders:
Liverpool and Manchester Railway.

4 **The "Derwent"**: an 1839 development of Timothy
Hackworth's coal engine for the Stockton and
Darlington Railway.

5 **Edward Bury's 2-2-0**, passenger engine for the
London and Birmingham Railway, 1837.

6 **The "North Star"**; Robert Stephenson's 2-2-2 of
1837, for the broad gauge Great Western Railway
(7ft).

7　**Crampton Type Engine "London"**; built by
Tulk and Ley, in 1847, for the London and Birmingham Railway.

8　**Allan's "Crewe" Goods**; a 2–4–0 of 1845 built at
Crewe for the Grand Junction Railway.

9　**Sharp 2 2 2**, passenger engine of 1842 for the
South Eastern Railway.

10　**"Firefly" class 2-2-2**, designed by Daniel Gooch
for the Great Western Railway, 1840.

11 **Stephenson Long-Boilered 4-2-0**, of 1847, for
the Southern Division of the London and North
Western Railway.

12 **The "Jenny Lind"**; David Joy's famous 2-2-2
built in 1847 by E. B. Wilson and Co. for the
Brighton railway.

13 **Gooch's Broad Gauge 8-Footer**; first introduced
1847 on the Great Western Railway, here shown
final form 1890.

14 **Joseph Beattie's 2-4-0**, express locomotive for the
London and South Western Railway, *Herod*. Built
1859.

15 **Stephenson's Long-Boilered Goods**; standard coal engine of the Stockton and Darlington section of the North Eastern Railway. One of the latest examples built 1874.

16 **A Furness Railway "Coppernob"**; a Bury type 0–4–0. An example of 1858, built by Fairbairn and Co.

17 **Hawthorn Type 2-2-2**; an 1852 express locomotive of the Great Northern Railway.

18 **The Cudworth "Mail" Engine**; crack South Eastern Railway 2-2-2 of 1862.

19 **Craven 2-2-2**, built 1862 for the Brighton railway, shown here as modified by Stroudley.

20 **A Broad Gauge Prodigy**; James Pearson's 9ft 4-2-4 tank engine of 1853, Bristol and Exeter Railway.

21 **A McConnell "Bloomer"**; one of the very celebrated 2–2–2 express locomotives of the L.&N.W.R.
Southern Division.

22 **Highland Railway 2–2–2**: A Scottish variant of
Allan's "Crewe" type, built 1863, here shown as
running in 1874.

23 **Lady of the Lake**; John Ramsbottom's 2–2–2 of
1859 for the Northern Division of the L.&N.W.R.

24 **Sturrock 0–6–0 with Steam Tender**; a heavy
mineral engine of 1863 for the Great Northern
Railway.

25 **Conner 8ft Single**; an express locomotive of 1859 for the Caledonian Railway.

26 **Great North of Scotland Railway**; one of the earliest British 4-4-os, designed by W. Cowan, 1865.

27 **Kirtley's "800" Class**; an outstanding 2–4–0
design of 1870 for the Midland Railway.

28 **Robert Sinclair's 2–2–2**; a picturesque and very
successful passenger engine of 1862 for the Great
Eastern Railway.

29 **A Stirling 8-Footer**; one of the most famous of all
19th Century locomotives, first introduced 1870
on the Great Northern Railway.

30 **A Stroudley "G" Class 2 2 2**; *Petworth*, a design
of 1880 for the London Brighton and South Coast
Railway.

31 **The Tay Bridge Engine**; designed in 1871 for the
North British Railway by T. Wheatley this engine
went into the river with the collapse of the first Tay
Bridge in 1879.

32 **North Eastern Railway "901" Class**; designed
by Edward Fletcher, 1872, for the Anglo-Scottish
expresses.

33 **David Jones's "F" Class**; a 4–4–0 of 1874 for the
Highland Railway.

34 **London Chatham and Dover Railway**; one of
Martley's "Europa" class 2–4–0s of 1873 used on
the Dover Mails.

35 **North London Railway**; an inside cylinder 4-4-0
tank engine of 1865, in original colours.

36 **A "Small Scotchman"**; a London Chatham and
Dover 0-4-2 tank engine of 1866, one of a class
distinguished by well-known Scottish names.

37 **The Steam Inner Circle**; one of the long-lived
Metropolitan 4–4–0 tanks, originally built in 1864,
here shown as running in 1948

38 **Great Western Railway**; 2–4–0 tank for the
Underground lines in London, and known as the
"Metropolitans".

39 **Dean's Standard Gauge 2–2–2**; a fine express locomotive of 1878 for the Great Western, here shown as running in about 1900.

40 **Webb's "Precedent" Class 2–4–0**; London and North Western Railway; introduced 1874 and 155 built at Crewe Works. *Snowdon* was the last to remain in traffic, withdrawn 1932.

41 **Glasgow and South Western Railway**; James Stirling's 4-4-0 of 1873.

42 **Dugald Drummond's N.B.R. 4-4-0** of 1876; designed specially to work the Waverley route between Edinburgh and Carlisle.

43 **A Caley "Jumbo"**; Drummond 0-6-0 of 1884 for
the Caledonian Railway.

44 **Webb's Standard Coal Engine**; a London and
North Western design of 1873, of which 500 were
built.

45 **The Dean "Goods"**; the very celebrated G.W.R.
0-6-0 of 1883 in its original livery.

46 **A "Skye Bogie"**; Highland Railway small-wheeled
4-4-0 of 1882 for the Dingwall and Skye line.

47 **Midland Railway**; A Johnson 2–4–0 of 1880 in the original green livery.

48 **The "Gladstone"**; the celebrated London Brighton and South Coast 0–4–2 of 1882, designed by W. Stroudley.

49 **Charles Sacre's 2-2-2**; for the Manchester, Sheffield and Lincolnshire Railway; a distinctive North Country design of 1883.

50 **South Eastern Railway "F" Class**; one of James Stirling's numerous standard 4-4-0s, first introduced 1883.

51 **Metropolitan District Railway**; a Beyer Peacock
4–4–0 tank of 1871, built to the Metropolitan
Railway design.

52 **London Tilbury and Southend Railway**; an
Adams 4–4–2 tank engine of 1882, as later modified
by Thomas Whitelegg.

53 **North London Railway**; an Adams 4-4-0 tank of 1868, as modernised, and running in the 20th Century.

54 **Maryport and Carlisle Railway**; a 2-4-0 passenger engine of 1867, running until 1921.

55 **Matthew Holmes's** 4–4–0, of 1890 for the North
British Railway, ran in the Race to the North in
1895.

56 **Great Eastern Railway**; James Holden's 7ft
2–2–2 of 1888.

57 **Lancashire and Yorkshire Railway**; an Aspinall
4-4-0 of 1891.

58 **W. Adams's Jubilee Class**; a London and South
Western 0-4-2 of 1887.

59 **Worsdell-Von Borries "J" Class**; North Eastern
2-cylinder compound 4–2–2 of 1889.

60 **Midland Railway**; a Johnson 4–4–0 of the "2183"
class, of 1892.

61 **The "Adriatic"**; a London and North Western
Webb 3-cylinder compound of 1889.

62 **Caledonian Railway**; one of the fast and efficient
Drummond 4–4–0s of 1884.

63 **A Dean 7ft 8in 4-2-2**; a classic Great Western design of 1892, of which 80 were built.

64 **Glasgow and South Western Railway**; one of James Manson's 4-4-0s of 1892.

65 **A North Eastern "Rail Crusher"**; nicknamed
thus because of their great weight, these 4-4-0s of
1892 were designed by Wilson Worsdell.

66 **A Johnson "Spinner"**; a Midland 4-2-2 express
locomotive of the 1886-97 period.   49

67 **London and South Western Railway**; an Adams outside-cylindered 4–4–0 of 1892.

68 **A Dunalastair 4–4–0**; of the Caledonian Railway, designed by McIntosh in 1896, this class was one of the most powerful of 19th Century locomotives.

69 **A Highland "Loch"**; one of David Jones's 4-4-0s
for the Perth – Inverness run. Built 1896.

70 **Great North of Scotland Railway**; engines of
this handsome design were first introduced in 1899.

71 **Webb 4-Cylinder Compound**; one of the longest-lived of all L.&N.W.R. compound designs. Of this 0-8-0 of 1901 a total of 170 was built.

72 **The First British "Atlantic"**; H. A. Ivatt's "990" class for the Great Northern, built 1898.

73 **The First British 4-6-0**; the "Jones Goods" of the Highland Railway introduced in 1894.

74 **The Aspinall Atlantic**; built 1899 for the Lancashire and Yorkshire Railway.

75 **Taff Vale Railway**; one of T. Hurry Riches' 0–6–2 tank engines of 1895.

76 **Barry Railway**; a handsome 0–4–4 passenger tank engine of 1892.

77 **Rhymney Railway**; a mixed traffic 0-6-2 tank
engine of 1909.

78 **Brecon and Merthyr Railway**; a mineral tank
engine of 1909.

79 **London Brighton and South Coast Railway**;
R. J. Billinton's "B4" class 4-4-0 of 1899.

80 **An Oil-Fired 4-2-2,** of 1898; James Holden's
locomotives for the Great Eastern Railway Cromer
expresses.

81 **Great Central Railway**; a Pollitt 4–4–0 of 1894 as
modified and superheated by J. G. Robinson.

82 **North Eastern Railway**; one of the celebrated
"R" class 4–4–0s of 1899, some of which were
in service for more than 50 years.

83 **Furness Railway**: a Pettigrew 4-4-0 express passenger engine of 1901.

84 **Cambrian Railways**; a passenger 4-4-0 of 1893 design.

85 **Somerset and Dorset Joint Railway**; a 4–4–0 of
1903 built at the Midland Railway works at Derby.

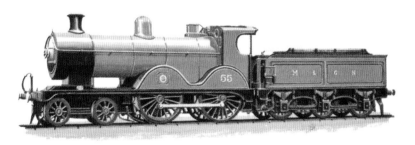

86 **Midland and Great Northern Joint Railway**;
an express passenger 4–4–0 of 1908, as rebuilt at
Melton Constable from a Midland design of 1894.

87 **Lynton and Barnstaple** narrow gauge railway;
one of the quaint little 2-6-2 tank engines of 1898.

88 **Leek and Manifold Light Railway**; one of the
handsome 2-6-4 tank engines of 1904.

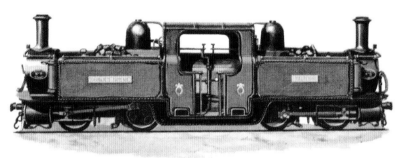

89 **Festiniog Railway**; one of the famous "double-engines", on Robert Fairlie's patent, as running today, but first introduced in 1869.

90 **Snowdon Mountain Railway**; one of the Swiss-built rack locomotives of 1895.

91 **The "Claud Hamilton"**; epoch-marking Great Eastern 4-4-0 of 1900, forerunner of more than 100 of this design.

92 **A Johnson "Belpaire" 4-4-0**, of the Midland Railway, as originally built in 1901 with large bogie tender.

93 **Hull and Barnsley Railway**; one of Matthew
Stirling's express passenger 4-4-0s of 1910.

94 **The "City of Truro"**; the Great Western record
breaker built 1903, attained 100 m.p.h. with an
Ocean Mail special in 1904.

95 **A "Precursor" Class 4 4 0**. of the London and North Western Railway, No. 1111 *Cerberus*, first introduced in 1904; eventually the class was 130 strong.

96 **Earle Marsh's "I3" Tank**; a very efficient 4 4 2 of 1908 for the London Brighton and South Coast Railway.

97 **The De Glehn 4 4 2 "La France"**. French-built
compound Atlantic for the Great Western Railway,
1903.

98 **Dugald Drummond's "T9" 4 4 0**, this London
and South Western Class of 1899, of which there
were 66, were nicknamed the "Greyhounds".

99 **Lancashire and Yorkshire Railways**; one of the numerous 2-4-2 side tank engines of 1889–1911.

100 **London and South Western Railway**; the "M7" 0-4-4 passenger tank engine of 1897.

101 **Stroudley's "D" Class 0–4–2 Tank**; originally built in 1873, here shown in the Marsh livery.

102 **Great Eastern Railway**; the 0–6–0 London suburban tank engine of 1890–1902.

103 **"Cardean" of the Caledonian**; one of the most
famous of all Scottish locomotives, built 1906.

104 **Glasgow and South Western Railway**; a Manson 4-6-0 of 1903 for the Midland "Pullman" trains.

105 **The Highland "Castle" Class**; a splendid design
of 1900, prepared originally by David Jones and
completed by Peter Drummond.

106 **A Reid "Atlantic"**; built 1906, later superheated,
the premier class of the North British Railway.

107 **A Great Northern "Atlantic"**; first introduced in 1902 by H. A. Ivatt, these engines were the mainstay of the Anglo-Scottish service south of York for 20 years.

108 **South Eastern and Chatham Railway**; Wainwright's "E" class 4–4–0 of 1905.

109 **A Great Western "Saint"**; outcome of a classic
locomotive development by G. J. Churchward,
begun in 1902.

110 **A Midland Deeley Compound**; developed from
the Smith-Johnson engines of 1902 the superheated
compound of 1913 represented the last word in
Midland locomotive practice.

111 **A "Jersey Lily" of the G.C.R.**; Robinson's handsome Atlantic design of 1904.

112 **The "Great Bear"**; Churchward's experimental
Pacific of 1908, Great Western Railway.

113 **A Brighton "Atlantic"**; Earle-Marsh's 4–4–2 locomotive of 1905 for the seaside expresses of the L.B.&S.C.R.

114 **North Staffordshire Railway**; John H. Adams's 4–4–2 superheated tank engine of 1911.

115 **The "Abergavenny"**; Earle-Marsh's 4–6–2 tank
engine of 1910, for the Brighton line.

116 **The "Immingham" Class 4–6–0**; Robinson's
express goods engine of 1907 for the Great Central
Railway.

117 **London Tilbury and Southend Railway**; Thomas Whitelegg's 4-4-2 express tank engine of 1907–9.

118 **The Class "X" Hump Shunters**; of the North Eastern Railway, built 1909 for work in marshalling yards.

119 **The "Coronation" Engine of 1911**; one of the
very celebrated "George the Fifth" class 4-4-0s of
the London and North Western Railway.

120 **A Great Central "Director"**; J. G. Robinson's
express passenger 4-4-0 of 1913.

121 **Midland Railway**; Fowler's Class 2 superheated 4-4-0 of 1913.

122 **Dugald Drummond's "D15"**; introduced 1912 on the L.&S.W.R. these handsome 4-4-0s were his last locomotive design.

123   **Great Eastern Railway**; the "1500" class 4-6-0 of 1912 (later known as L.N.E.R. "B12").

124   **A North Eastern "Z"**; one of Sir Vincent Raven's 3-cylinder Atlantics of 1911.

125 **A "Prince of Wales" 4-6-0**; a very successful
London and North Western design of 1911; engine
No. 1537 *Enchantress*.

126 **A Drummond 4-Cylinder 4-6-0**; one of the
"T14" class of 1911 (L.&S.W.R.) nicknamed the
"Paddleboats".

127 **A North Western "Claughton"**; Bowen-Cooke's
4-cylinder 4–6–0 first built at Crewe in 1913, engine
No. 668 *Rupert Guinness*.

128 **L. Billinton's Giant 4 6 4**; the *Charles C. Macrae*
of 1914 for the Brighton expresses.

129 **A Great Northern "Mogul"**; Gresley's "K2"
class 2–6–0 of 1914.

130 **A "River" Class 4–6–0**; originally built for the
Highland in 1915, but transferred to the Caledonian
and here shown in the C.R. livery.

131 **Churchward's Masterpiece**; the Great Western
4-cylinder 4-6-0 "Star" class, introduced 1907, and
superheated from 1909 onwards.

132 **A Pickersgill 4-4-0**; for the Caledonian Railway,
introduced 1916, of a class eventually numbering 48.

133 **Glasgow and South Western Railway**; Peter
Drummond's express goods 2–6–0 of 1915.

134 **A North British "Glen"**; a very powerful 4–4–0
of 1913 designed by W. P. Reid for the West
Highland line.

135 **Somerset and Dorset Joint Railway**; one of the special 2–8–0 freight engines designed and built at Derby in 1914.

136 **Caledonian Railway**; a Pickersgill outside cylindered 4–6–0 of 1916.

137 **A "Super D" 0–8–0 Goods**, of the London and
North Western Railway, introduced 1912; class
eventually 295 strong.

138 **North Staffordshire Railway**; Hookham's 0–6–4
passenger tank engine of 1916.

139 **A North Eastern "T2"**; a heavy mineral 0–8–0 of 1913.

140 **A Highland Railway "Clan"**; a 4–6–0 of 1919 designed by Christopher Cumming.

141 **The Gresley "K3" 2–6–0**; originally built for the
Great Northern, in 1920. The class became an
L.N.E.R. standard.

142 **South Eastern and Chatham Railway**; Maunsell's "N" class mixed traffic 2–6–0 of 1917.

143 **A Maunsell "E1"** **4-4-0**; rebuilt from class E in
1919 for the S.E.&C.R. Continental Boat trains.

144 **Furness Railway**; E. Sharples's 4-6-4 tank engine
of 1920 for heavy intermediate duty.

145 **The Lickey Bank Engine**; Midland Railway 4-cylinder 0–10–0 (Big Bertha).

146 **The "N2" Suburban Tank of 1921**; designed by H. N. Gresley for the Great Northern local services.

147 **Great Northern Railway**; Gresley's 3-cylinder 2–8–0 mineral engine of 1921.

148 **R. Whitelegg's Baltic Tank**; of 1922, for the Glasgow and South Western Clyde coast services.

149 **Metropolitan Railway**; Charles Jones's 4–4–4 express tank engine of 1920 for outer residential services.

150 **J. G. Robinson's Historic 2–8–0**; designed in 1911 for the Great Central Railway; adopted as a War Office standard, in 1914-18, and built to a total of 521 for army services overseas.

151 **A Great Western "Castle"**; a later example, the
Isambard Kingdom Brunel, of the famous design
introduced in 1923 by C. B. Collett.

152 **Lancashire and Yorkshire Railway**; a "Class
8" 4-cylinder 4–6–0 of 1920.

153 **The First Gresley Pacific**; No. 1470 *Great Northern* of the G.N.R. built 1922.

154 **Sir Vincent Raven's Pacific**; the climax of North Eastern locomotive design, built in 1922.

155 **The "King Arthur" Class**; Southern Railway express passenger 4-6-0 of 1925.

156 **An L.M.S. Standard Compound**; built from 1923 onwards as a result of the successful trials of the standard Midland type 4-4-0.

157 **An L.M.S. Standard Goods**; the "4F" 0-6-0, developed from Fowler's Midland design.

158 **The "Sandringham" Class 4-6-0**; built 1928, for the East Anglian services of the London and North Eastern Railway.

159   **The "Lord Nelson"**; Maunsell's 4-cylinder 4–6–0
for the Southern Railway, built 1926.

160   **The "Royal Scot" Class 4–6–0**; an L.M.S.R.
standard design of 1927 that became world famous.

161 **The "King George V"**; the ultimate development on the G.W.R. of the Churchward 4-cylinder 4–6–0 design, built at Swindon 1927.

162 **The Gresley Super-Pacific**; a very famous engine, *Papyrus*, of the L.N.E.R. "A3" class.

163 **An L.M.S. Horwich Mogul**; the 2–6–0 mixed
traffic design of 1926.

164 **The G.W.R. "Hall" Class**; a smaller wheeled
variant (1924) of the Churchward "Saint" class.

165 **Gresley's "Shire" Class 4-4-0**; a 3-cylinder
4-4-0 of 1927 for general passenger service.

166 **A Beyer-Garratt 2-6-0 † 0-6-2**; freight engine
for the L.M.S.R. introduced 1927.

167 **L.M.S. "5XP" (Baby Scot)**; of 1930, later known
officially as the "Patriot" class.

168 **A Southern "School"**; the most powerful 4–4–0s
in Europe, introduced by R. E. L. Maunsell in 1929.

169 **A Pannier Tank 0-6-0** of the Great Western Railway. Introduced in 1929 this class eventually consisted of 790 engines.

170 **A Stanier "Black Five"**; a standard L.M.S. mixed traffic 4–6–0 of 1934 design.

171 **A Gresley "P2" 2–8–2**, for the L.N.E.R., one of a class of 6, representing the only 8-coupled express locomotives to run in Britain; introduced 1934.

172 **A World Record Breaker**; Gresley's streamlined Pacific *Mallard*, which attained 126 m.p.h. in 1938.

173 **The "Princess Elizabeth"**; one of Stanier's "Princess Royal" class Pacifics of 1933 for the L.M.S.R.

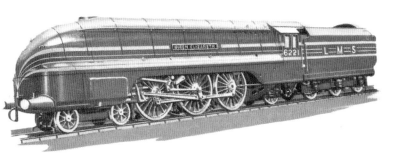

174 **The "Coronation" of 1937**; the L.M.S. stream-lined Pacific design for the Coronation Scot service.

175 **A "Green Arrow"** 2–6–2; Gresley's very successful mixed traffic design for the London and North Eastern Railway.

176 **A Stanier "8F"** 2–8–0; originally designed for the L.M.S.R. but adopted as a national standard engine in World War II.

177 **An L.M.S. "Jubilee" 4–6–0**; introduced 1934 by
Sir William Stanier, for general express service.

178 **"Sir William A. Stanier F.R.S."**; a Pacific of
1947 representing the final development of the
L.M.S. Stanier Pacifics.

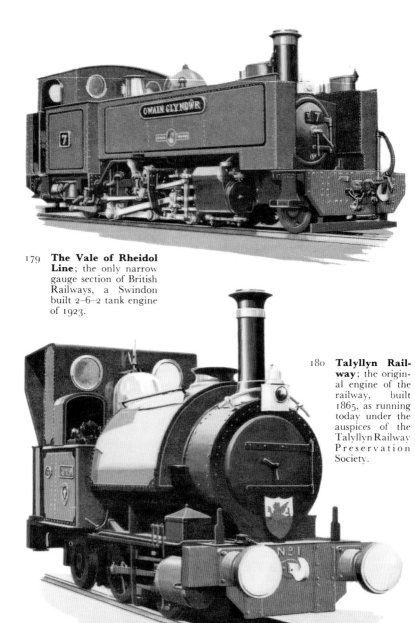

179 **The Vale of Rheidol Line**; the only narrow gauge section of British Railways, a Swindon built 2–6–2 tank engine of 1923.

180 **Talyllyn Railway**; the original engine of the railway, built 1865, as running today under the auspices of the Talyllyn Railway Preservation Society.

181 **Isle of Man Railway**; A Beyer-Peacock 2–4–0 tank engine of 1873, in the livery of today.

182 **Romney, Hythe and Dymchurch Railway**; a 15-inch gauge 4–8–2 express locomotive *Hercules*.

183 **"Merchant Navy" Class**; Pacific designed by O. V. S. Bulleid, in 1941, as originally built with air smoothed casing.

184 **A Thompson "B1" 4-6-0**; introduced by L.N.E.R. in 1942 for general utility service.

185   **The Rebuilt "Royal Scot"** of 1943, including many new features and the Stanier taper boiler.

186   **Austerity 2–8–0 of 1942**; built for wartime service at home and overseas to designs of R. A. Riddles.

187 **The Peppercorn "A1"**; the L.N.E.R. Pacific of
1947, here shown in British Railways colours.

188 **A "Britannia" Pacific**; a British Railways standard design of 1951, the *Hereward the Wake*.

189 **A "BR5" Mixed Traffic 4–6–0**; a general utility
engine developed from the Stanier "Black Five".

190 **A "West Country" 4–6–2**; formerly of the Bulleid
air-smoothed design, but here seen rebuilt with
conventional valve gear, and outer casing removed.

191 **A "BR4" Standard 2–6–0**; designed by R. A. Riddles for light general utility services.

192 **The "Evening Star"**; last steam locomotive built for service in Great Britain; one of the Riddles "9F" 2–10–0s.

1 **'Locomotion'**; engine No. 1 of the Stockton and Darlington Railway.

This celebrated engine, built in September 1825, was the first steam locomotive to be used on a public railway. It was a development of the type George Stephenson had worked up on the Killingworth Colliery lines, and included a number of features that were fairly common among the primitive, pioneer steam locomotives of what may be termed the pre-*Rocket* age. This engine is now preserved, and displayed on a pedestal in Darlington station. A point that immediately strikes the onlooker is the construction of the wheels – built up from a number of iron castings dowelled together. The valve gear was on the top of the boiler, and the two cylinders were mounted with their axes vertically, and the lower parts of each cylinder *inside the boiler*. There was one single flue 2 ft. in diameter, and at the front end this flue was bent round and continued upward as a chimney. The boiler pressure was 50 lb. per sq. in. When the engine was first put into service it would not steam, and the single flue had to be replaced by a return flue. The little tender was made entirely of wood, carrying a sheet-iron tank for water. This engine ran during the public opening of the railway, on September 27, 1825, and though it was far from successful in its original form its work was such as to provide encouragement and promise to all those who had faith in the establishment of a railway system operated by steam locomotives.

2 **The 'Rocket'**; Liverpool and Manchester Railway.

While very far from being the father of all steam locomotives the *Rocket*, winner of the ever-famous Rainhill trials of 1829, could certainly lay claim to be the very first one to be reasonably successful and reliable in service. In the Science Museum at South Kensington there are, virtually, two *Rockets*. One, an old and obviously well-used machine, is the original engine, though very much altered from the condition in which she won the Rainhill prize for George and Robert Stephenson. The second is an exact replica of the original, in her Rainhill condition, in the gay livery she sported for the trials. The *Rocket* as originally built, and as illustrated here, had her cylinders mounted at a steeply inclined angle high up on the side of the boiler. This gave her an awkward swaying action at speed, and some little time after she went into regular service on the Liverpool and Manchester Railway the position of the cylinders was changed. The other outstanding feature of the original *Rocket* was the use of the multitubular boiler, and the passing of the exhaust steam from the cylinders through a narrowing passage to an orifice in the smokebox. The blastpipe, for so it became known, produced a draught through the boiler tubes and assisted in accelerating combustion of the fuel, and the rapid raising of steam.

3 **Planet Type 2-2-0**; Liverpool and Manchester Railway.

One of the most marked characteristics in the working of the *Rocket*, observed very clearly during the Rainhill trials, and criticized by opponents of the Stephensons, was the swaying jerky action of the engine, attributable to the mounting of the cylinders high up on the side of the smokebox. Later engines of the 'Rocket' type had the cylinders mounted more nearly horizontal, but still outside the frames. The use of inside cylinders on the *Planet* in 1830 – probably the very first case in the world – was not wholly due to a desire to get smoother riding, but due to a suggestion made to Robert Stephenson by Richard Trevithick the great Cornish pioneer, who had found in repairing an old beam engine that he obtained an almost sensational economy of fuel by fitting a jacket round the cylinder to prevent loss of heat by radiation. On the *Planet* Stephenson enclosed the cylinders within the smokebox. The engine also incorporated the first use of 'sandwich' frames, which were formed of ash or oak, strengthened by iron plates inside and out. These gave flexibility and a great strength, and were a distinctive feature – for example – of many broad gauge locomotives on the Great Western Railway in later years. The *Planet* was thus very much a landmark in locomotive history.

4 The 'Derwent'; Stockton and Darlington Railway.

Hackworth had been associated with the Stephensons, father and son, from the very inception of the Stockton and Darlington Railway; but after its opening to the public circumstances arose to leave him very much on his own, and he was faced with the poor steaming qualities of the *Locomotion* and other engines working on the line. It was Hackworth who conceived the idea of putting a return bend in the flue, running it the length of the boiler twice, and so lengthening the time that the hot gases of combustion were in proximity to the water. After some experiments this idea was incorporated in a new engine, the *Royal George*, built in 1827, and in so doing Hackworth incorporated what we should now regard as a very quaint idea. The use of the return flue meant that the firebox had to be at the same end of the engine as the chimney. So Hackworth provided two tenders – one propelled in front of the engine carrying the coal and the fireman, and the second at the rear, carrying the water tank, or barrel, and the driver. A beautiful example of this type of engine has been preserved at Darlington, the *Derwent*, which was built by Alfred Kitching and Company, in 1839. Engines of this type were built down to the year 1846, and some were still in regular service on the Stockton and Darlington line in 1875.

5 Edward Bury's 2-2-0; London and Birmingham Railway.

Edward Bury was once described as a man strongly endowed with the commercial instinct. He certainly contrived to play, very successfully, the rôle of Locomotive Superintendent of the London and Birmingham Railway and contractor for the supply of locomotives at one and the same time. His engines were light, ingeniously constructed, and so very cheap; and in his rôle as user of them he saw to it that they were not overworked. The distinguishing feature of all his engines was the use of bar frames, which gave them a light, spidery appearance. They had circular fireboxes, with a steam dome and safety valve on the top. The passenger engines on the London and Birmingham were of the 2-2-0 type, while the goods, otherwise similar, were 0-4-0. If one engine were not enough to do the job he put on two, three, and sometimes even four on one train! It was all good for the locomotive trade. Like many engines of those early days the Bury's rode badly, partly because of the very short wheelbase, and the lightness of the tenders. The London and Birmingham nevertheless remained a home of these light four-wheeled engines long after all other main lines had abandoned them for longer and larger engines, and in view of the heavy traffic on the line, and the multitudes of engines necessary to work it, the four-wheeled Bury's, whether of the 2-2-0 or 0-4-0 type, have a special place in railway history.

6 The 'North Star'; Great Western Railway.

From its inception the Great Western Railway in many respects stood in isolation from the rest of the country, through its adoption of the broad gauge, 7 ft., in contrast to the standard gauge of 4 ft. 8½ in. used on most other railways in Great Britain. Brunel was the architect of the broad gauge, and at first he took direct responsibility for ordering the locomotives. It must be admitted that he saddled the G.W.R. with a poor lot – with one outstanding exception. The *North Star* came to the Great Western almost by accident, as it were. It was built by Robert Stephenson and Co. for service in America on the New Orleans Railway. It was actually shipped, but through business difficulties delivery was not taken, and it was returned to England. On its arrival back it was adapted to run on the 7 ft. gauge and sold to the Great Western. A replica of it is now housed in the G.W.R. Museum at Swindon, and looking on this one can quite appreciate Brunel's comment, that it would make a handsome ornament in the most elegant drawing-room. It was upon the general layout of the *North Star* that Daniel Gooch based the design of his very successful 'Firefly' class of 2-2-2 express locomotives. The original *North Star* was withdrawn from service in 1870, and for many years it was kept at Swindon. It was scrapped in 1906, and the present replica was constructed for the Railway Centenary celebrations in 1925.

7 **Crampton Type Engine 'London';** London and Birmingham Railway.
Thomas Russell Crampton was one of the great characters of early railway days. Unlike most of the great pioneers he was born in comparatively genteel circumstances, and it was not until he was 23 years of age that he took his first post as an engineer. From then onwards he proved himself a prolific, if rather fanciful inventor. He will always be remembered by the 'Crampton' type of locomotive, which has a single pair of large-diameter driving wheels at the extreme rear end. The idea was to leave the forward part of the locomotive completely clear of driving axles and running gear so as to use a large boiler. His engines were tried on many railways in Great Britain, but although they were fast runners they were not

generally successful. The engine illustrated in our picture was built in 1847 by Tulk and Ley, and had 8 ft. diameter driving wheels. It is credited with runs at over 50 m.p.h. on the London and Birmingham section of the L.N.W.R. main line. On the Continent of Europe Crampton had far greater success, and in France and Germany the type was well liked, and up to the year 1864 no fewer than 300 had been built. In France indeed the phrase 'Prendre le Crampton' was synonymous with 'going by train'! A magnificent example has been preserved, and today is still in full working order. It made some special runs as recently as the summer of 1963.

8 **Allan's 'Crewe' Goods;** Grand Junction Railway.
At the time of the great amalgamation of 1846, by which the London and Birmingham, the Grand Junction, and the Manchester and Birmingham Railways merged to form the London and North Western, Alexander Allan was 'foreman of locomotives' on the Grand Junction, at Crewe. To overcome difficulties with broken crank axles on the older engines Allan developed a new design using outside cylinders, with the cylinders themselves ensconced in a massive arrangement of double framing. This proved an extremely sound mechanical job, and large numbers of locomotives of both 2-2-2 and 2-4-0 types were built at Crewe for service on the Northern Division of the newly-formed London and North Western Railway. Engines of this type were the first to work over the formidable obstacle of Shap Summit, among the Westmorland Fells. In later years Allan was much in demand as a locomotive consultant, and engines of this same general type were used on various sections of the Caledonian Railway. On the L.N.W.R. all the old Crewe engines, both 2-2-2 passenger and 2-4-0 goods, were named; the nameplates were of the plain

brass plate type standard throughout the entire existence of the L.N.W.R., while the great majority of the names allotted to the Allan engines were handed down from one generation of Crewe locomotives to another. Between 1845 and 1858 a total of 396 engines of the Allan type were built at Crewe for service on the L.N.W.R.; 158 were of the 2-2-2 wheel arrangement, and 238 were 2-4-0s.

9 **Sharp 2-2-2;** South Eastern Railway. In contrast to the novel, almost freakish long-boilered express engines favoured by Stephenson's in the 1840s, some of the other locomotive builders concentrated on a simple, straightforward design, when they were left to their own predilections. Sharp, Roberts and Co., later Sharp, Stewart, and eventually a constituent of the North British Locomotive Company, developed a simple 2-2-2 design, with outside frames in which the characteristic feature was the curve of the running plate over the driving wheel axlebox. This was done to avoid leaving excessively-deep horn guides for the leading and trailing coupled wheels. The example illustrated is one of a batch used on the South Eastern Railway from the opening of the line. At that time the main line to Dover went via Redhill, and under a working arrangement with the London and Croydon Railway the locomotive stocks of the two companies were pooled. Nearly all the Sharp 2-2-2s contributed to the pool by the South Eastern Railway were named, and included such quaint Saxon titles as *Eadbald*, *Ethelred* and *Egbert* together with invaders of the Kentish shores like *Hengist* and *Horsa*.

10 **'Firefly' Class 2-2-2;** Great Western Railway.
When Gooch was appointed Locomotive Superintendent of the G.W.R. his chief, the great Isambard Kingdom Brunel had already ordered a number of locomotives. They proved to be a poor lot, and of the original deliveries only the *North Star* from Stephenson's, reference 6, had any degree of reliability. Gooch was authorized to purchase many more engines, and he took the *North Star* design, and incorporated in it many great improvements, particularly in the provision of a much more adequate boiler and firebox. The result was the very famous 'Firefly' class, of which the first examples were put on the road in 1840. They were enormous engines for the period, and striking in appearance not only for their great width, but by the huge bell-mouthed chimney, the boiler lagging of polished timber, and the haycock type of firebox, the top of which was covered in polished copper sheet. No fewer than 62 of these engines were built between 1840 and 1842, and they put the Great Western far in advance of any other company so far as engine power and speed was concerned. One of the finest recorded performances was in 1844 on the opening of the line throughout from London to Exeter. On the return trip, with the engine *Actaeon*, the entire journey was done in 4 hr. 40 min. at an average speed of 41½ m.p.h. over a distance of 194 miles. This was quite outstanding for the year 1844.

11 **Stephenson Long-boilered 4-2-0;** London and North Western Railway.
The long-boilered type of locomotive was used in many applications by Robert Stephenson and Co., and for passenger work the 2-2-2 wheel arrangement was at first adopted. Some were put into service on the York and North Midland Railway, others in East Anglia, and there was the notorious *White Horse of Kent*. All these engines were alike in having the wheels close together in the centre, leaving considerable overhangs at front and rear. And all were dangerously unsteady when they worked up to speed. The *White Horse of Kent* caused the death of several enginemen through derailments and overturning. Then Stephenson tried a different arrangement of the wheels, and the

London and North Western engine illustrated had the driving wheels at the back and two pairs of carrying wheels, spaced wide apart, under the front end of the engine. The middle pair of wheels were flangeless. Some engines of this type running on the L.&N.W.R. had driving wheels of no less than 7 ft. in diameter, the largest ever applied to a Stephenson long-boilered engine. But despite the re-arrangement of the wheels these engines were little better as vehicles than the 2-2-2 type, and their life was relatively short. They stand out as a curiosity, but one nevertheless that was at one time highly favoured by the pioneer firm of locomotive builders in the world.

12　The 'Jenny Lind'; Brighton Railway.

The designing of this famous and beautiful engine is one of the 'romances' of British railway history. Joy worked for E. B. Wilson and Company, of the Railway Foundry, Leeds, and after he had been sent to Brighton to gather particulars of the new express locomotives required the question was thrown into the melting pot, and Wilson's were told to supply whatever they liked. There was much dis-agreement among the directors as to what to build, and it was in a feeling of frustra-tion that Joy went home for the weekend. In the quiet of his own home he looked at the problem anew, began to sketch, and by Sunday evening the *Jenny Lind* was designed. Its particular features were the inside framing for the driving wheels, outside frames for the leading and trailing, and what was then quite a large boiler, carrying a pressure of 120 lb. per sq. in. The classical fluted style of the dome, and safety valve column was a feature of all Wilson's products at that time. After the success of the first engines of this type on the Brighton railway, Wilson supplied 'Jennys' to many other railways, and at the height of their popularity the Railway Foundry was building them at the rate of one per week. Some of the most picturesque, so far as outward finish was concerned, were those on the Oxford, Worcester and Wolverhampton Railway, which eventually became part of the Great Western. Others of the same general design were used on the York and North Midland Railway.

13　**Gooch's Broad Gauge 8-footer;** Great Western Railway.

Spurred by the exciting stimulus of the 'Battle of the Gauges', locomotive develop-ment on the Great Western Railway was extremely rapid in the eighteen-forties. Brunel had claimed superior travel in every way as the advantage of his 7 ft. gauge, and when its continuance was challenged to the extent of setting up a Royal Commission on Railway Gauges Daniel Gooch built a series of locomotives at Swindon Works that gave a perfor-mance far superior to anything then running on the standard 4 ft. 8½ in. gauge. The culmination of this rapid develop-ment was the *Iron Duke* of 1847. This remarkable engine was the forerunner of 23 more, built at Swindon in 1847 to 1851, and 7 more were added to the stock in 1854–5. These engines, rebuilt and no more than slightly modernized, lasted for the entire remaining period of the broad gauge, until May 1892, by which time their appearance had been changed to that shown in our picture of *Tornado*. Originally they had no cabs, and the boilers were clothed with varnished wood lagging. A peculiarity of the broad gauge was that none of the locomotives carried numbers. They were recognized only by their names – a fine lot, symbolical of the speed and prowess of the Great Western in broad gauge days: *Amazon, Courier, Rover, Swallow, Lightning, Warlock* and so on.

14　**Joseph Beattie's 2-4-0;** London and South Western Railway.

For many years the London and South

Western locomotive department, at Nine Elms, was ruled with a rod of iron by Joseph Beattie. He was not only a martinet but a lover of gadgets in engineering design, and his engines were fitted with innumerable fancy gadgets for improving their thermal efficiency. The 2-4-0 express locomotives with 6 ft. 6 in. coupled wheels were the nearest approach to a standard class at the period 1860–70. There were 62 of them in all, built between 1859 and 1875, and in that period they did the bulk of the express passenger work between London and Salisbury, and London and Bournemouth. They carried a most ornate and beautiful livery, but some of their names were rather forbidding – strongly suggestive of the hard, fiery-natured designer. Our picture shows *Herod*. Other Beattie engines had such titles as *Firebrand*, *Tartar*, *Plutus*, *Volcano*, *Vulcan*! Joseph Beattie followed a positive crusade towards coal saving, and his engines had some extraordinary designs of fireboxes, which certainly saved coal, but introduced many points of leakage. The drivers and firemen must have had many trials and tribulations in nursing Beattie's gadgets along. But it would have been more than their lives were worth to complain, or suggest alternatives!

15 **Stephenson's Long-boilered Goods;** North Eastern Railway.
By the end of the 'thirties' of last century many firms had entered the field of locomotive building, and at that early date in railway history the railway companies mostly had insufficient experience to specify their needs precisely. They had to choose between the specialities of different builders, and he who could claim novelty or increased efficiency got the most consideration. Robert Stephenson & Co. came out with the idea of the 'long-boilered' engine, in which all wheels were placed ahead of the firebox, so that there was no restriction on its size. But the firebox was not the only consideration,

and a long boiler needs a very fierce draught to make it steam freely. In main line express service the long-boilered type was a failure, but in heavy mineral service it was remarkably successful. In the latter kind of service one did not have to cater for continuous steaming. A coal train might be held up for half an hour or more, and then the long boiler proved a most useful reservoir for storing up a supply of steam for the next pull-away. On the Stockton and Darlington Railway the 'long-boilered' 0-6-0 was the standard freight engine down to the year 1875, and the engine illustrated, which has been restored to its original condition and preserved in the Railway Museum at York, was in regular service until 1922.

16 **A Furness Railway 'Coppernob'.**
Bury's design of bar-framed four-wheeled engine was adopted by a number of railways in the early days, and one of these was the Furness. Four engines of Bury's own manufacture were purchased in 1844–6, and one of these, No. 3, has fortunately been preserved and is now to be seen in the Transport Museum at Clapham. The engine illustrated is one of a larger type built later by Fairbairn. No. 3 has had a long and fascinating history. After 54 years' service on the Furness Railway it was taken out of traffic and enthroned on a pedestal at Barrow Central Station, surrounded by an enormous canopied glass case. Eventually there came the second world war, and in the sustained enemy attacks on the arms towns Barrow suffered severely and the central station was literally razed to the ground. *Coppernob*'s case escaped a direct hit, but all the glass was blown out, and the precious old relic left perilously exposed. In clearing up the mess, however, *Coppernob* was not forgotten, and she was removed to Horwich Works. For many years she remained safe, but occult from public gaze; but now, restored to her former glory, in the magnificent iron-ore

red of the Furness Railway, she is on show again, though still bearing some of the dents and scars as a memento of that terrible night at Barrow when the old station was destroyed.

17 **Hawthorn Type 2-2-2;** Great Northern Railway.
Before the locomotive superintendents of the leading railways began to develop a design style of their own one could usually tell the manufacture of any locomotive by the distinctive shapes of the chimneys, domes, safety valve columns and so on. The engine illustrated was one of a class of twelve very fine express locomotives built by R. & W. Hawthorn in 1852-3. On the G.N.R. they were always known as the 'Large Hawthorns', to distinguish them from a batch of 20 of generally similar appearance, but smaller dimensions, supplied in 1850. The 'Large Hawthorns' had 6 ft. 6 in. driving wheels, and what was a very large boiler for that period. They did excellent work on the line, and one of them was concerned in a most spectacular smash at Retford. This was engine No. 210, and on this occasion she was running the northbound Flying Scotsman. By some mischance a goods train of the Manchester, Sheffield and Lincolnshire Railway had been allowed to proceed right across the main line. The driver of No. 210 on sighting the obstruction realized he could not stop in time, so he did the only alternative thing – put on full steam, and charged full tilt into the goods train! He scattered the light wooden trucks like match splinters and took the express safely through.

18 **The Cudworth 'Mail' Engine;** South Eastern Railway.
The South Eastern Railway began its existence in a most complicated and roundabout way. Seeing that it formed the Royal Mail route to the Continent via Folkestone and Dover, and carried the mails from London to India and the Far East on the first stage of their journey, the original route to Dover, via Redhill, was a very poor one. East of Redhill, however, the line was direct enough, and laid out for fast running, but the working of the mail trains was complicated by the use of the old tidal harbour at Folkestone, which meant that the running of the boat trains had to be fitted in to suit the tides! Despite the difficulties and the handicaps some fine running was done with the 'Tidals', as the Folkestone boat trains were always known, and Cudworth's 2-2-2 express locomotives of 1862 were in the very front rank for their time. Such was their success that they were on the job for the best part of 20 years. The South Eastern had a reputation for sloth and inefficient working in Victorian times; and on the secondary and local services that criticism was justified. No such stigma was attached either to the Continental Mail Expresses that ran to the Admiralty Pier at Dover, or to the Folkestone 'Tidals'. The Cudworth 2-2-2s ran these trains up to the limit of speed permitted on the line, namely 60 m.p.h.

19 **Craven 2-2-2;** Brighton railway.
No set of illustrations of what might be termed the 'Middle Ages' of the Victorian railway development in Great Britain would be complete without at least one example of the work of John Chester Craven, Locomotive Superintendent of the Brighton Railway. The trouble is, there are so many examples to choose from. Craven's policy was the very opposite of standardization, and he built individual engines for special jobs. It seemed, indeed, that at one time he had a different kind of engine for each of the Brighton Railway's many country branch lines. His main line passenger engines were strong, reliable engines, and the one chosen for illustration was among the last built at Brighton under his superintendence. They were put to work in 1862. Certain features may be noted,

especially the shelter for the enginemen, which had no sides. To the travelling public these engines became more familiar in the form illustrated, when they had been modified by Craven's successor William Stroudley, who painted them in his famous yellow livery. The driving wheels were 6 ft. 6 in., and the cylinders 17 in. diameter by 22 in. stroke. The numerous different designs left by Craven did not appeal to Stroudley's ideas of standardization, and though these Craven 2-2-2s were good engines in their way they had relatively short lives, and the two of them were scrapped in 1888 and 1891.

20 **A Broad Gauge Prodigy;** James Pearson's 9 ft. 4-2-4 tank engine, Bristol and Exeter Railway.
Although the broad gauge main line south-westwards from Bristol had been strongly sponsored by the Great Western, it was at first an independent company, and its management enjoyed displaying its independence on many occasions – sometimes to the considerable embarrassment of the Great Western. James Pearson was locomotive superintendent, and he designed the extraordinary 4-2-4 tank engines, with a single pair of driving wheels 9 ft. in diameter. Eight of them were originally built, and they handled the express traffic between Bristol and Exeter for several years. Our picture shows their peculiar appearance from the rear end, but they were no less extraordinary at the front. The cylinders were partly enclosed in the base of the D-shaped smokebox, but the latter was so short from front to back that part of the cylinders protruded at the front. They had also a most unusual form of suspension of the main driving axles. The housing for the outer helical spring can be seen hanging down outside the driving wheel. The original engines were scrapped after a life of about 16 years, and four new engines with 8 ft. 10 in. driving wheels

were built in their place. After the Bristol and Exeter Railway was absorbed by the Great Western they were converted into 4-2-2 tender engines.

21 **A McConnell 'Bloomer';** L.& N. W.R. Southern Division.
For some years after the amalgamation of 1847 the London and North Western Railway was organized in two separate divisions, each with its own locomotive superintendent, and works. The practice of the Southern Division, at Wolverton, under J. E. McConnell, was the very opposite of that of Trevithick and Allan, at Crewe. The latter used the very smallest engines that would do the job, whereas McConnell 'built big', and put machines on the road that were generally ahead of their time. Technically his various 2-2-2 express locomotives were characterized by large boilers, and great freedom in running; but externally they created interest by having all the bearings inside. It was a time when Mrs Amelia Bloomer was advocating certain rather startling changes in female attire that shocked Victorian society, and McConnell's new engines, with all their wheels exposed, were immediately nicknamed the 'Bloomers'. There were three varieties: the original 'large' class of 1851, which is illustrated; a smaller variety, introduced in 1854, and three engines of 1861, which were known as the 'Extra Large Bloomers'. No less striking was the livery of the Southern Division – in its vivid scarlet. One has only to compare the Crampton engine *London* and one of the Bloomers, with the Allan 2-4-0 and the *Lady of the Lake* to appreciate the astonishing contrast between the contemporary styles of Wolverton and Crewe Works.

22 **Highland Railway 2-2-2.**
The success of the Allan Crewe-type locomotives, in their mechanical soundness and simplicity, tended to lead to the perpetuation of the design beyond the

point where it was really suitable. Of this there was no more striking case than that of the Highland Railway. Allan was consultant to the Inverness and Nairn Railway; but while his little 2-2-2s were ideal for the level run along the shores of the Moray Firth they were certainly *not* suitable for the line across the Grampians which attained an altitude of 1484 ft. above sea level in the Pass of Drumochter. Nevertheless no fewer than 54 locomotives of the Allan 6-wheeled type – 24 of the 2-2-2 type, and 30 of the 2-4-0 – were supplied to the Highland Railway between 1855 and 1871. At first they were supplied virtually identical in appearance to the Crewe engines, with their rather gaunt outline. But they were rendered much neater and prettier in appearance in Stroudley's day, and painted in the famous 'yellow' livery that he took to the Brighton Railway. Our picture shows engine No. 32 of the Highland, originally supplied in October 1863, but as running from 1874 onwards. She was originally named *Sutherland*, but took the name *Cluny* in 1874, exchanging names with No. 55, which was converted from a 2-2-2 to a 2-4-0 at that time. As shown, *Cluny* has the David Jones livery, and chimney with louvres. The cab dates from Stroudley's time. Originally these engines, like their counterparts on the L.N.W.R., had no cabs.

23 **Lady of the Lake;** Northern Division of the L.&N.W.R.
These dainty little engines, designed by John Ramsbottom, and built, to a total of 60, at Crewe between 1859 and 1865, were originally intended for the Irish Mail traffic between London and Holyhead. Ramsbottom was not a believer in large engines, and throughout the years of his chieftainship at Crewe he built machines that were about the smallest and lightest that would do the work. The 'Ladies' were ideal for the job when they were first introduced, and although they

had a peculiar lateral wobble when running at speed they were popular with their crews, and did good work. They were the first locomotives in the world to be equipped with apparatus for picking up water at speed, this system having been developed at Crewe under John Ramsbottom. Thus equipped, one of these engines, No. 229, *Watt*, was able to make what was then a record length of non-stop run, 103¾ miles from Holyhead to Crewe, with a special carrying despatches in connection with the famous Trent dispute with the U.S.A. in 1862. Engines Nos. 667 *Marmion* and 806 *Waverley* on alternate days worked the 10 a.m. Edinburgh express between Euston and Crewe during the exciting Race to the North in 1888. In later years these little engines did a good deal of very useful work as pilots to heavy express trains requiring an assistant engine. Our picture shows one of these engines as originally built, without cab, and in the green livery of the L.N.W.R. standard until 1873.

24 **Sturrock 0-6-0 with Steam Tender;** Great Northern Railway.
Archibald Sturrock, who became Locomotive Superintendent of the G.N.R. in 1850, was one of the boldest and most original railway engineers of his day. He had scarcely taken up his appointment before he was designing engines with unusually large boilers, and he was constantly striving to get more power per unit of weight. He had every reason to do so with his heavy goods and mineral engines, because the coal traffic southwards from Yorkshire was going up by leaps and bounds. So, in conjunction with one of the biggest boilers seen in Great Britain up to time, he patented an arrangement whereby the tender constituted a separate engine, taking its steam from the one large boiler. The tender was, in fact, a second 0-6-0. The first trials of these engines were very successful. Between

London and Peterborough, where the orginary goods engines could take 30 loaded coal wagons, the big engines with the steam tenders took 45. On the level stretches of the Lincolnshire loop line the single-engine load could be increased from 35 wagons to 60. But the engines proved too powerful. They were ahead of their time, and when not used at full capacity they were not economic. Furthermore they were not liked by the men, who felt it was asking too much of them to look after what was virtually a double engine. Consequently maintenance was not good, and the bold experiment had to be abandoned, after no fewer than 50 steam tenders had been in service.

25 Conner 8 ft. Single; Caledonian Railway.

Before the Caledonian Railway was ever built extreme controversy raged over the proposal to carry the line up the glen of Evan Water from Beattock to an altitude of more than 1000 ft. above sea level. Such gradients were not considered practical; yet after the route was settled, to include one of the worst inclines to be found on any main line in Great Britain – 10 miles at 1 in 75 – the superintendent who presided over the locomotive department from 1856 to 1876, Benjamin Conner, adopted as standard the 2-2-2 type for express passenger work, and moreover with driving wheels of no less than 8 ft. 2 in. diameter. This might have seemed the reverse of suitability for such a steeply graded route; but the engines were beautifully designed, superbly constructed, and did their work well. The first two were built at St Rollox works, Glasgow, in 1859, and the engine illustrated in our picture belongs to a slightly later batch, albeit of the same general design. It is interesting to recall that three engines of this same design were built by Neilson and Co. of Glasgow for the Egyptian State Railways. On the Caledonian, despite the great increase in the weight and speed of trains since their first introduction, the Conner eight-footers remained on the crack trains till 1884-5, and the last of them was not withdrawn until 1901.

26 Great North of Scotland Railway;

one of the earliest British 4-4-0s designed by W. Cowan, 1865.
The 'Great North', to give it the usual abbreviated title, was a curious railway. Its first locomotive superintendent was Daniel Kinnear Clark, an engineer perhaps better known for his treatises on railway machinery than for his work on the G.N.S.R. He did most of his work from an office in London, more than 500 miles away from the nearest point on the railway! There was a tradition of quarrelling in the management of the railway at Aberdeen, and Clark resigned precipitately when certain directors criticized his work. W. Cowan took over the job in 1857, and he developed Clark's design practice, and put on the road a number of interesting and gaily finished locomotives. The engine chosen for illustration is one of the first of the 4-4-0 type ever to run in Great Britain. It was one of a batch of nine built by Robert Stephenson and Co. in 1862-4. These had the dome placed immediately over the firebox, and a good point in design was the raising of the firebox above the level of the top of the boiler barrel, so as to give additional steam space in the hottest part of the boiler. A curious feature was the outside framing of the four-wheeled tender, which in its shape rather gave the impression that a centre pair of wheels had been left out. These engines did excellent work, and some survived in service until 1920.

27 Kirtley's '800' Class; Midland Railway.

A great locomotive historian, the late E. L. Ahrons, once described these locomotives as 'one of the most celebrated classes of express engines that ever ran n this country'. Our picture shows one of them as originally built, and carrying the handsome green livery that preceded the famous 'Derby red'. They were fast, powerful engines, with boilers that steamed very freely; and the 48 engines of his class were the mainstay of the Anglo-Scottish express services of the Midland for many years. They had about five years in their original condition, and then S. W. Johnson, Kirtley's successor, modernized them, putting on larger boilers and larger cylinders. They were immensely popular with the drivers and firemen, and they were that extremely rare species – an engine that is thermally efficient and yet a real 'drivers' engine'. Many of the men declared that the harder you thrashed them the better and more sweetly they responded. For many years they worked turn and turn about with the larger and newer engines built after them. When Johnson modernized them he fitted his own type of boiler mountings, and decked them in 'Derby red'. In many ways they looked finer than ever. The majority of them were still running at the time of the grouping, and so passed into L.M.S.R. ownership after 50 years of service.

28 **Robert Sinclair's 2-2-2;** Great Eastern Railway.
These celebrated engines, of which there were 30, did all the most important express working on the Great Eastern Railway for nearly 20 years. Even for their own day they were, theoretically, not very powerful, having cylinders no larger than 16 in. diameter by 24 in. stroke. The boilers were small, and carried only 120 lb. per sq. in. pressure. Nevertheless they were beautifully designed and constructed machines and did much finer work than their small dimensions would suggest. No fewer than four different firms were concerned in their construction. The first five came from Fairbairn and Sons, of Manchester; then came 10 from the Avonside Engine Company, of Bristol, in

the year 1864. Next, in 1865, came another ten from Kitson's of Leeds, and the last five (1866–7) were built in France, by the celebrated firm Schneider et Cie, of Le Creusot – makers of the once-deadly 75 mm. gun used in large quantities by the French Army. These French-built engines were, by general consent of the drivers, the best of the entire stud. In their hey-day they were divided between the four 'crack' sheds, Stratford, Cambridge, Ipswich and Norwich; but after larger engines were put on to the principal trains the old Sinclair singles were transferred to the G.N. and G.E. Joint line for working between March and Doncaster. There they continued the good work for another dozen years. The last of them were not scrapped until 1894.

29 **A Stirling 8-footer;** Great Northern Railway.
It is no exaggeration to say that these engines, the first of which was built in 1870 at Doncaster, are among the most famous express passenger locomotives of all time. Engines of this class were built at intervals from 1870 until 1895 with gradually changing and improving features of constructional detail, but all alike in the extreme elegance of their external proportions. The long domeless boiler, the beautifully shaped safety valve casing, the majestic sweep of the running plate over the driving wheel centre immediately caught the eye; and as one came to examine one of these engines in more detail one realized the numerous touches of beauty and distinction put into them by a designer who was at one and the same time an artist and a master craftsman. The earlier engines of the class had the picturesque slotted splashers as exemplified by No. 5 in our picture. Later engines had them closed in, and the last batch of all, built in the year that Stirling died, had a rather more generous canopy in the cab roof. They were no mere ornaments. They ran the fastest express service in the world,

during the 'eighties' of last century, and they climed the banks as well as they flew along at 70 to 75 m.p.h. on the downhill stretches. On the last night of the Race to the North, in 1895, engine No. 668 took the Aberdeen sleeping car train over the 105½ miles from Kings Cross to Grantham in 101 min. The pioneer engine of the class, No. 1, built in 1870, is preserved in the Railway Museum at York.

30 A Stroudley 'G' Class 2-2-2 'Petworth'; London Brighton and South Coast Railway.

William Stroudley, Locomotive Superintendent of the L.B.&S.C.R. from 1870 to 1889, developed a classic style in locomotive lineaments which, combined with the beautiful livery, made the Brighton engines unique for all time. But Stroudley was not merely an artist in styling and finish. His locomotives were soundly designed, superbly constructed and maintained, and very economical to run. Furthermore, he was ahead of most of his contemporaries in the degree to which all his engines incorporated standard parts and fittings. The 'G' class engines, of which 24 were built at Brighton during the years 1880-2, were the regular engines on the Portsmouth line. It is remarkable that Stroudley should have designed single-wheelers for that route, because it includes a good deal of sharp grading, and a distinctly stiff climb over the North Downs between Dorking and Horsham. Nevertheless these extremely pretty little engines did excellent work on this route for many years, and it was not until after 1895 that replacement of them commenced. They were nearly all named after beautiful country villages and resorts on the line, and in the Isle of Wight. A notable exception was No. 329, which was specially named *Stephenson*. As such it played a notable part in the Stephenson Centenary celebrations in Newcastle in 1881.

31 The Tay Bridge Engine; North British Railway.

The period was one in which the majority of railways in Great Britain were using six-wheeled passenger engines. The eight-wheelers were mostly 4-2-2. Engine No. 224 of the North British, with its sister engine No. 264, were the first of what became the most characteristic British passenger engine type of pre-grouping days, namely the 4-4-0 with inside cylinders, and inside frames throughout. They were big engines for the period, and apart from the unusual design of the boiler, with the dome over the firebox, they were also characterized by their solid bogie wheels. But if Nos. 224 and 264, were notable in conception and design No. 224 achieved a notoriety unique in British railway history. On the night of December 28, 1879, she was hauling the ill-fated train that entered upon the Tay Bridge at the moment that the high girders collapsed. Engine and train went down with the ruins of the bridge, and of the eighty persons on board there was not a single survivor. The engine, however, was the one thing that did survive the disaster. It lay for nearly four months at the bottom of the Firth of Tay, but was then recovered, and found to be so little damaged that it was taken to Cowlairs Works, Glasgow, for repair, travelling on its own wheels. After overhaul the engine went into service again, and lasted for another 39 years. It was eventually scrapped in 1919, just forty years after its plunge into the Firth of Tay.

32 '901' Class; North Eastern Railway.

Edward Fletcher was born and bred in the very cradle of the steam locomotive. He was serving his apprenticeship with George Stephenson at the time the *Rocket* was built, and he assisted in the trials at Killingworth Colliery, before that famous engine left for Liverpool, to win triumph and immortal engineering fame in the Rainhill trials. In 1854 he was appointed

Locomotive Superintendent of the North Eastern Railway and in that position he designed a host of striking and uniformly successful engines. There was no such thing as standardization in Fletcher's day. Engines were built to do individual jobs, and even when the close of his career was approaching and he produced, in the '901' class 2-4-0s, his masterpiece, there were numerous individual varieties. Some were built at Gateshead Works, others by contractors, and Fletcher allowed the latter to use their own standard types of boiler mounting and finish. But they were alike in being gorgeously arrayed, and the engine in our picture, No. 910, is today preserved and stands in the Railway Museum at York in all her original glory. Looking on No. 910 the visitor may well wonder what railways were like when locomotives were so gaily bedecked. But those elegant little engines hauled the Scotch expresses of their day, frequently attaining speeds of more than 70 m.p.h. They were very economical in working and immense favourites with their drivers and firemen.

33 David Jones's 'F' Class; Highland Railway.

From its inception the Highland Railway had used locomotives that were small in relation to the heavy gradients and hard work required in working over the 1484 ft. altitude of Drumochter summit, in the heart of the Grampian Mountains. Furthermore, though the company was served, from 1865 onwards, by engineers of high calibre, funds were not available for the purchase of larger and more suitable locomotives. By the year 1873, however, the position had changed, and David Jones was able to design and have built what was then one of the heaviest and most powerful passenger engines in Europe. A first order for 10 or these splendid machines was placed. The majority were named at first after counties through which the Highland Railway

ran, but others were named after personalities, and the country estates of directors and other gentlemen prominent in the management of the railway. Our picture shows the *Ardross*, named after the home of Sir Alexander Matheson, Chairman of the Company. The 'F' class embodied the heavy double-framing at the front-end that had been characteristic of Alexander Allan's designs whether at Crewe or in Scotland. This style was continued in later Jones engines on the Highland Railway for another eighteen years after the introduction of the 'F' class.

34 The 'Europa' Class; London, Chatham and Dover Railway.

In 1873 the Chatham Railway gained the exclusive contract for carrying the Royal Mail between London and Dover, and to ensure punctuality the Locomotive Superintendent, William Martley, was instructed to provide four new locomotives of enhanced power. Few engines of a small class have, in relation to their small numbers, gained praise or fame to a greater extent than these splendid little 2-4-0s, which were named *Europa*, *Asia*, *Africa* and *America*. They immediately became known as the 'Mail Engines', and became familiar and popular with the travelling public from their handsome appearance and excellent work. These trains stopped at Herne Hill, to attach or detach the City portions, and the 74 miles between Herne Hill and Dover Town were booked to be covered at an average speed of about 47 m.p.h. At the height of the Chatham Company's Continental mail traffic there were seven expresses daily booked to make an overall average speed of 44 m.p.h. between Victoria and Dover Pier. In 1873-8, the hey-day of the 'Europa' class, this was excellent going over a hilly road. They were fitted with new boilers in 1892 and survived to carry the gay S.E. & C.R. livery. In the present century they continued to be called upon for express work, and they were not finally withdrawn from traffic until 1907–8.

35 4-4-0 **Tank Engine;** North London Railway.

The North London, although originating as a protégé of the London and North Western, displayed a striking individuality so far as locomotive design was concerned. During mid-Victorian times it might indeed have seemed that the lowlier and dingier of the districts through which a railway ran the gayer and more ornate was the finish of the locomotive. The yellow Stroudley engines of the Brighton Railway worked through the Thames Tunnel, and these spanking little Adams 4-4-0 tanks worked around Canonbury, Islington, Dalston, and Poplar. If they are compared to their contemporaries on the Metropolitan and the Metropolitan District it will be realized how different in outward appearance it was possible to make a locomotive of the same wheel arrangement, of similar power, and capable of doing the same work! The gay livery was retained until 1882, when a change was made to the utilitarian 'black' of the London and North Western Railway. These pretty little 4-4-0 tanks were rebuilt in the 'eighties' to have cabs and more modern boiler mountings. Unlike the Metropolitan and the Metropolitan District Railways, the North London built their own locomotives, at Bow Works. In still later years some North London locomotives were overhauled at the Crewe works of the L.&N.W.R.

36 A **'Small Scotchman';** London, Chatham and Dover Railway.

The London, Chatham and Dover Railway was distinguished by the complexity and volume of its London suburban services; and these were not confined to its own metals. In its sustained drive to develop traffic it possessed running powers over the lines of several other companies,

and in 1866 more powerful locomotives were needed to cope, particularly, with the services over the Great Northern and Midland lines. These L.C.D.R. trains originated at Moorgate, and ran to Wood Green and Hendon respectively. Another very important service was that between the Crystal Palace and the London termini. Martley introduced the smart and workmanlike little 0-4-2 tank engines illustrated here. Not only were they built in Scotland, by Neilson and Co., but for some reason these London suburban tank engines all had Scottish place names, ranging from islands off the West Coast, like *Iona*, *Bute*, and *Arran*, to famous rivers like *Spey*, *Tay*, and *Nith*. They all put in nearly forty years of hard work in and around London. By the time they came into S.E.&C.R. ownership, and duly carried the new livery, they had been reboilered and so exchanged their picturesque, distinctive look, shown in our picture, for a more conventional domed boiler.

37 **The Steam Inner Circle;** Metropolitan Railway.

These famous engines, the first to be owned by the Metropolitan Railway, were not ready in time for the opening of the line in 1863. At that time the extent of this pioneer Underground railway in London was only from a junction with the Great Western at Bishops Road (Paddington) to Farringdon Street. The line was worked first by the Great Western, and later by the Great Northern Railway until the Metropolitan 4-4-0 tanks arrived. These latter were splendid engines and worked the Underground services without intermission until the Inner Circle was electrified in 1906. As originally built they had the characteristic features of Beyer-Peacock & Co. in the huge bell-mouthed domes, placed cheek-by-jowl with the chimney. The bogie had an exceptionally short wheelbase; the cylinders were steeply inclined, and they had no cabs.

Today it certainly takes a stretch of the imagination to picture what travelling on the Inner Circle was like, in steam days! Our picture shows one of these engines in their later form, with a more modern boiler, and the handsome livery of Metropolitan steam locomotives at the time when the inner-London sections of the line were electrified. One of these historic locomotives has been preserved, and is to be seen in the Transport Museum at Clapham.

38 2-4-0 tank for the Underground lines; Great Western Railway.
These delightful little engines were introduced to work the London suburban trains of the G.W.R., and particularly to work through the Underground lines of the Metropolitan Railway Inner Circle, to Liverpool Street. Engine No. 968, which is the subject of our picture, was one of the fourth batch, being built at Swindon in 1874. So successful were they in hauling the smartly-timed business trains that construction of them continued for 30 years after their first introduction. The later engines of the class had small cabs, but the majority had nothing more than weatherboards. In any case the cabe provided shelter only when they werr running chimney first. They were neves turned at journey's end though, and when running bunker first, which represented half their weekly mileage the men were quite exposed to the weather. No fewer than 110 of them were built, and the majority had large condensing pipes shown in our picture. When running over the Metropolitan line they were not allowed to exhaust their steam in the normal way, to minimize the effect of steam working in the tunnels. The exhaust steam was turned instead into the side tanks. Many of them were still at work in the London area in the late nineteen-twenties, but by that time they were painted plain green, without lining, and with black underframes.

39 Dean's Standard Gauge 2-2-2; for the Great Western.
While the broad gauge was still in existence provision had nevertheless to be made for the standard-gauge parts of the line, and of these none was more important than that to Birmingham, Chester and Birkenhead. Daniel Gooch had designed a class of ten 2-2-2s, with the usual sandwich frames, in 1861, and Dean thoroughly modernized these engines in 1877, giving them larger cylinders, but at first retaining a domeless boiler. They worked in the same link as the Armstrong 'Sir Alexander' class, which had the more conventional plate frames, and in due course their appearance was still further modernized by the closing in of their open splashers, and the fitting of new domed boilers. Our picture shows one of these engines as running about 1900. They were very fast and free-running engines, and did splendid work on the Paddington–Birmingham expresses, all of which at that time ran via Oxford. The drivers showed great skill in getting them away from a stop without excessive slipping, and they took loads of 300 tons, and sometimes more, with complete success. The form shown in our picture did not represent their final form. In the twentieth century some of them were fitted with the new type of Swindon domeless boiler, and high Belpaire fireboxes. In this form they outlasted the larger Dean 4-2-2 express engines, and No. 165 of the '157' class was the last single-driver locomotive to remain in regular service on the G.W.R. She was not withdrawn until 1915.

40 Webb's 'Precedent' Class 2-4-0; London and North Western Railway.
The 'Precedent' class was a development of John Ramsbottom's 'Newton' class of 2-4-0; but the improvements made by Webb extended to much more than the provision of larger cylinders, a larger boiler, and higher boiler pressure. The 'Precedents' were among the first loco-

motives in Britain – probably in the world – in which the arrangements for steam flow were made very short, and direct, with the result that these little engines developed power and speed out of all proportion to their size, and generally in advance of engines of the same wheel arrangement on which the cylinder and valve layout were more conventional – and at that time involved circuitous passages and ports. In the eighteen-nineties engine No. 2002 *Madge* of this class attained the high speed of 88 m.p.h., while during the Race to the North, in 1895, No. 790 *Hardwicke* ran the racing portion of the Euston–Aberdeen Tourist express over the 141.1 miles from Crewe to Carlisle at an average speed of 67 m.p.h. The engine illustrated, No. 2191 *Snowdon* was the last of the class to remain in regular passenger service, and was not withdrawn until 1932.

41 James Stirling's 4-4-0 of 1873; Glasgow and South Western Railway.

For 25 years, from 1853 to 1878 there was a Stirling in the chair at Kilmarnock Works. Until 1866 it was Patrick, who then left to attain eminence as the locomotive engineer of the Great Northern Railway. He was succeeded, on the G. & S.W.R. by his younger brother James, who continued the family tradition in that he built no locomotives other than with domeless boilers. In other respects he differed from his brother, particularly in the matter of coupling the driving wheels. Patrick to the very end of his long life never built a coupled engine for express passenger work. James Stirling not only built 4-coupled engines, but in 1873 put the Glasgow and South Western Railway in the forefront of British locomotive practice with the very fine 4-4-0 express engine illustrated in our picture. One engine only was built in 1873; but when the design was proved construction continued until 1877, by which time there were 22 of them on the road. They were

very large and imposing engines for their day, and included one innovation of detail, in James Stirling's steam-operated reversing gear. Hitherto all engines had a manually operated gear, which was often very hard to move – this being before the days of ball-bearings and other friction-reducing devices. The Stirling 4-4-0s ran the Midland Scotch expresses between Carlisle and Glasgow, from 1876 onwards, and they were among the fastest trains in the country at that time.

42 Dugald Drummond's N.B.R. 4-4-0 of 1876.

The year 1876 saw the opening of the Midland Railway Company's independent route to Carlisle – the far-famed Settle and Carlisle line – and through services were inaugurated from St Pancras to both Edinburgh and Glasgow. In the running of the former service the North British Railway was in partnership with the Midland, and for the new accelerated services, in keen competition with the established routes to Kings Cross and to Euston, some powerful new locomotives were put on the road. Known as the '476', or 'Waverley' class, they were the first of a remarkable series of 4-4-0 locomotives designed by Dugald Drummond, and his younger brother, Peter. Technically they were notable for the length of the coupling rods, namely 9 ft., which was most unusual at that time. Drummond developed the type in later years on the Caledonian and then on the London and South Western Railway, while his brother took the design to the Highland, and then to the Glasgow and South Western. Drummond was an earnest follower of Stroudley's practice, having worked under him at Brighton, and he took to the North British the practice of naming locomotives after the stations they served on the line. Ten out of the twelve engines of the '476' class were named after places on the 'Waverley' route, between Edinburgh and Carlisle.

43 A Caley 'Jumbo'; Drummond 0-6-0.
A great change came over the locomotive practice of the Caledonian Railway when Dugald Drummond was appointed superintendent in 1882. Until then practically all the locomotives, passenger and goods alike, had been fitted with outside cylinders, carrying on the traditions established in Scotland by Alexander Allan when he came north from the L.&N.W.R. at Crewe. But Drummond, following his success on the North British Railway, used a very much neater and more modern design, and the smart 0-6-0 goods engine, first introduced in 1884, was typical of his earlier work on the Caledonian. They proved splendid engines, not only for goods but for general service all over the line, and formed the basis of goods engine development at St Rollox for many years subsequently. Not only this: Dugald Drummond took the design with him to the London and South Western Railway, while his younger brother Peter adopted it, in almost exactly the same form, on the Highland Railway. In later years in Scotland the 'Caley Jumbos' could be seen doing all kinds of light and intermediate duty, and in years just before World War II they were frequently used for assisting heavy express passenger trains over the very severe gradients of the Callander and Oban Railway. At that time, painted in the L.M.S. plain black, it was difficult to distinguish the Caledonian and Highland varieties of the design, except by the numbers.

44 Webb's Standard Coal Engine; London and North Western Railway.
The L.&N.W.R. was well-known at one time as the largest joint-stock corporation in the world. Its princely revenue was derived very largely from its goods and mineral traffic, and the first new engine design of Francis W. Webb, after his taking office as Chief Mechanical Engineer in 1871, was an excellent 0-6-0 for heavy goods traffic. In later years the idea of a small 0-6-0, with cylinders no larger than 17 in. diameter by 24 in. stroke doing 'heavy' work would seem strange; but at the time of their first introduction, in 1873, the '17 inch coal engines', as they were always known, were among the most powerful freight engines in the country. They were extremely simple, in both design and construction, and very cheap and easy to build. As an experiment Webb set Crewe works a test to see how quickly one of these engines could be built. The result could be described as sensational, for the engine was built and left the erecting shop under her own steam in 25½ hours! This class was an L.&N.W.R. standard, and construction of them continued for 19 years (1873–92). Eventually there were no fewer than 500 of them at work. During this time there were no changes in design. Those built in 1892 were exactly the same as those of the first batch of 1873 – a striking tribute to the effectiveness of the original design. No fewer than 227 out of the original 500 were still in service in 1923, when the L.&N.W.R. passed into the London Midland and Scottish system.

45 The Dean 'Goods'; G.W.R.
This class, of which 280 were built in the years 1883–1898, proved to be perhaps the most notable design using the very common 0-6-0 wheel arrangement, ever to run in Great Britain. At the time of its first appearance something of a surprise was created in that it was the first Great Western engine design to have only inside frames. Hitherto outside frames, mostly using the sandwich form of construction had been universal. The first 20 engines of the class had domeless boilers; but after several batches there came the familiar huge polished brass dome, and the usual accompaniments of decoration characteristic of the Dean period, and applied alike to goods and passenger engines. At first, of course, the engines were non-superheated, but in more recent

years new superheated boilers have been fitted to many of them, and they have done remarkable work on the light and branch passenger trains, as well as in the haulage of goods. Many of them saw service overseas during the First World War, both in France, and in the Middle East, while during the Second World War no fewer than 109 of these veterans were requisitioned for war work. An engine of this class has been preserved, and is housed in the G.W.R. Museum at Swindon.

46 **A 'Skye Bogie';** Highland Railway. The original of the 'F' class passenger engines, shown in Plate 33, can be traced to a reconstruction of one of the earlier 2-4-0s made by David Jones in 1873. The Dingwall and Skye line, crossing the county of Ross, to reach the west coast, involved some exceedingly severe railway working with gradients steeper than anywhere else on the Highland system, and incessantly sharp curvature. To render the 2-4-0s already available more suited to these conditions Jones rebuilt one of them with a leading bogie. This engine was so successful that the bogie type was adopted for the Class 'F' main line passenger engines of 1874, and following this some similar engines, but with small coupled wheels, were built at Inverness specially for the Dingwall and Skye line. These proved to be remarkably handy and efficient engines, and some of them put in more than 40 years' service on the line. When originally introduced they carried the gay livery characteristic of all Highland engines, passenger and goods; but they were most familiar in their plain green of later years. They were the first Highland engines not to carry names. They did all the work over the very hilly and winding route to the Kyle of Lochalsh – passenger, goods and cattle alike. The men became so attached to them that when larger engines were eventually put on to the Dingwall and Skye line they

were at first regarded as clumsy and unnecessarily big!

47 **Midland Railway;** A Johnson 2-4-0.
Samuel Waite Johnson was one of the supreme artists of the locomotive engineering world. He designed engines that were simple, workmanlike, and efficient in traffic, yet having a beauty of 'line' that has never been surpassed. Every detail was perfectly proportioned, and one can see this in the handsomely-shaped chimney, the curves of the dome and of the brass safety valve casing. His earliest passenger engines were of the 2-4-0 type, after which he built 4-4-0s. But for general service on the Midland Railway he built further batches of the 2-4-0 type from 1879 onwards, and it is one of these that has been chosen to illustrate his earlier work. No. 1400 was the first of a batch of ten engines built at Derby in 1879, and painted in the light green colour then standard. The magnificent crimson-lake, 'Derby-red', of later Midland engines was introduced by Johnson some years later. The '1400' class engines were at first put on to the London–Leeds route, but after four years the entire ten of them were transferred to Lancaster and Carnforth sheds to run the important expresses between Leeds, Bradford and Morecambe on the one hand, and the connecting trains to the Furness Railway on the other. On this duty the ten engines put in 40 years of service, and even after displacement from those duties they continued in secondary service for many years afterwards.

48 **The 'Gladstone'.**
This was the first engine of the most celebrated of all Stroudley's designs. It was built at Brighton in 1882, but engines of this class continued to be built at intervals down to the year 1891, by which time 36 of them were at work. The outstanding

130

feature of these engines – designed for the fastest and heaviest traffic on the line – was the wheel arrangement, namely the 0-4-2. Engineers of other railways looked askance at the use of large diameter driving wheels (6 ft. 6 in.) at the leading end of an engine intended to run fast; but the 'Gladstones' proved very steady and smooth riding machines, with a gentle easy ride at speed. They proved exceptionally powerful for their size, and the the way they would start away from Victoria station, and take a heavy train up the 1 in 64 gradient on to the Grosvenor Road Bridge frequently confounded their critics. The pioneer engine has been restored to its original form, and its gorgeous colouring, and is now to be seen in the Railway Museum at York. It was withdrawn from service in 1927, after 45 years of hard work on the Brighton line.

49 **Charles Sacré's 2-2-2;** Manchester, Sheffield and Lincolnshire Railway.
The M.S.&L. was a curious and difficult system for which to provide locomotive power. It included the level lines east of Sheffield which ran across the Lincolnshire plains, and there were the relatively easy sections of the Cheshire Lines Committee, west of Manchester. But between these two groups was the very severe connecting line over the Pennines, between Sheffield and Manchester. Over this latter route the M.S.&L. were partners with the Great Northern in operating a fast and highly competitive through service between Manchester and Kings Cross, against the rival services of the London and North Western and the Midland. Although Charles Sacré had built a number of 4-4-0 locomotives from 1878 onwards, it was in 1883 that he turned out from Gorton Works the beautiful series of 7 ft. 6 in. 2-2-2s of which one is illustrated in our picture. These were clearly intended to make the best of both

worlds, and some of them were put to work on the Manchester–Liverpool and Manchester–Southport services of the C.L.C. while others were reserved for the Great Northern through expresses to Kings Cross. On these trains the M.S.&L. engines worked through between Manchester and Grantham, thus running for 33 miles over the Great Northern main line.

50 **South Eastern Railway 'F' Class.**
James Stirling was one of the earliest exponents of the practice of locomotive standardization, and during his tenure of office as Locomotive Superintendent at Ashford, from 1878 to 1898, he introduced no more than six classes, and three were relatively small in numbers. His three principal classes, 0-6-0 for goods, 0-4-4 tank for suburban passenger, and 4-4-0 for express passenger were built in relatively large numbers, and totalled eventually 122, 118, and 88 respectively. The 'F' class express passenger, illustrated here, was typical of James Stirling's style. They were striking rather than handsome; but they did some excellent work on the road, and they continued on main line work long after the newer engines of Wainwright's design had been introduced. James Stirling, like his elder brother Patrick on the Great Northern Railway, built no engines for the South Eastern Railway other than with domeless boilers. They steamed well, despite relatively poor fuel. Speed on the South Eastern was limited, by permanent way restrictions, to a maximum of 60 m.p.h. over the entire system, and so the highly competitive boat train services, to and from Dover, on which the S.E.R. was continually up against the enterprise of the London, Chatham and Dover Railway, had to be maintained by hard running, uphill. The 'F' class engines excelled in this respect. Two of them put in no less than 44 years' service.

51 Metropolitan District Railway;
a Beyer-Peacock 4-4-0 tank.

These engines were generally of the same design as those of the Metropolitan Railway, and our picture shows one of them in a very early form. In view of the way the two companies eventually became inter-connected on the Underground lines in Central London, and worked various services jointly, the actual ownership of the tracks may be mentioned. The 'District' owned the line from Earls Court over the south side of the Inner Circle, to Aldgate East and Whitechapel while the Metropolitan extended from Edgware Road to Gloucester Road, at the western end, and to Aldgate and Minories Junction at the eastern end. The Inner Circle in steam days was worked jointly, some trains by District and some by Metropolitan engines and stock in proportions equal to the respective mileages owned by each company. It worked out that *all* trains going clockwise round the Circle were Metropolitan and the majority going anti-clockwise were District. The District Railway had westward and south-westward extensions from Earls Court, to Richmond, Ealing, Hounslow, and Wimbledon. All these trains were worked by the 4-4-0 tank engines of which a total of 54 were built for the District Railway, between 1871 and 1886. They 'saw steam out' on the District, and with the 66 similar engines of the Metropolitan represented a remarkably efficient, if not very handsome stud.

52 London Tilbury and Southend Railway; an Adams 4-4-2 tank engine.

These engines, of which there were 36 in all, were designed by W. Adams, while he was Locomotive Superintendent of the Great Eastern Railway. They originally had very severe-looking stove-pipe chimneys, but were later modified to the handsome appearance shown in our picture. The first batch, built by Sharp, Stewart and Co. of Manchester, came south in charge of a young engineer named Thomas Whitelegg, who was later appointed superintendent of the L.T.&S.R., and was later succeeded in that office by his son, Robert. The Whiteleggs, father and son, had a great regard for handsome appearance in a locomotive, and successive enlargements of the basic 4-4-2 design enhanced rather than detracted from their graceful lines. All engines of the L.T.&S.R. were named after stations on the line, and while there was a certain distinction in names like *Southend, Shoeburyness, Upminster, Purfleet,* and the like, things became a little less interesting when locomotives were named after dingy places in the London suburban area such as *Whitechapel, Black Horse Road,* and *Commercial Road.* These engines lasted well into the L.M.S. era. The first of them was not scrapped until 1930, and the last was not withdrawn until October 1935.

53 North London Railway; an Adams 4-4-0 tank of 1868.

William Adams was one of the many locomotive engineers of Victorian times who moved rapidly from one railway to another. Examples of his fine work were eventually to be found not only on the North London, but also on the Great Eastern, on the London, Tilbury and Southend, and most distinguished of all, on the London and South Western. Generally he favoured outside cylinders and his 4-4-0 tank design for the North London was originally turned out in the same brilliant and ornate style as the inside cylinder 4-4-0 (see reference 35). This style of painting was continued on the North London Railway until 1882, after which a livery corresponding closely to that of the London and North Western Railway was adopted. It is in this form that the Adams 4-4-0 tank is illustrated. It was in such form that these powerful and efficient little engines became familiar to thousands of season-ticket holders travelling to and from the City terminus at Broad Street. They worked trains of little four-wheeled coaches, seemingly of caravan length, over the Great Northern main line to Potters Bar, and to High Barnet over a steeply graded branch. They were familiar on this duty well into the nineteen-twenties. On these trains they carried the destination on a huge board that extended almost to the full width of the buffer beam.

54 **Maryport and Carlisle Railway;** a 2-4-0 passenger engine.

The Maryport and Carlisle Railway was one of the most consistently properous of all the local railways in Great Britain. It served the northern part of the West Cumberland coalfield, and carried the coals to Carlisle. From 1859 onwards until the fateful year of 1914 it never paid a dividend of less than $5\frac{1}{4}$ per cent. Yet prosperity never went to the head of its astute management. There was no heavy capital expenditure on new works, or locomotives built for prestige purposes, and the example chosen for illustration in this book is a picturesque little thing added to the stock in 1867 but still retained in service until 1921. The engine R1 could not be classed as typical of the Maryport and Carlisle Railway, because there was nothing that could be called a standard design, or representative of standard practice. Locomotives were added to the stock in ones and twos, as required; and the earlier ones were carefully repaired and kept going. The smart green engines were familiar sights at Carlisle, and there was a time when it was a regular thing for the Maryport company to work the evening mail train southwards over the Furness Line. The bright green turnout made a strong contrast to the iron-ore red of the Furness locomotives, and was nevertheless an excellent travelling ambassador of one of the best-run small railways in the country.

55 **Matthew Holmes's 4-4-0;** North British Railway.

In 1890 the Forth Bridge was opened, and the North British Railway was immediately able to provide very much faster services from Edinburgh to Perth, on the one hand, and on the East Coast main line to Aberdeen. To provide suitable engine power for the new trains Matthew Holmes built a very much enlarged version of the Drummond 4-4-0s of the 'Waverley' class, with much larger boilers and cylinders. Externally they could be distinguished by the neat, lock-up safety valves on the dome, and by the style of cab, which followed that of Patrick Stirling, on the Great Northern Railway at Doncaster. The North British was fortunate in having such excellent engines when the time came for the great Race to the North in the summer of 1895. Then the 8 p.m. Tourist express from Kings Cross to Aberdeen was worked at ever increasing speed, until the final night of the race the $59\frac{1}{4}$ miles from Edinburgh to Dundee were covered in 59 min. In view of the incessant curvature of the line and of the stiff gradients this was a performance that can only be called venturesome, in the speeds at which many of the curves were taken. In normal working 80 min. was considered a fast time for this very awkward stretch of line; and to cut 20 minutes off this time was a marvellous tribute to Holmes's 4-4-0 locomotives and their crews.

56 **James Holden's 7 ft. 2-2-2;** Great Eastern Railway.

The existence of so many level stretches of line in Cambridge and Lincolnshire might suggest that the Great Eastern was an ideal line for single-driver locomotives. Actually the main line includes a number of sharp and severe gradients, not excepting the immediate start out of Liverpool Street up the 1 in 70 gradient of Bethnal Green bank. James Holden built 2-4-0 and 2-2-2 express locomotives of otherwise identical design with 7 ft. wheels, 18 in. by 24 in. cylinders and the same design of boiler. The 'singles' illustrated were exceptionally good engines in starting away, and taking quite heavy loads at the schedule speed demanded in the 1890s. These engines were used turn and turn about with the 2-4-0s of the 'T.19' class; but it was a time of quite rapid increase in train loads, and James Holden was soon required to build still larger engines. These '1000' class single-wheelers followed the precedent of the old Sinclairs, and went north for working on the Joint Line. Those stationed at Ely ran to York and back every day. Two of them were stationed at Harwich Parkeston Quay, and each of these ran to York with the North Country boat trains. At one time some of them were equipped for oil firing. Unfortunately the rapid advance in haulage requirements on the Great Eastern made larger locomotives necessary, and they were superseded sooner than their excellent performance really justified.

57 Lancashire and Yorkshire Railway; an Aspinall 4-4-0 of 1891.

For the greater part of the nineteenth century the Lancashire and Yorkshire was a slow, and generally rather shocking railway. But by the late 'eighties' there was a tremendous drive for all-round improvement and with the appointment of John A. F. Aspinall as Locomotive Superintendent some first-class engines were provided to run the vastly improved train services. The new 4-4-0 locomotives of 1891, built at Horwich works, were very speedy and reliable engines. They worked all over the system, as can be appreciated by the many depots at which they were stationed, namely Blackpool; Bolton; Fleetwood; Lostock Hall (Preston); Low Moor (Bradford); Newton Heath (Manchester); Sandhills (Liverpool); Southport; and Wakefield. They were the first real express locomotives that the Lancashire and Yorkshire Railway have ever owned, and they worked the famous 'Club' trains from Manchester to Blackpool and Southport; the cross-country expresses to Leeds; and the very fast inter-city services between Liverpool and Manchester. The latter trains had to cover the 36 miles between the two cities in 40 minutes, non-stop, and although the bulk of the trains consisted of no more than three coaches it needed very smart running. Although finished in black, these engines were always very smartly kept, with the fine coat of arms of the company, including the red and white roses of Lancashire and Yorkshire, on the leading driving wheel splasher.

58 W. Adams's Jubilee Class; London and South Western.

These celebrated engines, of which no fewer than 90 were built between the years 1887 and 1895, were designed for fast mixed traffic duties – excursions, troop trains, and fast goods. They were unique on the L.&S.W.R. in having the 0-4-2 wheel arrangement, and the fact that they followed so soon after the famous 'Gladstones' of the L.B.&S.C.R. suggests that Adams derived the idea of them from Stroudley. The cylinders were the same on both classes, namely 18 in. diameter by 26 in. stroke and both had the steam chests beneath the cylinders. The 'Jubilees' had 6 ft. coupled wheels. But though so similar in their capacity and alike in their excellent performance on the road they were as unlike as any two engine classes could be in their outward appearance. The 'Jubilees' with their stove-pipe chimneys, plain domes, massive splashers, and cabs tended to look altogether bigger engines than the *Gladstones*. They were nevertheless beautifully finished in the handsome pale green of the L.&S.W.R. But for the onset of the Second World War they would all have been withdrawn by the end of 1939, after lives of more than 40 years. A number of them were, however, restored to traffic for the duration of the emergency, and the last three were not scrapped until 1948. These engines, Nos. 618, 627 and 636, were all between 55 and 56 years old at that time.

59 **Worsdell-Von Borries 'J' Class.**
During his distinguished career as Locomotive Superintendent of the North Eastern Railway T. W. Worsdell developed the Von Borries system of compounding, using only two cylinders of different sizes, and both placed inside the frames. The low pressure cylinders were large, and on the biggest engines of the type built at Gateshead Works the valve chests were outside. The 'J' class 4-2-2s were the culminating point of this development. They had driving wheels of 7 ft. 7 in. diameter, and were designed to haul heavy trains at high speed. This was in anticipation of increased traffic following the opening of the Forth Bridge in 1890. Although the North Eastern locomotives worked no farther north than Edinburgh they would be conveying the traffic for the new shortened routes to Perth, Inverness and Aberdeen. They proved to be among the fastest engines of their day. One of them was recorded at 90 m.p.h. with a load of 18 six-wheeled coaches; another of them ran a train of 32 coaches (six-wheelers) from Newcastle to Berwick, 67 miles in 78 minutes. This was remarkable work in 1889–90. Unfortunately mechanical troubles developed, and when Worsdell's younger brother Wilson took charge of the locomotive department he altered these engines to two-cylinder simples. As such they did nearly 30 more years of excellent work on the line.

60 **Midland Railway;** A Johnson 4-4-0.
By the 'nineties' of last century Johnson's artistry in locomotive design was reaching its zenith in successive batches of 4-4-0 express passenger engines. These hand-

some machines all had the same general appearance, though there were variations in major dimensions and detail according to the different sections of the Midland Railway over which the engine had to run. Johnson had to provide for such diverse conditions as the mountain lines through the Peak District and among the Pennines; the fast stretches of the main line to London, and the long level roads in Lincolnshire. The 4-4-0s of whatever batch worked uniformly well, and the most recent of them, built about the turn of the century, performed feats of speed and load haulage that might well be thought scarcely possible from such slender looking engines. The example illustrated in our picture dates from 1892, and it was one of those with 7 ft. diameter coupled wheels, intended for the fastest stretches of the line. A feature of these engines, exemplifying Johnson's attention to neat and harmonious detail, is the flush-fitting smokebox door, with no visible fastening other than the central handle. The sweeping curves of the splashers over the driving wheels were another characteristic of all Johnson's 4-4-0 locomotives up to 1900.

61 **The 'Adriatic';** London and North Western.
The 'Teutonic' class compounds represented the third development of Webb's three-cylinder compound system, in which there were two high pressure cylinders outside, and a single, very large low pressure inside. The earlier engines of this series, known respectively as the 'Experiment' and 'Dreadnought' classes, were inclined to be sluggish in running, through defects in their valve gear. But the 'Teutonic' had a single loose eccentric for the low pressure cylinder, and in conjunction with a better design of valves it made all the difference. Although they were uncertain starters, the 'Teutonics', once under way, were fast and powerful engines. No. 1304 *Jeanie Deans* worked the

2 p.m. Scottish corridor express, between Euston and Crewe for a period of more than 9 years, every day of the week, while No. 1309 *Adriatic* made the running between Euston and Crewe on the last night of the Race to the North in 1895 when the entire 540 miles from London to Aberdeen was covered in 512 min. The share of the *Adriatic* was to run the 158 miles from Euston to Crewe at an average speed of 64½ m.p.h. Another spectacular run was that of No. 1305 *Ionic*, which ran non-stop over the 299 miles from Euston to Carlisle with a special train, in 1895. At the time this was the longest non-stop run that had ever been made anywhere in the world. Nevertheless the 'Teutonics' did not last long after Webb's retirement in 1903. Their uncertain starting could not be tolerated in twentieth-century traffic conditions.

62 **Caledonian Railway;** one of the Drummond 4-4-os.
Dugald Drummond, though a Scot by birth, education and early training, served some of the most impressionable years of his career under that early master of locomotive design, William Stroudley. He was in fact Works Manager at Brighton during those great years when the traditions of standardization and fine workmanship were being built up. When Drummond got his first independent appointment, that of Locomotive Superintendent of the North British Railway in 1875, he at once showed his appreciation of Stroudley's precepts, incorporated however in a locomotive type suited to Scottish needs, with the 4-4-0 wheel arrangement (reference 42). This design he used again, in a more highly developed form on the Caledonian, in the '66' class, first introduced in 1884. The East Coast companies were to learn to their discomfiture of the speedworthiness of these engines during the Race to the North in 1895, when several of the Drummond engines made remarkable records. Engine

No. 90, for example, ran from Carlisle to Perth, 150 miles non-stop at an average speed of 60 m.p.h., and at a time when 60 m.p.h. was the generally acknowledged speed of a British express train on level track these engines showed that they could run at 75 m.p.h. on the level between Perth and Forfar.

63 **A Dean 7 ft. 8 in. 4-2-2;** Great Western.
In these beautiful engines the cult for high finish and extensive ornamentation on Great Western locomotives seemed to reach its climax. There were many smaller 'singles' that were decorated in much the same style; but these engines reached the stage shown in our picture by a rapid process of evolution. The first examples were built at the time when the broad gauge was still in existence, and any new locomotives had to be designed with conversion from 7 ft. to 4 ft. 8½ in. gauge in view. With temporary running plates, and completely exposed driving wheels they looked positively ugly. Then came the narrow gauge 2-2-2 stage, which might have persisted had it not been for an alarming derailment of one of them in the Box Tunnel. In their final Dean stage, as depicted here, they did some splendid work on the long non-stop runs then worked on the G.W.R. There were 80 of them in all, and their usual runs were between Paddington and Newton Abbot, via Bristol; Paddington and Newport; and Paddington and Wolverhampton, the latter via either Banbury, or Worcester. Engine No. 3065 *Duke of Connaught* took part in the record run of the Ocean Mail from Plymouth to Paddington on May 9, 1904. The share of the Dean 'single' was to run the 118 miles from Bristol to Paddington in 99½ minutes – a wonderful achievement for that period.

64 **Glasgow and South Western Railway;** one of James Manson's 4-4-os.
Manson came to Kilmarnock in 1891,

having previously been Locomotive Superintendent of the Great North of Scotland Railway. He could be described as one of the most 'orthodox' of nineteenth-century Scottish locomotive engineers, relying upon the most simple and straightforward of designs, with the features most generally adopted at that time. Nevertheless, because of the essentially sound design of the detail parts, and of the care taken in maintaining the locomotives, his otherwise 'ordinary' 4-4-0s achieved an extremely high reputation. They were by no means nursed, or 'petted'. The Glasgow and South Western drivers of those days – particularly those on the Clyde coast and Stranraer trains – were very hard runners, and the engines had to stand up to the pounding of drivers who made it a point of honour to run their trains to time. On the main line from Glasgow to Carlisle rather different techniques prevailed. The distances run between stops were much longer, and the men were inclined to take their engines easily up the banks to save coal, and then to run as fast as they could downhill, on a light rein. But whatever the treatment – whether the 'coal-dodging' on the Carlisle road, or the pounding to Ayr and Stranraer – the Manson 4-4-0s of 1892 won golden opinions everywhere.

65 **A North Eastern 'Rail Crusher'.**
There was a time, during the 'eighties' of last century when it seemed as though the North Eastern Railway was becoming as thorough-going a compound line as the London and North Western, with T. W. Worsdell building many locomotives, passenger, goods and tank alike, on the two-cylinder Worsdell Von Borries system. But as soon as his younger brother took over there was a change, and the 'M' class 4-4-0 locomotives, built at Gateshead in 1893, were two-cylinder simples, fitted with W. M. Smith's piston valves. At the time of their construction they were the heaviest express passenger engines in the

country, and were nicknamed the 'rail crushers' on that account. But they were far from being clumsy or ponderous engines. They rode with the ease and buoyancy of a swing; they were extremely fast, and it was largely due to their use that the North Eastern Railway was able to play such a notable part in the Race to the North, in 1895. There was one memorable night, indeed, when engine No. 1620 took the Aberdeen sleeping car express, weighing 100 tons behind the tender, from Newcastle to Edinburgh, $124\frac{1}{2}$ miles, in 113 minutes. A feature of these engines, and in fact of all N.E.R. engines of the period, was the elegance of the cab interiors. Not only were all the metal fittings kept beautifully, but the sheet metal of the cab walls and sides was covered with a wood lining, which was always kept well polished.

66 **A Johnston 'Spinner';** Midland 4-2-2.
These beautiful engines represent a remarkable, if passing phase in the history of the British steam locomotive. Since he took office in Derby in 1874, Johnson had built none save coupled engines, 2-4-0 and 4-4-0 for express passenger work, until the year 1887. In that year five express engines of the 4-2-2 type, with a single pair of driving wheels 7 ft. 4 in. diameter, were built at Derby. This revival of the obsolescent 'single wheeler' was due to the invention of the steam sanding gear, which by sanding the rails allowed engines to get a better grip. Once this was done Johnson was glad enough to revert to the simplicity and speediness of a 'single-wheeler' for the fastest duties. Between 1887 and 1900 no fewer than 90 new locomotives of the 4-2-2 type were built at Derby, of gradually increasing dimensions. They were most graciously proportioned engines and could run extremely fast. Speeds up to 90 m.p.h. were recorded with them. Though they were great favourites with the men, because

of their smooth action and low coal consumption, they needed care in starting, with heavy trains, despite the use of steam sanding. The driving wheels would slip imperceptibly, without any of the clatter experienced on the footplate when a coupled engine slips; and for this reason they got their nickname of the 'Spinners'.

67 London and South Western Railway; an Adams 4-4-0.

The engine illustrated is one of a family of locomotives that were among the most powerful in the world at the time of their construction, and which by skilful design, and by superb workmanship put into them were amongst the most economical. Adams certainly did not turn his back upon compounding as a possible means of increased efficiency, and one of the Crewe-built Webb three-cylinder machines was tried on the L.&S.W.R. But Adams secured greater efficiency, and incomparably greater reliability by careful consideration in every stage of the circuit of the steam, from the regulator to the cylinders, and through the exhaust ports to the blast pipe and chimney; and the result was a free-running trouble-free engine. Externally these big 4-4-0s, whether of the 6 ft. 7 in. or of the 7 ft. varieties, had a style of their own that was striking, and tremendously impressive at the time of their construction. A stovepipe chimney may seem the very antithesis of handsome design; but it set these locomotives off to perfection – so much so that when Dugald Drummond, who succeeded Adams, replaced them by shapely chimneys in his own style much of the striking character of the Adams 4-4-0 disappeared.

68 A Dunalastair 4-4-0; Caledonian Railway.

Splendid though the work of the Drummond 4-4-0s had been it must be admitted that most of their spectacular running had been made with light trains. Traffic over the Anglo-Scottish routes was very much on the increase in the year of the Race, and the new Caledonian Locomotive Superintendent, John F. McIntosh, found it necessary to provide engines of far greater power. He took the Drummond 4-4-0, therefore, as a basis, and built on to it a very much larger boiler. Thus while the Drummonds had to be handled on 'a light rein' or else they would run short of steam, the new McIntosh engines could be worked hard for hours on end, if need be. The first of them, built at St Rollox Works in 1896, was named Dunalastair after the Highland home of the Caledonian Railway Chairman, and it can be said without exaggeration that no British locomotive class, of any period, has achieved greater fame. They proved themselves capable of running just as fast, and climbing the severe banks just as well as the Drummonds in the race of 1895 but with double the loads. The design was developed through four successive enlargements, known as the 'Dunalastair II', 'III' and 'IV' series, and finally there were the superheated developments of the Type IV. The 'Dunalastair II' series achieved an international reputation, because the design was accepted without any alteration for service on the Belgian National Railways.

69 A Highland 'Loch'; one of David Jones's 4-4-0s.

In his earlier 4-4-0 locomotives for the Highland Railway Jones had perpetuated the massive double framing at the front end, with the outside cylinders snugly ensconced between the two parts of the framing, and very rigidly secured thereby. This was a legacy from the practice of Alexander Allan, introduced at a time when locomotive construction had scarcely emerged from its infancy and there was difficulty sometimes in maintaining the cylinder fastening secure. In 1896 when the majority of British engines still favoured inside cylinders, Jones retained them outside, but with greatly improved constructional methods abandoned the double framing on the 'Lochs', and produced an extremely simple locomotive thereby. The 'Lochs' were in the very top flight among passenger engines of the day. Massively built, skilfully designed, and economical to run, they quickly became great favourites with their drivers. This, Jones's successor in office learned some years later. On a very special occasion the new engineer intended to run an express from Perth to Inverness with two of his own engines. The men demanded that on such an auspicious occasion they must have two Jones 4-4-0s; the newer ones were not *suitable*! Many years later, during World War I, when additional engines were needed for the Dingwall and Skye line for the wartime traffic, three more 'Lochs' were built, exactly to the original drawings of 1896. One could not wish for a finer tribute to an excellent design.

70 **Great North of Scotland Railway;** engines of this handsome design introduced in 1899.

Following the resignation of W. Cowan, the G.N.S.R. was served successively by two engineers who later moved to much larger Scottish Railways: James Manson, who went to the Glasgow and South Western, and W. Pickersgill, who went to the Caledonian. In 1899 Pickersgill designed a particularly handsome 4-4-0, and ten were ordered from Neilson and Co. of Glasgow. When the time came for delivery, traffic on the G.N.S.R. had declined to such an extent that the Company could not afford them, and five were purchased by the English South Eastern and Chatham Railway. But the five taken by the G.N.S.R. became the first of the final development of motive power on the railway, and eight further engines of the class were built at Inverurie Works between 1909 and 1915. After World War I when T. E. Heywood had

succeeded Pickersgill as Locomotive Superintendent, eight new 4-4-0s were added to the stock, similar to Pickersgill's 1899 class, but having superheaters. The eight engines of the new superheater class were all named, and it is one of these, the *Gordon Highlander*, that has been preserved. In Heywood's time the picturesque green livery of the locomotives was superseded by black, and in G.N.S.R. days the *Gordon Highlander* never carried the original green. When the engine was withdrawn for preservation and restored, it was painted in the green livery, as shown in our picture.

71 **Webb 4-cylinder Compound; L.&N.W.R.**
After building a large number of three-cylinder compounds, with the curious arrangement of having two small high pressure cylinders, and one huge low pressure cylinder, Webb turned to four-cylinder compounds. His 4-4-0 passenger engines with this arrangement were largely a failure, but in applying the principle to a heavy mineral engine Webb produced about the best and longest-lived compounds of his career. The valve layout that made his passenger compounds so sluggish was no handicap in a hard-slogging slow-moving coal engine, and these massive though rather ungainly engines did many years of excellent work. Out of the 170 built between 1901 and 1940 60 of them still remained as compounds in 1923. Others were converted into two-cylinder simple engines. But one of the interesting developments concerned the wheel arrangement. A mere glance at our picture is enough to suggest that there was considerable weight overhanging at the front end. All four cylinders were in line, and with some of the engines trouble was experienced from this overhanging weight. Webb's successor, George Whale, rebuilt a number of these engines by inserting a pony truck at the leading end, thus converting them from 0-8-0 to 2-8-0.

Some of the engines thus rebuilt were fitted with much larger boilers, and these latter engines formed the virtual prototype for the celebrated 'Super D' o-8-os of later years.

72   The First British 'Atlantic'; Great Northern.

The death of Patrick Stirling in November 1895, was followed by the appointment of H. A. Ivatt, from the Great Southern and Western Railway, of Ireland. Ivatt had, however, been trained at Crewe, and although in size and power his locomotives for the Great Northern came eventually to look very different from those of Stirling it was nevertheless a process of development rather than a metamorphosis. Within two years of taking office Ivatt had produced a huge engine, No. 990, the first British locomotive of the Atlantic type, though in so doing he beat Mr Aspinall of the Lancashire and Yorkshire Railway for the honour by no more than a matter of months. The first Ivatt 'Atlantics' appeared in the same year as the memorable 'Gold Rush' and were nicknamed the 'Klondykes' in consequence. They were handsomely proportioned, and immediately displayed a haulage capacity far above that of the Stirling 'singles'. The pioneer engine, No. 990, was named *Henry Oakley*, after the General Manager of the company, and a further 20 engines were built later. They did excellent work on the line, though in 1902 Ivatt to some extent superseded his own creation by producing a modified version with a greatly enlarged boiler. As the pioneer of the Atlantic type in Great Britain, of course, the *Henry Oakley* is a most historic engine, and it is preserved in the Railway Museum at York.

73   The First British 4-6-0; Highland Railway.

From the moment he was authorized to build new locomotives David Jones put the Highland Railway in the forefront of British locomotive practice; and from the honour of possessing in 1874 one of the heaviest and most powerful locomotives in Europe, Jones created something of a sensation 20 years later when he built the first British examples of the 4-6-0 type. In designing something very much larger than anything that had gone before, it might well have been thought that Jones was venturing into the unknown, and would have proceeded cautiously, with a single prototype – or two at the outside. On the contrary an order was placed with Sharp Stewart and Co. for 15 of these huge engines, straight off the drawing board. Moreover they proved absolutely 'right' from the very beginning. There were no teething troubles. To use motorcar parlance, the men 'stepped in and drove away'. Although primarily intended for goods traffic they were freerunning engines, and were used on passenger trains during the heavy traffic of the tourist season. It is believed that some of them, when new, were painted in the Stroudley style of old, with 'Brighton yellow' as the basic colour; but in our picture we have shown one of these engines in the standard Jones style, with a basis of apple green. Engine No. 109 of this class has been restored to a reproduction of the original condition, and has done a great deal of interesting work in Scotland in the haulage of special trains.

74   The Aspinall Atlantic; Lancashire and Yorkshire Railway.

It was a race between the Great Northern and the Lancashire and Yorkshire Railway as to which would produce the first Atlantic engine to run in Great Britain. The Great Northern won the race, but the Lancashire produced an engine of great character and distinction. In some ways the 'Highflyers', so called because of the high pitch of their boilers, could be described as an enlarged and elongated version of Aspinall's 4-4-0 of 1891. But the

'Atlantics' were notable in having a very large boiler, and a Belpaire firebox, both of which features placed them far apart from the 4-4-0s. They were designed for high speed running over all parts of the system with heavier trains than could be taken by the 4-4-0s. When they first appeared in 1899, locomotive enthusiasts and railwaymen alike were positively staggered by the size of these 'Atlantics', and their running, particularly on the Liverpool and Manchester service, was at times breathtaking, not only in the maximum speeds attained but in their acceleration from rest. With them it was nothing to pass Salford, a mere ¾ mile out of Manchester, at over 50 m.p.h. On a trial run from Liverpool to Southport, in 1899, with a 5-coach train, one of them is reported to have attained a speed of almost 100 m.p.h. All 40 of them passed into L.M.S.R. ownership, and the last of them was not scrapped until October 1933.

75 **Taff Vale Railway;** One of T. Hurry Riches' 0-6-0 tank engines.
The Taff Vale was an amazing railway. Its main line ran from Cardiff to Pontypridd, and there forked – one line going up the Rhondda Valley and the other to Merthyr. At its greatest extent it had a route mileage of little more than 110, and yet it owned, in 1922, no fewer than 271 locomotives. At the zenith of the coal export boom its trains positively queued up at the entrance to the Cardiff Docks, but amid the teeming coal traffic the company managed to run a swarm of local passenger trains. As on the other railways in South Wales, the 0-6-2 tank was a very popular type. It was equally handy for goods and pasenger working, and the fashion for this type in South Wales can well have been set by the fine engine illustrated in our picture. Eventually the Taff Vale had no fewer than 150 locomotives of this wheel arrangement. Riches was locomotive superintendent of

the railway from 1873 to 1910, and it was indeed a measure of his stature in the engineering world that he was elected President of the Institution of Mechanical Engineers in 1906–7, a very high honour for a man from so relatively small a railway. Our picture cannot show in any detail the striking coat of arms of the Taff Vale Railway, which includes a positively riotous example of the Red Dragon of Wales

76 **Barry Railway;** handsome passenger tank engine.
It is perhaps inappropriate to have, as representative of one of the South Wales 'coal' railways, a locomotive used exclusively in passenger service. But the passenger activities of the Barry Railway were so typical of the unbounded enterprise of the company, and the 0-4-4 tank engines were so brilliantly turned out that they have been chosen in preference to the less ornate, work-horse engines that handled the coal trains. The Barry Railway owed its origin to the congestion of traffic on the Taff Vale and Rhymney lines, and was built primarily to carry coal. And from its opening in 1888 it did this in great quantities. But having started on the way to establishing a new town at Barry Island a passenger service was inaugurated, and soon became an important item in the company's activities. The Barry Railway was indeed the only one of the local South Wales to participate in the running of a main line service – the celebrated 'Ports to Ports Express', between Barry and Newcastle-upon-Tyne. This service was operated in conjunction with such giants of the railway world as the Great Western, the Great Central, and the North Eastern. The Barry locomotives hauled this express between Cardiff and Barry, and the smart little 0-4-4 tanks were used for this duty. They were certainly not the least handsome of the locomotives that hauled that express on its long journey.

77 Rhymney Railway; a mixed traffic tank engine.

The Rhymney Railway was a purely local concern in South Wales, a child of the prodigious boom in the coal trade during the Victorian Era. It began at the head of the Rhymney river valley, among high mountains, and it ended at the Cardiff docks. The coal it conveyed for export reached at times to astronomical quantities, but there was also a thriving passenger business between such centres of population as Caerphilly Ystrad Mynach, Bargoed, and Rhymney. The locomotives therefore had all to be general purpose machines, and the engine illustrated is typical of the workmanlike 0-6-2 tank designs introduced from 1906 onwards by Mr C. T. Hurry Riches. This able engineer was a son of the famous locomotive superintendent of the neighbouring Taff Vale Railway. The new superintendent of the Rhymney Railway came to Caerphilly Works from the Great Central Railway, and in the Welsh valleys he imparted much of the grace and smart turnout of Gorton to the goods and passenger engines of the Rhymney. Both classes of engine carried the green livery, lined out, and having chocolate brown underframes, while the engines particularly allocated to passenger working had polished brass domes, and brass pedestals for the safety valves. Unlike its neighbour, the Brecon and Merthyr, the Rhymney Railway used the Westinghouse brake.

78 Brecon and Merthyr Railway; mineral tank engine.

This railway, despite its name, does not actually enter Merthyr on its own metals, but it provides a long and important link in the chain of communication between the mining valleys of South Wales and the fine farming country north of the Brecknock Beacons. There are some extremely heavy gradients on the way, particularly in the long descent from Torpantau Tunnel to Talybont-on-Usk, where the gradient is 1 in 38 for many miles. A humorist once declared, indeed, that the Brecon and Merthyr Railway would do well as a toboggan run! These fine engines, built by Robert Stephenson and Company to the design of James Dunbar, had 4 ft. 6 in. coupled wheels – ideal for the heavy grades – yet even these engines were limited to a maximum load of 10 loaded wagons and a brake van up the 1 in 38 gradients. It can be well imagined how much double-heading was necessary with the freight trains before the introduction of these powerful locomotives. They were not confined to freight. At one time there was a brisk passenger business over this route, with through carriages from Cardiff (Taff Vale line) via Merthyr to Brecon and the seaside resorts on Cardigan Bay. This was additional to the regular passenger service from Newport via Bargoed. These engines were equipped with the automatic vacuum brake so that they could assist in the passenger traffic.

79 London Brighton and South Coast Railway; 'B4' class.

When Billinton succeeded to the office of Locomotive Superintendent of the L.B.&S.C.R. in 1889, after the death of Stroudley, he at once abandoned the principle of front-coupled express locomotives, and in his first design, the 'B2' class of 1895, he used the conventional 4-4-0 wheel arrangement. This first class, nicknamed the 'Grasshoppers', were not successful. The boiler was too small, and on the Portsmouth line the new engines did very little better than the old Stroudley 'singles' of 1880. But in his second 4-4-0 design, the 'B4' class of 1901, Billinton made no mistake. They were splendid engines in every way, and had no difficulty in running the 51 miles between Victoria and Brighton in the hour – sometimes considerably less. When they were newly built they carried the beautiful Stroudley livery, with all its gay colouring in addition to the famous 'yellow'. But they were best known in the handsome chocolate brown of later Brighton days, set off with much black and yellow lining out. Engine No. 70 was originally named *Holyrood*, and she made a record run from Victoria to Brighton with the Sunday Pullman train on July 26, 1903: 51 miles in 48¾ min. start to stop. In later years, when she was carrying the chocolate livery, the engine was named *Devonshire*, as illustrated. The 'B4' class went generally by the name of the 'Scotchmen', because most of them were built in Glasgow, by Sharp, Stewart and Co. Ltd.

80 **An Oil-Fired 4-2-2, of 1898;** Great Eastern Railway.
The last single-driver express locomotive built for the Great Eastern was designed specially for the accelerated Cromer expresses of 1896. Until then, passengers for that rising resort of the Norfolk coast had to change at Norwich. At first the new Cromer expresses stopped at Ipswich, but later the run was made non-stop. In the season the loads were particularly heavy, including a dining car and some bogie corridor vehicles. But not many of the latter had then been built, and a typical load of one of these Cromer expresses would be 12 six-wheelers, 4 bogie coaches, and a 4-wheeled fruit van. To handle these long and heavy trains, at an average speed of 49 m.p.h. throughout, James Holden built ten of the very handsome 4-2-2 locomotives illustrated. On their first introduction these trains had been worked by the '1000' class 2-2-2s, but the big 4-2-2s took over in the summer of 1898. Four of the latter were stationed at Ipswich, and four at Norwich. The London–Cromer non-stops were all worked as lodging turns, by Ipswich and Norwich men on alternate days. The Ipswich engines started at their home shed, worked to London, and then

took the Cromer non-stop. Then they worked back to Norwich and lodged. On the following day they did the trip in reverse. In their later years they followed their predecessors to the Joint Line, and finished a short but brilliant career running the York expresses of the Great Eastern Railway.

81 **Great Central Railway;** a Pollitt 4-4-0.
In 1893 the Manchester, Sheffield and Lincolnshire Railway obtained its Act authorizing the extension to London, and in 1897 the title of the railway was changed to Great Central. In readiness for the London express services Harry Pollitt designed a class of 4-4-0. These engines proved very successful, but in later years the new locomotive superintendent, J. G. Robinson, greatly improved them by adding superheaters, and a commodious canopied cab. These engines were soon displaced by larger machines on the London Extension but they then became the mainstay of the Cheshire Lines passenger services. In rapid acceleration, and fast running between stops they earned such a reputation for reliability that the Liverpool and Manchester trains became known as the 'Punctual' expresses. On this duty the rebuilt Pollitt 4-4-0s were in competition with very fast rival services on *two* other routes between Liverpool and Manchester namely those of the London and North Western, and of the Lancashire and Yorkshire. All three routes provided a 40-minute service between the two cities, though on the Cheshire Lines in some ways the hardest work was involved on those trains making an intermediate stop at Warrington, and completing the 34 miles from Manchester to Liverpool in 45 minutes, inclusive of the stop.

82 **North Eastern Railway;** One of the 'R' class 4-4-0s.
The turn of the century on the railways

of Great Britain was a time of greatly increased train loads, and of a growing realization that operation must be more economically performed. Following the great success of the 'M' class engines, by the standards of the nineteenth century, Wilson Worsdell set out to design an enlarged version that should be capable of taking much heavier loads, but which would also be capable of a much longer day's work. It was still a time for each driver to have his own engine, but in the 'R' class each engine had two regular crews, who worked in two shifts. The 'R' class were not only excellent engines in hard weight pulling, but they proved capable of doing practically double the daily mileage previously considered normal for an express locomotive. They were immensely popular with their crews, and so far as the double-manning was concerned, a typical day's work would go from Newcastle to Edinburgh and back with the first crew, and then from Newcastle to Leeds and back with the second. Among other duties they ran what was then the fastest start-to-stop run in the country: 1.9 p.m. Darlington to York, 44.1 miles in 43 min. The trip was frequently done at much higher speeds, and a record was made by engine No. 1672, when the start-to-stop time was 39½ min. Some of these engines lasted for more than 50 years.

83 **Furness Railway;** Pettigrew 4-4-0.
Although no more than a local railway, the Furness was held in unusually high esteem, partly because of the great importance of its traffic, and still more so because of the status of its Locomotive Engineer. Pettigrew was associated with William Adams of the London and South Western Railway in some of the most important and comprehensive tests carried out on British locomotives in the nineteenth century. He was also the author of the standard work on locomotive constructional practice at the

time. One looks with particular interest, therefore, to the locomotives he designed for the Furness Railway, and one is not disappointed. The handsome and powerful 4-4-0s, of which an example forms the subject of our picture, could be described as an inside cylinder version of the famous Adams 4-4-0 of the L.&S.W.R. While the Furness line did not give an opportunity for sustained fast running there were certainly some very smartly timed trains, particularly the early morning mail, booked to run the 19 miles from Carnforth to Ulverston in 24 min. Although level, the line makes a winding course, very close to the sea, and to keep such a schedule involved very rapid acceleration, and a steady 60 m.p.h. thereafter. These 4-4-0s also did well on the heavy gradients experienced in crossing the Barrow isthmus. An attractive feature of all Furness locomotives was the pleasing shade of red that was the basis of their livery – 'iron-ore red' – very appropriate to the district in which they worked.

84 **Cambrian Railways;** a passenger 4-4-0.
The Cambrian Railways – always in the plural – was a difficult system to manage, with its main line running from Whitchurch up the Severn Valley, and then through mountainous country to the sea at Aberystwyth, and some very long and meandering branches. Furthermore, its administrative headquarters and locomotive works was clean outside Wales, at Oswestry, in Shropshire. From Dovey Junction a line made its way right round the northern arc of Cardigan Bay to Pwllheli, while from Moat Lane Junction another line followed a chain of valleys in Central Wales, to Brecon. And yet, for all its far flung extent the Cambrian had much more of a main line character than the busy local railways of South Wales. Its trains savoured of long-time, if not long-distance travel, and this was re-

flected in the locomotive power employed. Very few tank engines were used, and on the main line trains a change was made from the 2-4-0 to the 4-4-0 type of tender engine in 1878. The engine shown in our picture is of a later and much larger class, designed by Mr Aston and first built by Sharp, Stewart and Company in 1893. They were excellent machines, and for many years hauled the main line trains, carrying through carriages from Aberystwyth to Manchester, Birmingham and London. The Cambrian engines, although painted black, had the distinction of carrying the insignia of the Prince of Wales on their tenders.

85 Somerset and Dorset Joint Railway; a 4-4-0 of 1903.

The Somerset and Dorset was a joint concern of the London and South Western, and the Midland Railway. Its main line ran from Bath to Bournemouth, and it involved some exceedingly heavy gradients in the crossing of the Mendips. Because of the joint ownership engineering responsibility for the working of the line was divided; the L.&S.W.R. maintained the track and the signalling, while the Midland had the responsibility for locomotives. Between Bath and Evercreech Junction the ruling gradient is 1 in 50, and for the S.&D. working it was considered desirable to modify the standard Midland express engines by providing them with smaller wheels to cope with the inclines involved in crossing the Mendips. The engine chosen for illustration is, however, particularly interesting. Instead of being an adaptation of a Midland design to suit S.&D. conditions it was virtually a new Derby design, of which a subsequent adaptation with *larger* coupled wheels became a Midland Railway standard. It was the first time Derby had used this particular type of boiler on a 4-4-0 locomotive. The coupled wheels were 6 ft. in diameter, and when subsequently it was decided to

rebuild a number of the older Midland 4-4-0 locomotives with larger boilers, this S.&D. boiler was applied to engines with 6 ft. 6 in. coupled wheels.

86 Midland and Great Northern Joint Railway; an express passenger 4-4-0.

This interesting joint line, now completely closed and dismantled, at one time carried a considerable traffic from the East Midlands to East Anglia. It was an amalgamation of a number of smaller local railways, and was jointly owned, as its name implied, by the Midland and the Great Northern Railways. Some of the locomotives were precisely of standard Midland design, though instantly distinguished by the handsome mustard-yellow livery. The locomotive works of the Joint Line were at Melton Constable, and there, under the supervision of William Marriott, Locomotive Superintendent, the locomotives we illustrate were rebuilt from a Midland design of 1894. At the same time the rebuilding made use of many parts that were standard Derby fittings at the time, such as the chimney tapering outwards from the base, the safety cover, and the canopied cab. The curious thing is, however, that these features never appeared simultaneously on a contemporary Midland engine. The M.&G.N. main line from Norwich to its point of junction with the Midland Railway near Saxby, includes much heavy grading, and these engines worked through between Norwich and Leicester, each engine and crew working the fast expresses on alternate days, and lodging at Leicester overnight.

87 Lynton and Barnstaple narrow gauge railway; one of the tank engines.

The Lynton and Barnstaple was one of the unluckiest of light railways. It was built to provide rail communication of a kind, to the remote twin towns of Lynton and Lynmouth, approached by only rough and indifferent roads. The line to Barnstaple was opened in 1898, but there had been much miscalculation in the estimates and the line cost far more than had been allowed for. Once opened, it proved a very popular line for summer visitors; but it never really paid its way, and for some years after grouping the Southern Railway lavished money upon some publicity, but still operated it at a loss. Eventually in the autumn of 1935 it was closed. This sad event was long before the days of amateur preservation societies for these picturesque little railways. It would have formed an unrivalled object for such attention had closure been threatened some ten or a dozen years later. The 2-6-2 tank engines were built specially for the line by Manning, Wardle and Co. of Leeds. The first three were delivered for the opening of the line, and were happily named after 3-letter Devon rivers *Yeo*, *Exe* and *Taw*. Another engine of the same type, *Lew*, was added after the Southern Railway had assumed responsibility in 1923. They were then painted in standard livery, with the name SOUTHERN extending from end to end of the side tanks.

88 Leek and Manifold Light Railway; one of the tank engines.

Towards the end of the Victorian era the policy was formed of constructing cheaply-built light railways in rural districts to act as feeders to the main line systems, in areas where the prospective traffic did not warrant the building of ordinary branch lines. Certain relaxations from the ordinary Board of Trade requirements were permitted as a result of an Act of Parliament dated 1896, and great hopes for success were expressed as a result of this legislation. The Leek and Manifold Light Railway was built under the provisions of this Act, amid the beautiful hills and dales of the south-western corner of the Derbyshire Peak

District. It was opened in 1904, and worked by two picturesque 2-6-4 tank engines. Our picture shows one of these in the handsome chocolate livery originally used. Later the North Staffordshire Railway livery was adopted, and when the latter company came within the L.M.S. group the two little Manifold tank engines were painted in Midland red. Unhappily the railway never paid. After World War I local buses provided a much more convenient service, though the railway was kept going, at a considerable loss, until 1934. One notable feature of the locomotives was their huge headlight, needed because much of the line was unfenced, and unprotected by gates at level crossings.

89 Festiniog Railway; one of the 'double-engines'.

The Festiniog Railway was built to convey slates from the quarries of Blaenau Festiniog to Portmadoc for shipment, and while heavy loaded trains could be worked down the valley without difficulty there was congestion on the line because of the limited loads of empties that could be hauled up the steep gradients from the coast. Robert Fairlie then devised the famous double-engine, consisting of two engine units, back to back, with two boilers fed from a central double firebox. Although the double boiler is built as a single unit structurally, there are actually separate fireboxes and separate firedoors. The water and steam space is continuous throughout. The first 'double engine', the *Little Wonder* showed its ability to haul more than twice the load of any engine already on the line, and after 1869 a number of double engines were put to work. Two of them still survive today, and after lying derelict in the Boston Lodge Works for very many years both have been restored to first-class working order, and are giving excellent service on the railway today. The Fairlie articulated engines of the Festiniog

Railway represent a most historic development in steam locomotives. The principle of articulation, so putting what is virtually an assembly of two engines under the control of a single crew, was developed strikingly in the Beyer-Garratt type of locomotive, to which reference is made later.

90 **Snowdon Mountain Railway;** one of the Swiss-built rack locomotives. Tremendous interest was created when the Snowdon Mountain Tramroad and Hotels Co. Ltd. – to give the concern its original title – was incorporated in November 1894. The line climbs from Llanberis to the summit of Snowdon, 3500 ft. above sea level, in 5 miles, with a maximum steepness of ascent of 1 in 6. The gauge is 2 ft. 7½ in. and there is a double steel rack for engaging the locomotive pinions. The locomotive *Wyddfa* is one of three supplied by the Swiss Locomotive Company of Winterthur, for the opening of the line, in 1895; but of that trio, one was destroyed in a sensational accident, in which the locomotive left the rails on a high, exposed ridge, and plunged thousands of feet to destruction. Following that, additional safety devices were included, and the line has been operated with complete safety since its opening to regular traffic in April 1897. There are seven locomotives in service, all of the 0-4-2 type, but varying in detail. In addition to the two survivors of the original trio, both of which are still doing good work, there are two dating from 1896, and three newer ones supplied from Switzerland in 1922–3. Each 'train' consists of one coach, seating 60 passengers, and on the upward journey it is propelled by the locomotive. By reason of the exceptional steepness of the ascent, and the need for the utmost caution when descending the mountain, speed is limited in both directions to a maximum of 5 m.p.h.

91 **The 'Claud Hamilton';** epoch-making Great Eastern 4-4-0. For upwards of 40 years successive locomotive superintendents of the Great Eastern Railway had built little save single-driver express locomotives. Where there had been coupled engines, as with the otherwise identical '1000' class 2-2-2, and 'T.19' 2-4-0 of James Holden, the singles had proved as good as, if not better than, the coupled engines. But by the turn of the century something considerably larger was needed. The crack expresses were being equipped with corridor coaches throughout, and restaurant cars, and the loads of the holiday trains were rising from 250 to 350 tons. Under James Holden's supervision the *Claud Hamilton* engine was designed and built at Stratford, in 1900. It was much larger and more powerful than anything previously seen on the G.E.R., and where the 'singles' had tackled trains up to 250 tons in weight, the 'Claud Hamilton' class 4-4-0s could, when really extended, take *four hundred* tons. Again, while most of the 'singles' had a very short life some of the 'Claud Hamiltons', through various processes of rebuilding, lasted for more than fifty years. The first engine, No. 1900, was the only one to be named, after Lord Claud Hamilton, the Chairman of the Great Eastern Railway. The original design had a boiler with a round-topped firebox, but later varieties were fitted with Belpaire types. They rank among the most successful 4-4-0 express passenger locomotives ever built.

92 **A Johnson 'Belpaire';** Midland Railway. Throughout the nineteenth century the Midland had been a railway with locomotives of slender proportions and exceedingly graceful appearance, and a study of the examples shown under our references 47, 60 and 66 makes it clear that they had a strongly characteristic style of their own. At the turn of the

century train loads were very much on the increase; the stimulus of competition demanded accelerated service, and these demands were reflected in a profound change in the traditional appearance of Midland locomotives. The large-boilered 4-4-0s built at Derby at the turn of the century had the square-topped Belpaire fireboxes, and large bogie tenders, to enable them to make long non-stop runs with heavy trains. As the first engines on the Midland to have this particular type of firebox they were always known as the 'Belpaires', even in later years when there were many locomotives of other types running with Belpaire fireboxes. When the Midland decided to instal water troughs the large bogie tenders became unnecessary, and these engines were fitted with a standard six-wheeled non-bogie type. In later years they were renumbered in the '700' series, and their usefulness was further increased in the nineteen-twenties when they were fitted with superheaters.

93 **Hull and Barnsley Railway;** Matthew Stirling's express locomotive.
The Hull and Barnsley Railway was built as an alternative, highly competitive route for conveying coal from the South Yorkshire coalfield to Hull, for export to Scandinavia and the Baltic states. At the same time this enterprising line attempted to build up a fast passenger service between Hull and Sheffield. From 1885, until the railway was absorbed into the L.N.E.R. group, the locomotive superintendent was Matthew Stirling, son of the celebrated Patrick Stirling of the Great Northern, and nephew of James Stirling. Like his father and his uncle, Matthew Stirling was firmly attached to locomotives with domeless boilers. His freight engines were 0-6-0s and 0-8-0s, but until the year 1910 he had not found it necessary to build anything larger than 2-4-0s for passenger traffic. Then, however, he introduced the handsome 4-4-0 design

shown in our picture. Though not so richly endowed with flowing curves and nineteenth-century elegance as one of his father's engines, this 4-4-0, of which design five were eventually in service, represents a worthy development of the Stirling tradition in locomotive constructional practice. They did admirable work on the Sheffield–Hull expresses, from 1910 until the re-arrangement of the train services some time after grouping, in 1923.

94 **The 'City of Truro';** Great Western Railway.
These locomotives, although relatively few in number, gained great fame for their designer, for the G.W.R., and for British railways in general. Technically they represent an important link in the chain of development of locomotive practice at Swindon, from the Victorian traditions of the Dean period to twentieth-century standards. They retained the outside frames of former days, and cylinders with slide valves, but they incorporated the very important advance of the tapered-barrel boiler, and Belpaire firebox. In high-speed express traffic with trains of moderate weight they were outstandingly successful, improving upon the new standards of running set by immediate predecessors of the 'Atbara' class, which were similar, but with parallel boilers. Engine No. 3433 *City of Bath* set up a new record for the London–Plymouth run made non-stop, via Bristol, in 233½ min. for the distance of 246.6 miles; this record was made with an advance portion of the Cornishman express in 1903. Engine No. 3440 *City of Truro* reached a maximum speed of slightly over 100 m.p.h. near Wellington, with an Ocean Mail special in May 1904. In ordinary service these engines were responsible for the first regular running of the Cornish Riviera Express non-stop in each direction between Paddington and Plymouth 245.6 miles in 267 min.

The *City of Truro* has been preserved, and is now in the Great Western Railway Museum at Swindon.

95   A 'Precursor' Class 4-4-0; London and North Western Railway.

Webb's large scale experiment with compound locomotives had left the L.N.W.R. short of powerful and reliable engines, and the first task of his successor, George Whale, was to provide for that deficiency. Under his direction a simple, straightforward 4-4-0 was designed in record time at Crewe Works; in some ways it was a much larger version of the 'Precedent' class 2-4-0, but with the important difference of having Joy valve gear instead of the Allan straight-link motion. Within 10 months from the time of Webb's retirement the first engine of the new class, No. 513 *Precursor* was on the road, and it proved an immediate and outstanding success. There were no teething troubles, and after a first batch of ten, constructed at intervals between March and June 1904, quantity production began in earnest, and a level 100 of them were completed at Crewe between October 1904 and May 1906. At times they were turning them out at the rate of 2 per week! And what engines they were. They proved an absolute godsend to the Running Department, by their almost unfailing reliability, taking loads of 350 to 400 tons on schedules demanding average speeds of 52 to 55 m.p.h. from start to stop. Twenty more of them were constructed in 1907. The engine illustrated, No. 1111 *Cerberus*, was the first of eight engines of the class completed at Crewe in the one month of March 1905, when production of them was at its height.

96   Earle-Marsh's 'I3' Tank; London Brighton and South Coast Railway.

Basically these engines, introduced by D. Earle-Marsh in 1907, could be des-cribed as a tank engine version of the Billinton 'B4' express passenger 4-4-0 (reference 79). The 'I3' class were express locomotives in every way, with 6 ft. 6 in. coupled wheels, and for the relatively short runs of the Brighton railway they were handier and more compact than a tender engine at the terminals. But when Marsh equipped some of these engines with the Schmidt superheater he trans-formed them into one of the most economical locomotive classes ever to run south of the Thames. In 1909 one of them, No. 23, was engaged in comparative trials on the 'Sunny South Special' express service, as between Rugby and Brighton. The competing engine was a L.N.W.R. non-superheated 'Precursor' type 4-4-0, and although the circumstances for the two engines were not necessarily identical the Brighton engine showed a remarkable economy in both coal and water con-sumption, while running the trains with conspicuous ease. It is generally con-sidered that the working of the 4-4-2 tank engine No. 23 influenced the decision of the L.N.W.R. to introduce superheating on a considerable scale. The Brighton tank engines had a long and arduous life, and some of them were still doing excellent work on the non-electrified sections of the Southern Railway as recently as 1947. The last survivor was scrapped in 1953.

97   The De Glehn 4-4-2 'La France'; Great Western Railway.

At the turn of the century much attention was focussed upon current French loco-motive practice by the very successful running of the various classes of four-cylinder compound on the Northern Railway. These engines were designed upon the system of Mr Alfred de Glehn, an English engineer, who was then Chief Engineer of the Société Alsacienne of Belfort. The introduction of the Nord compound Atlantics made some quite spectacular accelerations of the English boat trains possible, as between Paris and

Calais, and many English engineers gave consideration anew to the use of the compound system. On the Great Western Churchward arranged for a French-built compound 'Atlantic' to be purchased, and the *La France*, delivered in 1903, ran a series of trials on the principal Great Western expresses in competition with Swindon-built engines. For the most part these were not 'set' trials, but they involved the careful observation, month in, month out, of general performance, reliability, running costs, fuel consumption and so on. While these did not show any superiority over the Swindon-built ten-wheelers *La France*, and the two larger French compounds purchased in 1905, included some features of detail design that became standard practice on the G.W.R., notably the bogie, and design of big-end for the inside cylinder connecting rods. The principal feature that was copied, however, was the division of the drive between two axles – the inside cylinders driving on to the leading pair of coupled wheels.

98 **Dugald Drummond's 'T9';** London and South Western Railway.
This class, of which 66 were built between the years 1899 and 1901, represented the culmination of Dugald Drummond's 'small' 4-4-0 design, which was initiated on the North British Railway in 1876, was developed on the Caledonian and brought to its final and most successful form on the London and South Western. A smaller-wheeled variant of the same design was put into service on the Highland Railway by Peter Drummond. The engine illustrated, No. 714, belongs to the second batch of 1899, which had cross-water tubes in the firebox, designed to promote more rapid circulation of the water, and quicker steam raising. The cover over the ends of these tubes is seen between the coupled wheel splashers. Although slender in appearance these engines were capable of very hard work on the road. The

coupled wheelbase (10ft.) was exceptionally long, and permitted of a large firebox grate area. In consequence the capacity for steam raising was good, and enabled the engines to haul heavy trains and do work that belied their slender appearance. They could run very fast, and on the Salisbury-Exeter road frequently attained speeds of 85 m.p.h. and over. In later years a number of them were rebuilt with extended smokeboxes, superheaters, and stove-pipe chimneys, and one of these latter has been preserved, and is painted in L.&S.W.R. colours.

99 **Lancashire and Yorkshire Railways;** one of the side tank engines.
In addition to its many and various main lines the Lancashire and Yorkshire had numerous branches, some extending into very hilly country on the Lancashire side of the Pennines. Aspinall introduced the 2-4-2 side tank type of locomotive in 1899, indeed engine No. 1008 was not only the first of the class, but also the first engine to be built new at Horwich Works. No fewer than 210 of the original type were built, down to the year 1898; but after that, the type was developed to the very efficient superheater version of 1911. Our picture shows an engine of 1905 vintage, originally built to use saturated steam, but modernized by the addition of a superheater in 1921. In this, their final form, they were remarkable little engines, pulling heavy loads on the longer-distance residential trains from Manchester. One of the hardest runs was an evening non-stop from Salford to Colne, on which the usual load was one of 10 non-corridor carriages, filled almost entirely with first-class season ticket holders. In climbing into the hills there is a stretch where the gradient averages 1 in 118 for 15 miles, and these little tank engines used to run that heavy train with the punctuality of chronometers. Altogether the Lancashire and Yorkshire Railway owned 330 of these 2-4-2 tank engines. Many of them

put in more than 50 years of service, and some lasted for over 60 years.

100 **London and South Western Railway;** the 'M7' tank engine.
This class, of which no fewer than 105 were built between 1897 and 1911, can be considered among Dugald Drummond's 'small' engine designs. They represent the only example on the L.&S.W.R. of an affinity, so far as wheel arrangement was concerned, to Stroudley's front-coupled types on the Brighton railway. They were splendid engines in every way, and many of them have put in more than 60 years of service. They originally ran the London suburban trains, and locals on many country branches. Although their coupled wheels were only 5 ft. 7 in. diameter as against 6 ft. 7 in. on the express passenger engines they could run very freely, and were used on the longer-distance residential trains from Waterloo in addition to purely suburban services. Beautifully constructed, they were veritable little 'Rolls Royces' among tank engines, and rode with a quietness, ease, and silence that would have been the envy of many a driver on a far more spectacular main line passenger engine. In their later days they were still very familiar sights at Waterloo, working trains of empty coaches between the carriage sidings at Clapham and the terminus.

101 **Stroudley's 'D' Class 0-4-2 Tank.**
This was another very successful Stroudley design, used in heavy suburban and branch line passenger service all over the Brighton system. The first of them was built in 1873, and it was undoubtedly the favourable experience gained with these engines in semi-fast traffic that led Mr Stroudley towards the use of front coupled driving wheels in the 'Gladstone' class. There were no fewer than 125 of the 'D' class, built between the years 1873 and 1887, and all of them were named after stations on the line. It must be admitted that this system of naming was applied both to these engines and to the smaller 'A' class with the 0-6-0 wheel arrangement in a somewhat unimaginative way. One feels also that those concerned either had their tongues in their cheeks, or were devoid of a sense of humour – otherwise one of these splendid little engines would never have been named *Crawley*! They were strongly built, almost unfailingly reliable, and in consequence long-lived. After the L.B.& S.C.R. became part of the Southern Railway many of the 'D' class were drafted to country branches far from the old Brighton line, and some of them reached the ripe old age of 70 years before they were finally withdrawn from service. Originally they were painted in the Stroudley yellow livery.

102 **Great Eastern Railway;** the London suburban tank engine of 1890–1902.
At the time of the grouping, in 1923, the Great Eastern Railway was operating, entirely by steam, the heaviest suburban traffic in London. The development of the outer residential districts coupled with the increase in local traffic had placed a tremendous strain upon the traffic-handling capacity of Liverpool Street Station, and the Operating Superintendent, F. V. Russell, remodelled the entire timetables, in addition to making a large number of small but significant alterations to the track layout, so as to run many more trains in the rush hours. To cut down the time spent at intermediate stations the carriage doors were painted different colours to denote the three classes, so that passengers could quickly recognize the whereabouts of the class they wanted. These services became known as the 'Jazz trains', in consequence of the coloured doors. They were worked by small, but very sturdy and reliable 0-6-0 tank engines, having small wheels

for rapid acceleration from many stops. From Liverpool Street they worked the 'Jazz' service to Enfield, Palace Gates, Walthamstow and Chingford, and did remarkable work for many years. The design was originally introduced in 1890 by James Holden, though an improved version, with higher boiler pressure and larger side tanks, dates from 1902. No fewer than 134 of them were still in service on the nationalized British Railways in 1949.

103 'Cardean' of the Caledonian.
It is doubtful if any single locomotive built in the first decade of the twentieth century achieved, at the time, a fame greater than that enjoyed by the first of this small class of 5 locomotives. No. 903 was named *Cardean*, after the country estate of the Deputy Chairman of the Caledonian Board at that time, and in accordance with the practice of the day, so far as big engines on the Caledonian were concerned, it was allocated to one particular duty, and one only. *Cardean* had that veritable queen of Anglo-Scottish expresses, the 2 p.m. from Glasgow to Euston, which she took down to Carlisle. Then, after handing over to the L.&N.W.R., she brought the corresponding northbound express from Carlisle to Glasgow. And except for the very few occasions when she was under repair *Cardean* made that round trip every weekday for the best part of ten years! It was her unfailing reliability and excellent timekeeping that made the engine something of a legend – not only in Scotland but wherever there were railways. Technically *Cardean* and her four sister engines, none of which bore names, were a very large 4-6-0 development of the 'Dunalastairs', and their performance was enhanced in 1911–12 when they were fitted with superheaters. Simply and massively built, they were in every way an epitome of the neat, graceful British locomotives of the pre-1914 era.

104 **Glasgow and South Western Railway;** a Manson 4-6-0.
The Anglo-Scottish expresses following the Midland route from St Pancras to Carlisle were sharply timed, and greater engine power was needed than that afforded by the Manson 4-4-0s of 1892. The 4-6-0s built in 1903 were in every way a typical Manson design, in their neatness of outline and simplicity of detail. The drivers took to them at once, because they responded so readily to traditional methods of working between Glasgow and Carlisle. The new engines ran with the utmost freedom and steadiness downhill, and speeds of 85 m.p.h. and more were common. At the time these 4-6-0s were introduced there were no Pullman cars on the Anglo-Scottish trains; but since the inauguration of the through Midland service between St Pancras and Glasgow in 1876, service to and from England was invariably referred to as the 'Pullmans'. The Manson 4-6-0s were economical engines on any count; but they were made even more so by the techniques of driving used by the men. At a later date two additional engines were built by Manson having superheaters, and these were probably the lightest engines on coal to be found anywhere in Great Britain at the time. All the Manson 4-6-0s passed into L.M.S.R. ownership; but by that time their day was practically over, and they were barely equal to the demands of the traffic.

105 **The Highland 'Castle' Class.**
David Jones, who had enjoyed so distinguished a career as Locomotive Superintendent of the Highland Railway since 1870, had the misfortune to sustain a serious injury on the footplate of one of his epoch-making 4-6-0 goods locomotives (see Plate 73). This so affected his health that he had to resign, many years before what would have been his normal retiring age. He had, however, prepared a design

for an express passenger version of his famous goods 4-6-0, and it fell to his successor, Peter Drummond, to place this splendid engine in service. There was time for Drummond to include a number of the specialities for which he and his elder brother Dugald were well known, such as the steam reverser, compensated bogie, and the large double-bogie tender with inside frames. The boiler mountings and cab were those of the Drummonds. But in the fundamentals of the design the 'Castle' was a Jones product, and it was accorded the popularity common to every engine design Jones had produced while at Inverness. The 'Castle' class became the mainstay of the passenger service between Inverness and Perth, and remained so for nearly 20 years. A modified form of the class was introduced by F. G. Smith in 1913, and three more engines, with coupled wheels, 6 ft. diameter instead of 5 ft. 9 in. were built in 1917 to cope with the heavy wartime traffic on the Highland Railway. Our picture shows the original livery of 1900. In later years they were finished in plain green without any lining.

106 **A Reid 'Atlantic';** North British Railway.
In the early years of the twentieth century, as from its inception in 1876, the Midland and North British joint Anglo-Scottish service made heavy demands upon engine power between Edinburgh and Carlisle. In view of the gradients and the loads to be hauled a six-coupled engine would have seemed desirable; but because of the very bad curvature W. P. Reid decided upon an 'Atlantic', and he built the most powerful engine of the type ever to run in Great Britain. The first examples of the class were non-superheated, but after these had been modified their work became remarkable; both on the 'Waverley' route, and on the East Coast main line between Edinburgh and Aberdeen they took heavy loads, and climbed the steep gradients with a sureness and efficiency that helped to make the North British one of the most punctual railways in Great Britain. These massive engines, which all had fine Scottish names, looked their best in the original North British brown livery; but in London and North Eastern days they remained among the selected few pre-grouping types to be painted in the new standard apple-green, when most others were relegated to 'black'. In all they put in thirty years' work on the Aberdeen route, though they were displaced from the Waverley route a little earlier.

107 **A Great Northern 'Atlantic'.**
Until the end of the Stirling régime Great Northern engines, despite the very fast and hard work they did on the line, were distinctly slender in appearance. Ivatt, in consequence, caused something of a surprise with his first 'Atlantic'; but that surprise was nothing compared with the veritable sensation that followed the building of his first 'large' Atlantic, No. 251, in 1902. The boiler and firebox were actually the only points of difference between No. 251 and the 'Klondykes' as the cylinders and all else remained the same. Although capable of very good work, the potentialities of these massive engines were not realized in their original state, and it was left to Ivatt's successor, the celebrated H. N. Gresley – later Sir Nigel Gresley – to make those modifications and additions that transformed them into truly wonderful engines. Gresley fitted them all with high-degree superheaters and some of them with slightly larger cylinders and piston valves. As such they could do extraordinary work. One of them ran the Queen of Scots Pullman from Leeds to Kings Cross in a net time of 176 min. for the run of 187 miles, while another of them, called upon to replace a disabled Pacific at Grantham at a moment's notice, ran the afternoon Scotsman over the $82\frac{3}{4}$ miles from

Grantham to York in 86½ min. with a very heavy train of *seventeen* bogie coaches, 585 tons. Our picture shows one of them in G.N.R. days. There was very little change externally, when they had been transformed by Sir Nigel Gresley.

108 **South Eastern and Chatham Railway;** Wainwright's 'E' class.
The working union of the South Eastern and the London Chatham and Dover Railways under a Managing Committee as from the year 1899 was accompanied by complete integration of the engineering and operating departments of the two former railways; and one outcome was the production of a range of very fine and exceedingly handsome locomotives, under the superintendence of H. S. Wainwright. The 4-4-0 of Class 'E' which is illustrated herewith was first introduced in 1905 and shared with the earlier engines of Class D all the heaviest work on both the former South Eastern and London Chatham and Dover routes until 1914. The Continental boat expresses, especially the mails, were heavy trains for that period, frequently loading up to 350 tons or more, and the 'E' class engines in particular did some excellent work with them. In a period when locomotives were still *objets d'art,* and cleaning was a ritual rather than a chore, the engines of the S.E.&C.R. were unusually ornate. One of the 'D' class has been preserved and is on show to the public in the Museum of Transport at Clapham. There one can study the beautiful painting and decorative work put into an ordinary workaday passenger locomotive of the early nineteen-hundreds.

109 **A Great Western 'Saint'.**
The standard G.W.R. express passenger two-cylinder 4-6-0 was the outcome of a classic locomotive development at Swindon. Churchward had set himself a performance target of a locomotive that would exert a drawbar pull of 2 tons at 70 m.p.h., and moreover a pull that could be sustained for an hour or more, if need be. The development took two definite lines: the designing of a boiler that would steam very freely, and would be trouble-free in service, albeit more expensive than a conventional one in first cost; a cylinder and valve gear that would use the steam to the best advantage. Most of the way towards these ideals had been attained when the second G.W.R. express 4-6-0 No. 98, was built at Swindon in 1903; but the final touch on a design-masterpiece was achieved with the third engine, No. 171, in which boiler pressure was increased to 225 lb. per sq. in. This engine gave a superior all-round performance to the French compound *La France*. The 'Saint' class came to include the original proto-type 4-6-0s; further engines of the same general type originally built as 'Atlantics'; the series named after 'Ladies', and the final 25 named after 'Courts'. The latter were built new with the Swindon super-heater, and all the earlier engines were similarly equipped in due course. Our picture shows engine No. 2914 *Saint Augustine*, as originally built, non-super-heated.

110 **A Midland Deeley Compound.**
The development and ultimate success of the 'Midland Compound' is one of the romances of British locomotive history. Leaving out of account its progenitor on the North Eastern Railway, W. M. Smith's patent locomotive of 1898, it went through four distinct phases: the original Smith-Johnson compound of 1902; the Deeley development of 1905; and the superheated rebuilds from 1913 onwards. These early varieties, which numbered 45 in all, had 7 ft. coupled wheels. Then, after grouping there came the L.M.S. development with 6 ft. 9 in. coupled wheels of which 195 were built. The variety chosen for illustration is the superheated compound, dating from 1913, when No. 1040, one of the original

Deeley engines was rebuilt by Sir Henry Fowler. The standard L.M.S. type will be noticed later on. The superheated compounds represent the highest development of express passenger locomotive practice on the Midland Railway. Between the time of the first rebuilding in 1913, and the summer of 1923 it was subject to various trials and modifications, but after the valve gear tests of March 1923 it was finalized as a magnificent motive power unit, particularly suitable to very hard work over the mountain gradients of the Derbyshire Peak District, and of the picturesque main line to Scotland between Settle and Carlisle.

111   A 'Jersey Lily' of the G.C.R.

In attempting to build up traffic on the London Extension line, in the face of severe competition from railways to east and to west, the Great Central used publicity in all its forms; one of these was to build 'prestige' locomotives. Certainly the actual demands of the traffic in the years 1903-4 did not demand anything so large or powerful as Robinson's beautiful 'Atlantics', though their excellent design and massive construction was to stand the L.N.E.R. in good stead 20 years later. The 'Atlantics' were nicknamed the 'Jersey Lilies'; but this allusion to the famous actress of the day, Lily Langtry, was not, as is sometimes thought, a tribute to the handsome appearance of the G.C.R. engines. The first of the class was a huge engine compared to everything that had gone before, and it so happened that at the time of its introduction one of the local public houses near Gorton Works included as one of its attractions an enormously fat woman, weighing, it is said, some 20 stones, and nicknamed, sarcastically, the 'Jersey Lily'. When the first Robinson 'Atlantic' took the road its vast size led to its being nicknamed immediately the 'Jersey Lily', and the engines were known thus throughout their existence. They were very fast and powerful engines, and ran the evening express from Marylebone to Bradford with great distinction until the year 1936.

112   The 'Great Bear'; Great Western Railway.

The great majority of the locomotives illustrated in this book have been representatives of large classes, or prototypes, the performance of which has had a marked influence on the future practice of the railway concerned. *The Great Bear*, designed by Churchward, and built at Swindon in 1908, was an outstanding case of a 'might-have-been'. It was built at a time when the G.W.R. was in the midst of a remarkable development programme in which great emphasis was laid on the production of large boilers that could be steamed efficiently, and which had low maintenance costs. *The Great Bear*, which remained the only British tender engine of the 'Pacific' type for a period of 14 years, had a steaming capacity far in advance of anything needed for the traffic of the day. It was more than a prestige symbol; it was a prototype built against the time when much larger locomotives might be required. That time never came during the period when Churchward was Chief Mechanical Engineer, and so 'The Bear', as it was affectionately known on the G.W.R., remained an isolated engine, and a difficult one to use to the best advantage. Because of its length and weight it was restricted to the main line between London and Bristol. In 1924 the boiler needed renewing; but because of the limited route availability of the engine it was decided to rebuild it as a 'Castle' class 4-6-0. The old number, 111, was retained, but it was renamed *Viscount Churchill* after the Chairman of the G.W.R.

113   A Brighton 'Atlantic'; L.B.& S.C.R.

Following the famous régime of William

Stroudley at Brighton the old traditions were carried on by his successor R. J. Billinton. But when the latter engineer was succeeded by D. Earle-Marsh, who had previously been on the Great Northern Railway, at Doncaster, there was a considerable change, and an early departure from previous practice was the introduction of some large Atlantic engines very similar in general appearance to H. A. Ivatt's large boilered Atlantics on the G.N.R. (reference 107). Five of these engines were put to work on the Brighton line at first, and did well in the haulage of seaside trains and residential expresses of ever increasing weight. They were followed by a superheated version of 1911. In the handsome dark brown livery they looked especially fine at the head of the 'Southern Belle', the all-Pullman 60-minute express between London and Brighton. After grouping of the railways in 1923 they were painted in the standard Southern livery of dark green, and at a later period they were all named, after headlands on the south coast of England. Some of these, such as *St Catherine's Point, The Needles, Hartland Point, Trevose Head* were excellent names; but on the other hand the name of engine No. 38, *Portland Bill*, had its unintentionally humorous side!

114 **North Staffordshire Railway;** John H. Adams's superheated tank engine. The North Staffordshire Railway was primarily a local line serving the district indicated by its name. Much of its traffic originated in the Potteries, and the local services were excellently run. At the same time the Company had a very enterprising management, and a number of working arrangements with neighbouring companies led to extensive locomotive journeys well beyond the confines of the North Staffordshire. On holiday expresses N.S.R. locomotives worked as far afield as Llandudno. But one of the most interesting duties arose from the routing

of certain expresses between Manchester and London via the North Stafford line, so as to serve Macclesfield and Stoke-on-Trent, and on these important duties North Staffordshire locomotives hauled the trains between Manchester and Stoke. These were heavy restaurant car expresses, and it was a point of honour with the N.S.R. drivers to hand the trains over to the London and North Western, at Stoke, on time. Adams designed the handsome 4-4-2 tank engines shown in our picture specially for these trains. The line is a hilly one, and in consequence the coupled wheels, were made rather smaller than usual for ordinary express working, namely 6 ft. instead of the more popular 6 ft. 6 in. to 6 ft. 9 in.

115 **The 'Abergavenny';** Earle-Marsh's tank 4-6-2 engine. A natural sequel to the success of the 'I3' class of 4-4-2 tank engine (reference 96), was the development of the design into something considerably larger to cope with the increasing loads of the fast trains between London and the South Coast towns. From the four-coupled 'I3' Marsh adopted the 4-6-2 wheel arrangement, in company with a much longer and larger boiler, and larger cylinders. The latter needed to be of a size such that they could not be accommodated within the frames, but in the tradition of the period the outside cylinders, crossheads and connecting rods were arranged very neatly, and a very handsome engine resulted. Only two of these engines were built, for trial purposes, one in 1910 and the other in 1912, and they differed from each other in respect of the valve gear. Engine No. 325 *Abergavenny*, as illustrated, had the Stephenson's link motion between the frames whereas No. 326 *Bessborough* had the Walschaerts radial valve gear, outside. Both engines did excellent work, and but for Marsh's retirement they would probably have become the standard express locomotives

for the line. But Marsh's successor, L. B. Billinton, introduced still larger tank engines in later years. Although *Abergavenny* and *Bessborough* remained thus an isolated pair of engines they had a long life and did much valuable work. They were still on the steam-hauled Tunbridge Wells trains in 1947–8, and were not scrapped until 1951.

116   **The 'Immingham' Class 4-6-0;** Great Central Railway.

J. G. Robinson, in the years between 1900 and 1912, provided the Great Central Railway with a series of locomotives for every kind of duty, and whether they were for the most spectacular main line express trains or for heavy mineral service, each was an artistic masterpiece, as well as a supremely good engineering job. In this period the Great Central Railway was developing trade with Scandinavia and with the Baltic, via Grimsby, and a great new port was under construction at Immingham Dock. In readiness for handling express goods traffic Robinson built a smaller wheeled variant of his 6 ft. 9 in. express passenger engines, some of which latter were of the 'Atlantic' type and some 4-6-0. The 'Immingham' class, as they were known, had 6 ft. 6 in. coupled wheels. Like Robinson's Atlantic (*Jersey Lilies*), these 4-6-os were exceptionally strong and reliable engines. Their normal livery in Great Central days was black with a handsome amount of lining out in white and red, with the company's coat of arms on both engine and tender. In L.N.E.R. days the 'Imminghams' was painted apple green, and did much excellent work on the Kings Cross–Leeds expresses over the heavy gradients of the West Riding north of Doncaster, where the large Pacifics were not then allowed to run.

117   **London Tilbury and Southern Railway;** Thomas Whitelegg's express tank engine.

By the turn of the century residential traffic was rising to enormous proportions on the L.T.&S.R. line. The business trains were made up to the maximum length that could be accommodated in the platforms at Fenchurch Street station, and the most precise timekeeping prevailed. A late arrival of a Southend express had 'news value'. To keep abreast of traffic requirements Thomas Whitelegg reconstructed a batch of ten 4-4-2 tank engines originally put in service in 1897–8, giving them much larger boilers, new cylinders, and the very handsome appearance shown in our picture. These rebuilt engines did splendid work on the heavy business trains, and they were reinforced by four new engines to the same dimensions added to the stock in 1909. *Thundersley* was one of the 1909 batch, and was distinguished by having a polished casing to the safety valves. On all the other engines of the class this mounting was painted over green. The Midland Railway absorbed the Tilbury line in 1912, and after the former company had become part of the L.M.S. system in 1923 twenty-five more were built in 1923–7, and a final ten as comparatively recently as 1930. This in itself is a great tribute to the efficiency of Thomas Whitelegg's design of 1907.

118   **The Class 'X' Hump shunters.**
The North Eastern Railway was fortunate in having a very heavy coal traffic, and much of the output from the Durham and Northumberland coalfields was shipped from ports large and small along the North-east coast. At the points of heaviest concentration hump marshalling yards were laid in, and there shunting engines of exceptional power were needed. Wilson Worsdell, in his handsome Class 'X' shunters, followed the precedent set two years earlier on the Great Central Railway by using three-cylinder propulsion. This provided a very even starting effort, and enabled the locomotive

to propel a heavy train from rest without slipping, and jerking. Ten of these engines were built in 1909–10, and a further five were built by the L.N.E.R. in 1925 – a sure proof of their great success. The earlier ones put in more than 45 years' work. Each engine used to be in continuous service for 24 hours at a stretch, and their bunker capacity of 3 tons was enough to provide all the fuel for this long term of duty. They had one very interesting constructional feature that was later adopted by Sir Nigel Gresley in some of his modern L.N.E.R. three-cylinder locomotives, in that the three cylinders and their associated valve chests were made in a single casting. This in itself was a fine tribute to the foundry techniques in use at Gateshead works.

119 **The 'Coronation' Engine of 1911;** London and North Western Railway.
These engines, designed and built at Crewe under the direction of C. J. Bowen-Cooke, are sometimes dismissed as nothing more than a superheated version of the Whale 'Precursor'. It is true that the chassis, wheels, boiler barrel, and firebox were the same; but the application of the Schmidt superheater was accompanied by a re-design of the cylinders, and by the use of piston valves instead of slide valves, and the improvement in haulage capacity and thermal efficiency was very striking. In relation to their size and weight the 90 engines of this class did some phenomenal work. It was nothing unusual for them to take trains of 390 tons behind the tender up the 1 in 75 of Shap Incline without assistance, and at the southern end of the line they would make start-to-stop average speeds of 55 to 58 m.p.h. between Euston and Crewe with loads up to 450 tons. By the standards of 1910–1916 – their hey-day – they were economical in fuel and repairs, though in recognition of the very hard work they were called upon

to do the day-to-day maintenance was very good. Because of the success of the 'George the Fifth' class many of the non-superheated 'Precursors' were rebuilt, with piston valves, superheaters and extended smokeboxes, making them identical to the 'George the Fifths' in everything except the quite superficial difference of the separate splasher for the leading pair of coupled wheels, instead of the continuous splasher.

120 **A Great Central 'Director'.**
The introduction of superheating led many locomotive engineers towards consideration of smaller engines to do the work previously entrusted to 'Atlantics' and 4-6-os, and the Great Central 'Director' class, of 1913, was an expression of this trend. These engines were designed to work through between London and Manchester, whereas the 'Atlantics' had usually to be changed at intermediate points. The first ten, built in 1913, were all named after directors of the company, though in the course of their long life two were re-named. Another 11 of a slightly enlarged design were built by the Great Central Railway in 1920, and it is one of these, No. 506 *Butler-Henderson* that has been preserved, and is housed in the Museum of Transport at Clapham. After grouping, another 24 of these fine engines were built specially for service in Scotland. Because of the reduced height of the loading gauge on the former North British Railway the Scottish engines had very much reduced chimneys and boiler mountings, and did not look so handsome in consequence. They all had names taken from characters in the Waverley novels, such as *Flora MacIvor*, *Haystoun of Bucklaw*, *Wizard of the Moor*, and *The Fiery Cross*. The original 'Directors' continued to do excellent work on the old Great Central line down to the year 1936, while the Scottish variants worked between Edinburgh, Dundee, Perth and Glasgow.

121 **Midland Railway;** Fowler's Class 2 superheated 4-4-0.

The traffic policy of the Midland Railway from the year 1907 onwards was to run a frequent service of fast, lightly loaded trains on all main routes, and because this did not demand the building of large new locomotives a programme was initiated for modernizing many of the older 4-4-os of Johnson's of the type illustrated on Plate 60. In Deeley's time a number of these engines were rebuilt with larger boilers of similar design to those provided for the Somerset and Dorset 4-4-os built at Derby in 1903, and illustrated on Plate 85. But from 1913 onwards a further stage in modernization was commenced, with the production, on the old chassis, and using the same wheels and motion, of a superheated rebuild, with a still larger boiler. Within their power class these proved excellent engines. Naturally they were limited in the loads they could take, but with this reservation they were fast, efficient, and very light on repairs. They worked all over the Midland system, including the heavy road from Leeds to Carlisle, and after the grouping of the railways the design formed the basis of a new L.M.S.R. standard, for light passenger working, having 6 ft. 9 in. coupled wheels against the 7 ft. of the Midland No. 2 Class engines. The Midland 7 ft. design was adopted for express passenger working on the Somerset and Dorset Joint Railway, and some engines of the design were painted in the handsome blue livery of that railway, and bore the initials S.D.J.R. on their tenders.

122 **Dugald Drummond's 'D15';** L.&S.W.R.

Following the conspicuous success of his 'T9' 'small' 4-4-os Dugald Drummond built several classes of 4-4-o for the L.&S.W.R. with larger boilers, and the class chosen for illustration is the 'D15', of which 10 were built in 1912. These very handsome engines included all the features of the 'T9' class, and as originally built they had the firebox water tubes. Like the 'T9s' they were very fast runners, but the enlarged boiler and proportions did not seem to give them as much extra capacity as was expected, and they did not really come into their own until Drummond's successor, R. W. Urie, fitted them with Eastleigh superheaters, accompanied by an extended smokebox. Their very graceful appearance at the front end was somewhat impaired, but their performance was vastly improved. The 'D15' class was the last of a group of three large-boilered 4-4-os of Drummond design, of which the others were the smaller-wheeled 'S11' class, designed for working on the hilly routes west of Exeter, and the 'L12', built in 1904-5. These latter were really a modified version of the 'T9', having the same chassis and machinery but with a larger boiler. In appearance they were very similar to the 'D15' class. Both the 'L12' and the 'D15' classes were long-lived; all the engines of both classes worked throughout the second World War, and passed into the ownership of the nationalized British Railways in 1948.

123 **Great Eastern Railway;** The '1500' class 4-6-0.

For twelve strenuous years the 'Claud Hamilton' class 4-4-os did excellent and most reliable work on the heaviest Great Eastern passenger services. So far as they were concerned the adjective 'heavy' was no mere comparative term. In the summer holiday season the express trains from London to Yarmouth and Cromer were among the heaviest in Great Britain. Then, in 1912, Stratford Works brought out the splendid superheater 4-6-0. This could be described as an enlarged 'Claud Hamilton', and the new engines very quickly proved themselves very strong and free-running. They were put on to the Norfolk Coast Express, and the

Continentals, and did very fine work from the outset. But some of their finest performance took place after the end of World War I when pre-war speed was restored, with still heavier loads. The work of the link of drivers at Parkeston Quay on the Hook of Holland boat express will live in locomotive history. In later years many of them were transferred to the former Great North of Scotland line, for service between Aberdeen and Elgin, and on the fish trains from the Buchan ports. Although the earliest engines of the class carried the beautiful G.E.R. blue livery shown in our picture, this was not restored after the war. Instead they ran in a plain unlined slate grey, until the grouping, after which they looked bright and cheerful again in the L.N.E.R. apple green.

124   A North Eastern 'Z'.

From the beginning of the twentieth century a variety of large ten-wheeled engines for express passenger traffic were built by the North Eastern Railway. There were 4-6-0s, two-cylinder 'Atlantics', and two experimental four-cylinder compound 'Atlantics'; and in 1908 there was even a reversion to the 4-4-0 type, in the very large and powerful 'R1' class. What proved, however, to be the company's standard large express passenger engine appeared in 1911, in the form of the handsome three-cylinder simple 4-4-2 of the 'Z' class. These engines combined the high steaming capacity of a boiler with an outside diameter of 5 ft. 6 in., with the smoothness of action of a multi-cylindered layout. The result was that they ran well, pulled very heavy loads, and were much appreciated by the men for their comfort and smoothness in travelling. On the fine racing stretch of the East Coast main line between Darlington and York they took the Anglo-Scottish expresses of 350 to 400 tons at sustained speeds of well over 70 m.p.h., and there are recorded instances of loads,

taken punctually and without assistance, of up to 550 tons on the standard schedules of the day. They were still engaged on first-class express work up to the summer of 1934. A total of fifty was built, and historically they rank as one of the finest sets of engines designed and built for service in the North-East of England.

125   A 'Prince of Wales' 4-6-0; London and North Western.

These engines, like the 4-4-0 'George the Fifth' class, were a superheated development of a Whale design, and they proved the most generally useful passenger class the L.&N.W.R. ever possessed. At the time of grouping of the railways at the end of 1922 the company had no fewer than 245 of them in service. In their early days they were classified for traffic purposes as the same as the 'George the Fifths', and indeed there was little to choose between the maximum efforts of the two classes. The 'Prince of Wales' was quite a small 4-6-0, though it was potentially the more powerful of the two classes in having a somewhat larger boiler and firebox. The 'Prince of Wales' became generally favoured on the heavy gradients of the line between Lancaster and Carlisle, and by the time of grouping it was rare to see a 'George the Fifth' north of Preston. Engines of the 'Prince of Wales' class were engaged in competitive trials against Midland, Caledonian, and Lancashire and Yorkshire engines after the grouping. Although they did well so far as weight haulage was concerned the coal consumption was greater than that of the Midland compounds. The first 90 of the engines were named, in the old tradition of the L.& N.W.R. But in the difficult days after the end of World War I, when brass was in short supply, naming was discontinued in the 155 engines built after the war. These engines were turned out in plain black, without any lining, and the only adornment was the company's crest on the splashers.

126 A Drummond 4-Cylinder 4-6-0; L.&S.W.R.

As a locomotive designer Dugald Drummond was outstandingly successful with his smaller engines, but his essays into machines of greater power were beset by difficulties. The engine illustrated, however, was one of a class that did some good and very fast running on the West of England and Bournemouth routes. By reason of their very large splashers with the circular inspection cover they were nicknamed the 'Paddleboats' – the splashers being referred to as the 'paddleboxes'. Their performance on the crack trains were variable, but this was in some measure due to the rather awkward technique required in firing, rather than to any inherent fault in the basic design. The firebox was large, and very shallow, and great care was needed in spreading the coal evenly beneath the brick arch. Like all Drummond engines they were handsomely proportioned, though at a time when the majority of engineers were adopting superheaters Drummond was content with his own 'steam dryer', which raised the temperature of the steam to no more than 400 deg. Fah., where other engineers were using temperatures of 550 to 600 deg. Fah. The 'Paddleboats' were twice modernized: first by Urie, who fitted them with Eastleigh superheaters, and secondly in Southern Railway days by R. E. L. Maunsell, who followed his own dictum of making everything get-at-able by removing the 'paddlebox' splashers, and fitting forced lubrication for the coupled wheel axleboxes.

127 A North Western 'Claughton'.

Herculean though the work of the superheated express locomotives of the 'George the Fifth' and 'Prince of Wales' classes was in the years 1910–13, C. J. Bowen-Cooke had no sooner succeeded George Whale as Chief Mechanical Engineer than he was planning a far larger express locomotive than either of the two previously mentioned classes. It was a time when most locomotive engineers were restricted by the dead weight they could carry on any one axle, but Bowen-Cooke hoped to secure some relaxation in this respect by designing an engine in which the reciprocating parts were perfectly balanced. Following the practice that had developed in South Germany, where he had been very impressed by some 4-cylinder compound 4-6-0s on the Bavarian Railways, Bowen-Cooke arranged for all four cylinders in his new design to drive on to the leading axle. He secured a very smooth and fast running engine; but relaxation of weight restrictions was not forthcoming, and the 'Sir Gilbert Claughton' class had smaller boilers than was originally intended. Nevertheless they did some fine work, and it is a tribute to their success that no fewer than 130 were built. They needed a careful technique in firing, and with inexpert treatment in this respect they steamed poorly. But with proper handling their feats of weight haulage at high speed were unsurpassed in Great Britain up to the end of World War I, and they took loads up to 440 tons unassisted on the Shap incline.

128 L. Billinton's Giant 4-6-4.

The ultimate development of express passenger locomotive power on the Brighton railway is represented by L. Billinton's 4-6-4 tank design, of which the first examples were built in 1914. These engines were intended to provide an ample, almost overwhelming amount of power for the South Coast trains, so that a high average speed could be maintained without excessive maximum speed downhill. Only two of these huge engines were built at first. The incidence of war, in 1914, halted the traffic developments that made them desirable. Of the original engines No. 327 was named *Charles C. Macrae*, but the second remained nameless. After the war further engines of the class were built and the last of the series, No. 333, was notable in being finished specially in grey, and given the name *Remembrance*, in honour of the men of the L.B.&S.C.R. who fell in World War I. After grouping the remaining engines of the class, Nos. 327 to 332 were renamed after locomotive engineers famous in the early history of the constituent companies of the Southern Railway. At a still later period, when all the main lines of the former Brighton railway had been electrified, these one-time 4-6-4 tanks were converted to 4-6-0 tender engines, and continued to do good work on the former London and South Western section of the Southern Railway.

129 A Great Northern 'Mogul'.

The first Great Northern 'Mogul' engines, of 1912, caused a considerable stir in the locomotive world, but while they did good work on fast goods trains Gresley found they had insufficient boiler capacity for the heavy mixed traffic duties envisaged, and in 1914 he built a new series, similar so far as the cylinders and machinery were concerned, but with a much larger boiler. These proved to be splendid engines, and no fewer than 65 were built. In addition to fast goods services they also worked on passenger trains. Though having driving wheels no larger than 5 ft. 8 in. diameter they were fast runners, and frequently exceeded 70 m.p.h. Our picture shows one of them in the G.N.R. passenger livery, in which they originally appeared. They were painted in the goods grey after World War I and still later in L.N.E.R. black. In the nineteen-thirties a number of them were transferred to Scotland. These were fitted with enlarged cabs, giving a better protection against the weather, and thirteen of them working on the magnificently-scenic West Highland line were named after lochs lying within sight, or relatively near to the railway. These Scottish 2-6-0s put in many years of very hard work on this steeply graded and sharply curved route. Although in many ways so different from the indigenous Scottish locomotives they became great favourites with the enginemen from their solid reliability.

130 A 'River' Class 4-6-0.

When Peter Drummond secured the post of Locomotive Superintendent of the Glasgow and South Western Railway in 1913, he was succeeded by F. G. Smith, who had been Works Manager at Inverness since 1905. Smith was a first-rate locomotive engineer, and immediately began to make plans for a new passenger engine design that would once more put the Highland Railway ahead of all the other Scottish companies for both power and efficiency. But by some extraordinary mischance certain civil engineering restrictions had been overlooked; they were, in fact, not fully appreciated until the first of the engines had actually arrived at Perth, from the builders' works in Newcastle. It was only then found inadvisable to run the engines on the Highland Railway, and they were sold to the Caledonian. Our picture shows one of these engines in the livery of the latter company, for which they did good work for 12 years. After grouping, when the civil engineering restrictions had been removed, the six engines were put on to the Highland section, and they took up the work they were originally intended to do. It is a sad story, because in 1928 the locomotives that would have been a tremendous asset to the Highland Railway in 1915 were becoming obsolescent. Nevertheless they were able to show their mettle, albeit belatedly, and were at once accorded their original class name, the 'Rivers', by the men. On the Caledonian they were always known as the 'Highlandmen'.

131 Churchward's Masterpiece; the Great Western 4-cylinder 'Star' class.

The 'Star' class was the outcome of a most important series of experiments and researches at Swindon Works, during which the latest features of American and French locomotive practice were studied. (See also the *La France* reference 97.) The 'Star' embodied the divided drive, as in the French compound, but with all four cylinders taking high pressure steam. It had the same outstanding boiler as the 'Saint', using 225 lb. per sq. in. in pressure, and an interesting detail of French practice in the de Glehn big-end for the inside cylinder connecting rods. The 'Stars', of which 72 were built between 1907 and 1922, did magnificent work in traffic. One of their finest feats was that of the *King Richard*, No. 4026, in 1925, hauling an up West of England express weighing no less than 550 tons from Taunton to Paddington, 143 miles in 152 min. Successive batches of the 'Stars' were named after 'Knights', 'Kings', 'Queens', 'Princes', 'Princesses' and 'Abbeys'. No. 4003 *Lode Star* is preserved in the Great Western Railway Museum at Swindon. The 'Star' formed the basis of design of the still larger 'Castles' and 'Kings' of the G.W.R.

132 A Pickersgill 4-4-0; Caledonian Railway.

These handsome engines, of which 48 were built between the years 1916 and 1922, were a development of the famous 'Dunalastair' family of engine classes introduced by J. F. McIntosh. In the new engines, although the likenesses to their predecessors was strong, there were numerous relatively small evidences that a different personality was in charge at St Rollox Works. Moreover, Pickersgill was not a Caledonian man, but one who had previously held the post of Locomo-tive Superintendent on the Great North of Scotland Railway. There he had been responsible for some excellent, though small 4-4-0s. Nevertheless, the 'Pickersgill bogies' on the Caledonian included much detail design that had been traditional at St Rollox from the days of Dugald Drummond, and some items could be traced back to Drummond's association with Stroudley at Brighton, more than forty years before the appearance of the Pickersgill 4-4-0s. They did some hard work on all parts of the Caledonian main line, and with the stud eventually numbering 48 locomotives they were the largest passenger class numerically on the line. Many of them were still hard at work in Scotland forty years after their first introduction, and some of them were still on the active list as recently as the autumn of 1961.

133 Glasgow and South Western Railway; Peter Drummond's express goods.

The Drummond brothers between them made a very notable contribution to British locomotive practice, serving four Scottish and one English railway. On the Highland Railway the younger brother, Peter, followed closely along the lines of Dugald Drummond's work; but his transfer to the Glasgow and South Western Railway came almost at the same time as Dugald's death, and the period from 1912 to 1918 at Kilmarnock thus represents the final phase of the Drummond school of design. Many details were at once changed from the practice of James Manson, including that always-controversial point, the position of the driver on the footplate. The G.&S.W.R. had always driven from the right-hand side; the Drummonds insisted on left-hand drive. But details apart, Peter Drummond provided the Glasgow and South Western Railway with some excellent main line engines: 0-6-0 goods, 4-4-0 passenger, and then a superheated development of the o-6-o. Because of the increased weight at the front end a pony-truck was inserted, thus making the superheated goods a 2-6-o. These engines had all the traditional neatness of a Drummond design, but with the massiveness of a machine suited to twentieth-century needs, and moreover that of a heavy wartime traffic. These 2-6-os did excellent and economical work and many of them were still in service in the early nineteen-thirties.

134 A North British 'Glen'; West Highland line.

The locomotive department of the North British Railway, like that of the rival Caledonian had been given a tremendous fillip by the fine 4-4-os designed for them by Dugald Drummond, and at Cowlairs, as at St Rollox, the Drummond design formed a basis for the developments of many years thereafter. W. P. Reid built some powerful express passenger 4-4-os with names taken from characters in the 'Waverley' novels, and he followed those with a so-called 'intermediate' class, unnamed, with 6 ft. diameter coupled wheels. It was when these were followed by a superheated version of the same series that Reid produced one of the most outstandingly successful 4-4-os ever to run in Scotland. They were intended particularly for the West Highland line, with its incessant curvature and 1 in 60 gradients extending from Helensburgh on the Firth of Clyde, to Fort William and Mallaig, and the engines were all named after glens, lying on or near the route. They proved ideal engines for this strenuous duty. They could be pounded up the long gradients without the slightest ill-effects; they steamed freely, and suffered no trouble from the heating of bearings that might have been expected on so severe a route. To travel in a long train of 11 or 12 coaches hauled by a pair of them was an experience never to be forgotten.

135 Somerset and Dorset Joint Railway; one of the special freight engines.

In meeting the responsibility for providing and maintaining locomotive power for this very difficult route the Midland Railway had to cope with grading conditions far worse than anything on their own line. Under reference 85, mention was made of a new type of 4-4-o which with suitable adaptation subsequently became a Midland Railway standard; and again, in 1914, the Derby drawing office designed, for the S.D.J.R., a freight engine larger and more powerful than anything used on the Midland Railway proper. These very successful 2-8-os, which came to put in nearly 50 years' service on the Somerset and Dorset line, were to some extent a synthesis of standard parts. They used the boiler of the standard superheated compound 4-4-o, though of course the use of outside cylinders and Walschaerts valve gear was new to Midland practice. To provide tractive power for hauling the freight trains on the 1 in 50 banks the cylinders were very large, 21 in. diameter by 28 in. stroke. and these could not easily have been accommodated inside. In their last years these engines, surprisingly enough, have done a considerable amount of passenger working, on summer Saturdays. Their high tractive power has enabled them to take heavier trains without assistance than the modern 4-6-os, and this was invaluable at a time when there was a serious shortage of locomotives.

136 Caledonian Railway; a Pickersgill 4-6-o of 1916.

From the time of Dugald Drummond, who came to St Rollox in 1882, the Caledonian had been a line of inside-cylinder locomotives. Considerable interest was aroused in 1916 when the new locomotive engineer, W. Pickersgill, from the Great North of Scotland Railway, put on the road a series of six new 4-6-os with outside cylinders. Dimensionally they could be regarded as a half-way house between two varieties of large-boilered McIntosh 4-6-0: the 5 ft. 9 in. express goods class and the famous express passenger 'Cardeans' (reference 103). But Pickersgill introduced many changes in detail, as well as the change to outside cylinders, and these handsome and powerful engines never established any particular reputation for *speed*. They steamed well, and climbed the banks in excellent style. Furthermore they were so strongly and soundly constructed that they were very light on repair costs. This feature attracted the attention of the L.M.S.R. management, and a further batch of these Caledonian engines was built in 1925 after the grouping of the railways. One of these latter was put through a series of tests between Carlisle and Preston in 1926, and gave quite satisfactory results. The post-grouping engines of this class were painted Midland red when new; but at a later date, as mixed traffic engines they were painted plain black.

137 **A 'Super D' 0-8-0 Goods;** London and North Western Railway.
Whatever success may have attended the running of the Webb compound 0-8-0 coal engines, when new locomotives were required, after Webb's retirement, his successors turned to a simple two-cylinder 0-8-0 with a large boiler, and a very straightforward cylinder and valve layout. There came to be many varieties of this excellent and long-lived class, all having their own distinguishing class letters; but the general term by which the engines were known among the men was derived from Whale's first rebuild, with large boiler, of the Webb three-cylinder compound coal engines. These were non-super-heated, and were known as Class 'D'. When the superheater version of this class appeared in 1912 it was no more

than natural to call it a 'Super D', though the actual class name was 'G1'. At the time the L.&N.W.R. was merged into the L.M.S.R. system there were 295 of these engines, including some with higher boiler pressure classed officially as 'G2'. As a willing, reliable work-horse of a locomotive the 'Super Ds' have scarcely been surpassed. They were in their element hauling trains of 800 to 900 tons on the main line between Preston – Crewe and London; but in emergency they were sometimes put on to passenger trains and a record exists of one of them running up to 58 m.p.h. with a fast express between Watford and Euston.

138 **North Staffordshire Railway;** Hookham's passenger tank engine.
The increasing weight of the Manchester–London expresses running via Stoke constituted something of a problem for the North Staffordshire locomotive department. Notwithstanding the fine work done by the Adams 4-4-2 tanks, a four-coupled engine was not ideal for such a steeply graded route, and in consequence J. A. Hookham designed a six-coupled engine with ample boiler capacity. It is interesting that he should have chosen the 0-6-4 type, because on some other railways engines of this wheel-arrangement had not been notably successful, or smooth in riding at express speed. The North Staffordshire engines on the Manchester–London expresses had not only to climb well, particularly on the heavy ascent that comes immediately after the restart at Macclesfield, but they had to run freely at speeds of over 60 m.p.h. The allowance for the 19.9 miles from Macclesfield to Stoke was only 27 min. The big 0-6-4 tanks did their work well, and amply upheld the reputation of the North Staffordshire Railway. It is notable that the locomotive department at Stoke produced two engineers that came to render most distinguished service to the L.M.S.R. First there was T. Coleman,

who became Chief Draughtsman to Sir William Stanier, and who worked out the design of the 'Coronation' Pacific of 1937, and then there was H. G. Ivatt, the last Chief Mechanical Engineer of the L.M.S.R. Both were at one time North Staffordshire men.

139 A North Eastern 'T2'.

As a line with so heavy a coal traffic the North Eastern had an excellent record of heavy mineral engine performance. From Fletcher's o-6-os, and the Worsdell von Borries compounds of Class 'C', the younger Worsdell introduced eight-coupled coal engines in 1901. It is remarkable to recall that when first built these splendid, hard-slogging 'colliers' were decked in the full passenger engine livery of pale green, smartly lined out, and with polished brass safety valve casings. They did a great deal of tremendously hard work, and in due course they were followed, in 1913, by a superheated version, with still larger boilers. By that time the finish of freight engines was much plainer, and the 'T2' class, as they were designated, was in plain black, without any lining. They were considerably less handsome in outline. But if ever a locomotive class has earned its keep, in hard, unobtrusive, continuous duty, it is the North Eastern 'T2'. Altogether 120 of them were put into service between 1913 and 1921. There was no finesse about the working of these engines; they were down-to-earth freighters, that clanged and banged their way along. But they were utterly reliable, and after doing yeoman service in the 1939–45 emergency they were often referred to as 'the engines that won the war'.

140 A Highland Railway 'Clan'.

The Highland Railway should have added to its stock six exceptionally large and well-designed 4-6-0 locomotives in 1915. The mischance that led to their not being put into service has been told

(reference 130) and as a wartime expediency recourse was had to more 'Castles'. But the new locomotive superintendent, Christopher Cumming, designed some excellent new 4-6-os, the first four of which were put into service in 1919. While including modern features new to the Highland Railway, such as Walschaerts valve gear, superheaters, and Belpaire fireboxes they were nevertheless built in the well-established traditions of Inverness, which required an engine that would steam constantly while being pounded, for half an hour or more, up the heavy gradients of the Perth-Inverness line. The new engines, named after some of the greatest of the Highland clans, fulfilled this need admirably, and put in many years of hard work. After grouping when larger engines of English design were put on to the Highland section of the L.M.S.R. the eight engines of the 'Clan' class were transferred to the former Caledonian line to Oban. This was a route in many ways more severe than the Highland itself, and one which was in need of powerful and reliable engines. The 'Clans', still carrying their honoured names, became great favourites with the Oban men, and proved so useful that the last of them, the *Clan Mackinnon*, not was withdrawn from service till 1949.

141 The Gresley 'K3' 2-6-0.

This was originally a Great Northern design, introduced by Gresley in 1920. It was the first class on which the standard form of the Gresley conjugated valve gear was used, in which only two sets of the gear are required to actuate the valves of all three cylinders. The original batch, G.N.R. Nos. 1000–1009, were painted in the standard 'passenger green' livery, with the handsome lining out, and light red underframes. They also had the old style of G.N.R. cab, as on the 'K2' Moguls. But when the design was adopted as an L.N.E.R. standard, and many more locomotives were built, up to a total for the class of nearly 200, they were finished in the black lined livery. The tenders varied in detail. The one illustrated is that fitted to the original G.N.R. engines. They were general utility machines in every way, hauling heavy goods, express passenger of a class below that of the top link Pacifics, and proving very speedy and economical. Although the coupled wheels were no more than 5 ft. 8 in. diameter they frequently attained speeds of 75 m.p.h. Perhaps their finest work was done on the through fully-fitted express goods train services of the L.N.E.R. The afternoon 'Scotch Goods' from Kings Cross was booked to average 45 m.p.h. non-stop over the 112 miles from Peterborough to York, and on this duty the 'K3s' were scheduled to take a load of 55 wagons.

142 **South Eastern and Chatham Railway;** Maunsell's 'N' class.
The retirement of Wainwright in 1913 led to a complete reorganization of the locomotive department of the S.E.&C.R. and although war conditions imposed serious restrictions upon all development work Maunsell and his staff did manage to produce, during the war, two new locomotives that proved the prototypes of much new construction afterwards. One of these was the 'N' class 2-6-0, a powerful general-utility design, which showed the influence of Great Western practice in the tapered boiler barrel, and the use of a long-lap, long-travel layout in the valve gear. In exterior design the pioneer 'N' class engine No. 810, had the plain, essentially functional look that characterized Maunsell's work in S.E.& C.R. days. Engine No. 810 was a great success in fast goods and intermediate passenger working, and multiplication of the design began soon after the end of the war. The 'N' class became a Southern Railway standard, and formed the basis of a development of a family of similar engines, some with larger wheels, designed for light express traffic on heavily graded

routes. The 'N' class had been used all over the Southern Railway system, and until 1945 it was responsible for the heaviest passenger workings west of Exeter. Although steam is being replaced so rapidly many of these engines are still in service today.

143 **A Maunsell 'E1'** 4-4-0; S.E.& C.R.
Immediately after the end of the First World War the management of the S.E.&C.R. took a decision to concentrate in future all boat train traffic upon Victoria Station. This at once created a serious problem for the locomotive department, because civil engineering restrictions on the Chatham line precluded use of the powerful superheated 4-4-0s of 'L' class which had been introduced in 1914. Nothing larger than the non-superheated 'D' and 'E' class were permitted, and these would not have been able to handle the 300-ton trains required by the traffic department. R. E. L. Maunsell, who had succeeded Wainwright in 1913, thereupon carried out a very clever rebuilding of one of the 'E' class engines, No. 179: fitting a superheater, modernizing the design of the valve gear, and cutting down weight wherever possible. The result was an engine of considerably enhanced capacity that was no heavier than the original engine. The secret of success lay in the valve gear, but at the same time the engine was given an entirely 'new look'. In the austere livery of wartime there could not be greater contrast between these rebuilt engines and the originals, decked in all their finery (reference 108). Looks apart, the rebuilds were, for their size, some of the finest working engines ever to run in Great Britain.

144 **Furness Railway;** E. Sharples's 4-6-4 tank engine.
Apart from the mail trains, and the connections to London and North Western

long-distance expresses at Carnforth, most of the passenger working on the Furness Railway consisted of smartly-timed stopping trains. Before the large-scale introduction of private motoring there was a surprising amount of station-to-station passenger business. Various types of locomotives were used ranging from Pettigrew's latest 4-4-0s, to 0-6-2 tank engines, and after World War I the need was felt for larger engines. On short runs a tank engine has a considerable advantage, and E. Sharples prepared designs for the neat and powerful 4-6-4 that is illustrated. Much larger than anything that had preceded them on the Furness Railway these engines made short work of all kinds of traffic. They accelerated from rest with great rapidity, and ran freely at speeds of 50 to 55 m.p.h. They were well liked for their smooth riding and easy action, but their life in the Furness Railway livery was short. After grouping they were painted in Midland red, and as such looked very handsome; but after a short time 'red' was reserved only for the top-link express locomotives, and all other classes were painted in black. But whether in 'iron-ore' red, 'Midland red', or black, the 'Big Jumbos', as they were known, filled a very useful niche in Furness Railway operating.

145 The Lickey Bank Engine; Midland Railway.

The Lickey Incline has always formed a very formidable obstacle in the path of northbound trains on the West of England main line of the Midland Railway. The gradient is 1 in 37½ for 2 miles between Bromsgrove and Blackwell, and while 4-4-0 engines of the No. 2 Class would bring loads of 250 tons or even more up from Bristol, substantial assistance in rear was always needed up the Lickey Incline. A number of 0-6-0 tank engines were kept in steam at Bromsgrove to assist every north-bound train, pas-

senger and goods alike, and with the heavier trains two and sometimes even three bank engines were necessary. The 10-coupled tender engine, nicknamed 'Big Bertha', was designed as an experiment: as a machine that would do the work of two 0-6-0 engines. She was by far the largest and heaviest locomotive ever built by the Midland Railway, and fully justified the claims made for her. It certainly needed careful management of the fire before an ascent to keep those four large cylinders adequately supplied with steam during the 7 or 8 minutes of heavy pounding up the incline. But from her construction in 1919, she did the job for 30 years. She must have been unique among main line engines in having so limited a sphere of activity. All her work throughout those 30 years was done between Bromsgrove South and Blackwell – a distance of less than 3 miles. The only times when she went further afield were her periodic visits to Derby Works for overhaul.

146 The 'N2' Suburban Tank of 1921; Great Northern Railway.

The London suburban lines of the Great Northern Railway are uniformly difficult for the operation of heavy and fast passenger traffic. The immediate start out of Kings Cross is severely graded, and while the main line continues to Potters Bar on a long steady incline of 1 in 200 the branches, and particularly that to High Barnet, are very much more severe. Again, the City Widened Lines, of the Metropolitan Railway, over which Great Northern trains work between Kings Cross and Moorgate, required locomotives to condense their exhausts in the tunnels, and the climb between Kings Cross (underground) and the main line, in tunnel throughout and round the severe 'Hotel Curve', is a very awkward piece of railway. In H. A. Ivatt's time, 8-coupled tank engines were tried for a time, but ultimately the 0-6-2 type prevailed, and it was in producing a powerful superheated development of the Ivatt 0-6-2 that Gresley secured such marked success, in 1921. Sixty of them were put into service in that year, all fitted with the prominent condensing pipes on the side of the boiler. To such an extent were these engines on top of their job that they outlasted steam in the London area of the L.N.E.R. and all put in some forty years of hard work. After grouping of the railways, a further batch, without condensing apparatus, were built for service on the L.N.E.R. suburban lines around Edinburgh and Glasgow.

147 **Great Northern Railway**; Gresley's 3-cylinder 2-8-0.
The Great Northern, from its very inception, was a line of long-haul heavy goods and mineral traffic. Archibald Sturrock first tackled the problem with his famous but unsuccessful steam tenders (reference 24). H. A. Ivatt very quickly adopted eight coupled engines, which Gresley developed, with much larger boilers, into a 2-8-0. The first batch of these had two cylinders, outside; but having regard to the very heavy trains regularly worked, and the need frequently for starting on a heavy gradient, Gresley felt that a 3-cylinder layout would give smoother and easier starting, and in conjunction with these he developed his well-known conjugated valve gear, in which only two sets of motion are needed to actuate the valves of all three cylinders. A first and rather complicated version of this arrangement was fitted to one 2-8-0 engine, No. 461, in 1918, but the finalized gear was incorporated in the '02' class of 1921 beginning with engine No. 477. These locomotives proved ideal for the heavy coal traffic from South Yorkshire and Nottingham to London, and eventually more than fifty were built. The earliest examples were painted in the standard Great Northern 'freight-grey', as shown in our picture. The later ones,

built after the grouping, had modified cabs, giving a much better protection from the weather.

148 **R. Whitelegg's Baltic Tank;** Glasgow and South Western Clyde coast services.
Robert Whitelegg was the son of the Locomotive Superintendent of the London Tilbury and Southend Railway, and was brought up in the tradition of the handsome engines and impeccable service referred to in connection with plate 117. He duly succeeded his father in office on the L.T.S.R., and built some remarkable tank engines of the 'Baltic' (4-6-4) type. But after the L.T.S.R. was taken over by the Midland he resigned, and went to the Glasgow and South Western after the death of Peter Drummond, in 1918. There he repeated his earlier essay in 'Baltic' tank engine design, though on a still more powerful scale. Once again, however, he had no sooner produced his great engines than the railway concerned was absorbed in a far larger combination – this time when the G.&S.W.R. passed into the L.M.S.R. group. Rather than remain as a mere divisional chief Whitelegg resigned to become General Manager of the famous locomotive building firm of Beyer, Peacock and Co. The Glasgow and South Western Railway 'Baltic' tanks, although doing much good work, did not have the same attention as if their designer had still been in office at Kilmarnock. Furthermore, the policy of the L.M.S.R. was one of standardization, and a small class of 6 locomotives was doomed to early extinction. Nevertheless they were fine engines, and in other circumstances would no doubt have had a distinguished career.

149 **Metropolitan Railway;** Charles Jones's 4-4-4 express tank engine.
Beginning with the purely Underground section from Bishops Road to Farringdon Street, opened in 1863, the Metropolitan

Railway extended far out beyond the northern suburbs of London, to Aylesbury, and Verney Junction through a delightful part of the Chiltern Hills, in Buckinghamshire. Claiming it for themselves the railway exhorted town-dwellers to live in 'Metroland', and a number of very attractive services were run from Verney Junction, Aylesbury, and Chesham to the City. Luxurious bogie coaches were introduced and some trains even had a Pullman car. They were electrically hauled as far as Harrow-on-the-Hill, and then there was a change-over to steam. Some smart running was required on these popular residential trains, and after a trial of 0-6-4 tank engines, Jones introduced the handsome and efficient 4-4-4 tanks shown in our picture. These engines had to run fast, but were also required to climb well, because the line north of Rickmansworth mounts into the Chiltern Hills on a continuous gradient of 1 in 100. Though there was much express running on the London side of Rickmansworth, beyond that point the Metropolitan trains called at all stations, and hard work was involved in getting away from Chorley Wood, and Chalfont Road, against the continuous rising gradient. These engines did the job most competently.

150 J. G. Robinson's Historic 2-8-0.

Although passenger traffic on the London Extension never developed to the extent hoped for, in the north the freight and mineral traffic of the Great Central Railway was enormous. In 1911 Robinson built the first of a new design of large 2-8-0, and it was put through extensive trials. Proving thoroughly successful, an order for no fewer than 70 engines was placed with the North British Locomotive Company, and delivery of these was taken in 1912–13. The Great Central eventually had 127 of these tough, hard-working engines, but during World War I the design was chosen for general service on

military railways abroad, and a total of 521 were built by various firms for service with the Railway Operating Division of the British Army. Our picture shows one of these engines fitted with the Westinghouse brake, unlike the Great Central examples, which used the vacuum. After war service many of these R.O.D. engines were purchased by British railways other than the Great Central, and numbers of them were put to work on the London and North Western, the Caledonian, and the Great Western. On the last mentioned line they were so well liked as to become almost a G.W.R. standard type. After the grouping no fewer than 273 of them were acquired by the L.N.E.R., and used all over the system. This Robinson design must be set down as one of the most successful heavy freight engines of all time.

151 A Great Western 'Castle'.

It is no exaggeration to state that the 'Castle' is one of the most famous and successful locomotive designs the world has ever seen. Engines of this class, to an unchanged design, were built at intervals from 1923 to 1939, and after the end of World War II construction continued, to a design modified only to the extent of a different superheater, and altered arrangements for lubrication, until 1950, by which time no fewer than 171 were running. They were a development of the Churchward 'Star' class, and included all the virtues of the latter, plus the advantages of improved manufacturing techniques at Swindon, and precision methods in repair. Fast and economical in service, many notable records were claimed by the 'Castle' locomotives, including the fastest-ever start-to-stop run from Swindon to Paddington by the Cheltenham Flyer in 1932: 77.3 miles at an average speed of 81.6 m.p.h. with the *Tregenna Castle*; a run non-stop to Plymouth in 1925 with the *Caldicot Castle* and with the maximum load of the

Cornish Riviera Express when the arrival at North Road was 15 min. early, and a maximum speed of 100 m.p.h. down the Honeybourne bank by the *Builth Castle*. The pioneer engine, No. 4073 *Caerphilly Castle* is now in the Science Museum, South Kensington.

152 **Lancashire and Yorkshire Railway;** 'Class 8' 4-cylinder 4-6-0
In 1908 George Hughes had put on the road a class of non-superheated four-cylinder 4-6-0 locomotives of huge and impressive appearance. They were intended for rapid acceleration and heavy work on the main lines; but it is perhaps no exaggeration to say that gradually they gained a reputation for being 'the world's worst'. In 1920 a most intensive rebuilding was carried out, including a redesigned front-end, and the adding of a superheater. The engines were transformed and did excellent work. They had scarcely got into their stride when the grouping of the railways came in 1923, and their designer George Hughes was appointed Chief Mechanical Engineer of the L.M.S.R. In addition to the rebuilding of all the original L.&Y.R. engines of 1908, another 55 were built between 1921 and 1925. Many of them were allocated to working on the northern section of the former London and North Western Railway where they did good work over Shap. Always masters of their work they were nevertheless very heavy coal burners, and in comparative trials with various locomotives, in 1925, they proved considerably less economical than the London and North Western 'Claughton' class, with which they were classified on equality so far as loading was concerned. Our picture shows one of the original engines of 1908, as rebuilt. Later, all the class were painted in 'Derby red'.

153 **The First Gresley Pacific;** G.N.R.
It is no exaggeration to say that the building of the two prototype 'Pacific' engines Nos. 1470 and 1471 at Doncaster Works in 1922 marked the beginning of a new locomotive era in Great Britain. Although an experimental Pacific had been built by the Great Western Railway as long previously as 1908 that engine, No. 111 *The Great Bear*, had been an isolated unit, and formed no part of the standard pattern of locomotive operating on the G.W.R. On the other hand the Great Northern 'Pacifics' were destined to become an L.N.E.R. standard for all important express train working between London and Edinburgh, and with their success and ever increasing prowess the term 'big engine' took on a new meaning in the nineteen-twenties. But to revert to their first introduction, in size and tractive power they represented just as great an advance over the Ivatt 'Atlantics' as the latter engines did over the Stirling eight-foot 'singles'. Yet revolutionary though they were in size they represented an entirely logical step in the development, and their design was entirely in the Doncaster tradition. In the case of so great an advance in size it could hardly be expected that finality in design would be achieved at once. After some years alterations to the valve gear were found desirable. But from 1927 onwards after these changes had been made, the design, in its performance no less than its bold conception, became one of the classics of British steam locomotive history.

154 **Sir Vincent Raven's Pacific.**
The North Eastern Railway had a very long tradition of excellent and individualistic locomotive design, and just before the railway itself became merged into the L.N.E.R. group, the last Chief Mechanical Engineer, Sir Vincent Raven, produced the first of his huge Pacifics. These engines, of which five were built at Darlington Works, were a natural development from the very successful three-cylinder Atlantics of Class 'Z'. In this respect they were

unlike the contemporary 'Pacifics' of Sir Nigel Gresley, on the Great Northern. The latter represented an entirely new concept in design from Doncaster works rather than a straight enlargement of the previous 'Atlantic' engines. The Raven Pacifics were a pure enlargement in boiler and length, and in the perpetuation of the use of three sets of Stephenson link motion for actuating the valves. When Gresley was appointed Chief Mechanical Engineer of the L.N.E.R. he had to decide which 'Pacific' design to adopt as a future standard. Other things being equal he would naturally be inclined to favour his own design; but in trials with the dynamometer car between Doncaster and Kings Cross in 1923 the Great Northern engine showed a definite superiority over her North Eastern rival. Nevertheless the N.E.R. did some excellent work, and as the final expression of North Eastern design practice these Raven 'Pacifics' occupy a notable place in locomotive history.

155 The 'King Arthur' Class; Southern Railway.

This famous class of locomotives, one of the most generally successful of any during the Grouping Era of 1923–48, had its origin on the London and South Western Railway in 1918, when R. W. Urie built the first of 20 very powerful two-cylinder 4-6-0s. They were designed in what might be termed the Eastleigh-Scottish tradition of massive frame design, and complete immunity from running troubles. In heavy express service however their performance left a little to be desired, and after grouping R. E. L. Maunsell and his staff made a number of small, but highly important modifications. The draughting was altered; there were changes to the valve gear, and the boiler pressure was raised. The result was to produce a masterpiece. Many of these engines were built subsequently for general use on the Southern Railway. The example illus-

trated, No. 768 *Sir Balin* was originally a boat train engine working between Victoria and Dover. Then it was transferred to the West of England, and earned a fine reputation on the heavy road between Salisbury and Exeter, while since nationalization it has been back at its original station, Stewarts Lane, Battersea, for working Kent Coast trains. Our picture shows the six-wheeled tender fitted to a number of these engines when engaged on services such as the Brighton and Ramsgate lines where the length of turntable at one time precluded use of the standard bogie tender.

156 An L.M.S. Standard Compound.

Following the finalization of the Midland superheated compound design (reference 110), and its very successful performances in tests against other locomotives of comparable power within the L.M.S. group, certain modifications were made to the design to make it suitable as an L.M.S. standard. In the first post-grouping batches trials were made with slightly enlarged cylinders, and a reversion to the original valve setting. But further comparative trials over the very severe main line between Leeds and Carlisle confirmed the dimensions as established on the Midland Railway as most suitable, except that the coupled wheels were 6 ft. 9 in. instead of 7 ft. in diameter, and that the appearance of the engines was somewhat changed by the need to use shorter chimneys and dome covers to suit the reduced height of the loading gauge in Scotland. The driver's position was changed from the right-hand to the left-hand side of the cab. As thus standardized, the three-cylindered compounds did many years of splendid work. Especially fine was their performance on the heavily graded routes of the Scottish Border country. There were 190 in all of the 'standard' compounds, and they worked as far afield as Aberdeen, Stranraer, York, Holyhead, Lincoln, and Bristol, in addition of course to running the principal main lines from London.

157   An L.M.S. Standard Goods.

The Midland Railway, in pre-grouping days, had one of the heaviest coal and mineral traffics in Great Britain. As in passenger working, the company favoured the use of locomotives of moderate power, and although some powerful 2-8-0s were built at Derby for the Somerset and Dorset Joint Line the Fowler superheater 0-6-0 of 1911 was the largest freight locomotive built for purely Midland Railway usage. These very simple and economical engines were cheap to build and cheap to run, and 191 of them were built prior to the grouping. The general usefulness of the class led to its being adopted as an L.M.S.R. standard, and the engine illustrated is one of 580 built for general use all over the L.M.S. system from 1924 onward. It differs from the Midland design of 1911 only in having reduced height chimney and dome. The relatively large diameter of the coupled wheels, namely 5 ft. 3 in., enabled these engines to show a good turn of speed when required, and in consequence they were frequently called upon for passenger work on branch and secondary routes. On the Highland section, on the Somerset and Dorset, and on the Furness line they were often used on passenger trains. Five of them were built new for the Somerset and Dorset in 1922. While they were naturally not up to main line express passenger service they could otherwise be described as maids of all work.

158   The 'Sandringham' Class 4-6-0;

London and North Eastern Railway.

After the grouping of the railways, in 1923, the loading of express trains in many parts of the country was very much on the increase due to the use of more luxurious stock, the introduction of additional amenities, and so on. While this could be met on the trunk lines to the north by building larger and more powerful locomotives it could not be done in East Anglia. Over the lines of the former Great Eastern Railway restrictions did not only apply to axle loading and clearances. The turntables set a limit upon the overall length unless a cumbersome process of uncoupling engine from tender was to be followed. To provide enhanced power within the existing civil engineering restrictions Gresley introduced the 'Sandringham' class, in 1928. By use of three cylinders a better arrangement of balancing was obtained, thereby permitting a heavier dead weight per axle, than with a two-cylinder machine having the same amount of balance of the reciprocating parts. The 'Sandringhams', of which the first examples were named after country houses and estates in East Anglia, were very successful. Many additional engines of the class were built subsequently for the Great Central line, and as the latter railway did not suffer from turntable restrictions it was possible to fit larger tenders. The engines allocated to the Great Central line were mostly named after well-known football clubs. They were very fast and economical machines and frequently attained speeds of 90 m.p.h. In all, 73 of them were constructed.

159   The 'Lord Nelson';   Southern Railway.

While the 'King Arthur' class 4-6-0s were capable of excellent work they were no more than medium-powered engines by the standards of the mid-nineteen-twenties, and when the Traffic Manager of the Southern Railway announced his intention of running express trains of 500 tons weight at average speeds of 55 m.p.h. it was evident that locomotives of considerably enhanced power would be necessary. Maunsell and his staff carried out the most careful investigations before deciding on the main features of the new design. With the assistance of the Great

Western and of the London and North Eastern Railways James Clayton personally studied the working of the 'Castle' class 4-6-os, and of the first Gresley 'Pacifics', and eventually a four-cylinder 4-6-o was decided upon. Its unusual feature was the setting of the cranks at 135 deg., giving eight exhausts per revolution, instead of the usual four. Named after great Naval commanders, the 'Lord Nelson' class proved very fast and powerful engines, though they needed greater skill and experience in driving and firing than the general utility, workaday 'King Arthurs'. After he succeeded Maunsell as Chief Mechanical Engineer of the railway, O. V. S. Bulleid improved the 'Nelsons' by fitting multiple jet blastpipes and an improved design of cylinders. Our picture shows the 'Lord Nelson' as originally built in 1926.

160 The 'Royal Scot' Class 4-6-o; L.M.S.R.

Rarely can a famous locomotive design have been evolved in more curious and roundabout circumstances than the 'Royal Scot'. Sir Henry Fowler was planning a 4-cylinder compound 'Pacific', while other influences on the L.M.S.R. considered that a 4-6-o was large enough for all requirements. In the autumn of 1926 a 'Castle' class 4-6-o was borrowed from the Great Western and tested between Euston and Carlisle, with the result that a decision was taken to have 50 3-cylinder 4-6-os built at top speed by the North British Locomotive Company. So urgently were the new engines needed that in Glasgow the order was divided between the Hyde Park and the Queens Park Works of the manufacturer – 25 apiece. The 'Scots' were an immediate success, and did a great deal of very hard work between Euston and Glasgow. Originally, half of them were named after Scottish regiments – a gesture by the L.M.S.R. that created much interest and satisfaction in Scotland; the remainder

were named after historic locomotives ranging from the *Lancashire Witch* to the *Lady of the Lake*. The 'Scots' were much improved in detail by Sir William Stanier who incorporated some important features of Great Western practice after his arrival on the L.M.S.R. in 1932; and between that time and the outbreak of World War II these engines were among the most effective express passenger 4-6-os in the country.

161 The 'King George V'.

The 'King' class, which represents the ultimate development of the historic Churchward four-cylinder 4-6-o design, had the greatest nominal tractive effort of any British 4-6-o express locomotive, and was in fact equal in this respect to the much larger and heavier Pacific locomotives of the other British railways. The 'Kings', apart from the technical features of the design that made such a tremendous concentration of power possible, had several other great distinctions. The first engine of the class, No. 6000 *King George V*, virtually made its *début* in the U.S.A. For after a very short period of 'running in' it was shipped to America to represent Great Britain at the Centenary celebrations of the Baltimore and Ohio Railroad; and while in the U.S.A. the engine did some very notable work. At home the introduction of the 'Kings' made possible some accelerations of the West of England services, despite ever-increasing loads, and the thirty engines of this class spent the entire 32–35 years of their lives in the heaviest express passenger traffic. No. 6000 *King George V* is now preserved, and will be housed in the Great Western Railway Museum at Swindon.

162 The Gresley Super-Pacific; L.N.E.R.

The original Great Northern 'Pacifics' were designed in the Doncaster tradition of old, and had a boiler pressure of 180 lb.

per sq. in. As a result of the Interchange Trials with the Great Western Railway in 1925, when a 'Castle' class 4-6-0 carrying a pressure of 225 lb. per sq. in. proved the more economical, Gresley began experimenting with higher boiler pressures on his 'Pacifics', and of two trial engines one, No. 2544 *Lemberg*, had its cylinders reduced in diameter so that its nominal tractive effort, using 220 lb. per sq. in., was the same as that of the standard 180 lb. engines. A series of trials with the dynamometer car was run between Doncaster and Kings Cross, running *Lemberg* against a standard engines No. 4473 *Solario*. Taken all round there was very little in it, but Gresley was sufficiently impressed with the work of *Lemberg* to make 220 lb. per sq. in. his new standard for 'Pacific' engines, and in a new series, built at Doncaster in 1930, he used cylinders slightly larger than those of the experimental *Lemberg*. The new series, known as Class 'A3' thus had a higher tractive effort than the original Gresley 'Pacifics'. They proved very fast, powerful, and economical engines, and in 1935 No. 2750 *Papyrus*, in the course of a trial run from London to Newcastle and back, broke many world records for steam traction including the attainment of a maximum speed of 108 m.p.h. In due course, as the boilers became due for renewal, all the original 180 lb. Pacifics were converted to Class 'A3'.

163 **An L.M.S. Horwich Mogul.**
After the grouping of the railways in 1923, George Hughes of the former Lancashire and Yorkshire Railway was appointed Chief Mechanical Engineer of the L.M.S.R., and his former headquarters at Horwich, Lancashire, became H.Q. for the entire L.M.S.R. for a time. A general service locomotive, capable of taking fast goods or intermediate passenger trains was urgently needed, and the powerful 2-6-0 illustrated in our pic-

ture was designed and the first examples built at Horwich. To accommodate the very large cylinders outside they had to be located high up, and inclined at quite a steep angle. This feature, together with the working of the outside valve gear, led to these engines being nicknamed the 'Crabs'. When first introduced they were finished in the passenger livery of 'Derby red'; but our picture shows them in the guise familiar in later years. Despite their relatively small coupled wheels they were free running, and frequently attained speeds of 75 m.p.h. But they were at their best in hard slogging with heavy freight trains, or in working passenger trains on heavily graded routes. Some of them were used with success on the Highland line in Scotland, and they were much in demand for excursions, football specials, and suchlike traffic.

164 **The G.W.R. 'Hall' Class.**
During the nineteen-twenties 4-6-0 locomotives with four cylinders were standardized for express passenger work on the G.W.R., and to the 73 engines of the 'Star' class were added many new 'Castles' and the very powerful 'Kings'. But the two-cylinder 4-6-0s of the 'Saint' class, fitted with Churchward's very effective setting of the Stephenson link motion, were exceptionally smart in getting away from rest, and in C. B. Collett's time it was decided to use this engine design for an intermediate passenger and fast mixed traffic engine. An experiment was made by rebuilding engine No. 2925 *Saint Martin* with 6 ft. wheels, instead of the original 6 ft. 8½ in.; and the rebuilt engine did so well that she became the prototype of a new and ultimately very numerous class, named after country estates. So many of these engines were built eventually that the list of 'stately homes' in Great Western territory became completely exhausted, and some of the later engines of the class had names taken from as far afield as

Lancashire, the Lake District, and the East Riding of Yorkshire. In all, 330 of these engines were built. They were extremely fast runners, having regard to their wheel diameter, and on one occasion, in emergency, one of them ran the Bristolian, more than keeping the very fast sectional times then scheduled. The engine illustrated, No. 5930 *Hannington Hall* was one of a series built before the war.

165 Gresley's 'Shire' Class 4-4-0.

In building standard locomotives for use on many different sections of the L.N.E.R. Gresley used three-cylinder propulsion, with the conjugated valve motion that he had developed on the Great Northern Railway prior to grouping. The 'D49' was an interesting example of the application of a 3-cylinder layout to a large modern 4-4-0. The first engines of the class, designated D49/1 were built in 1927, and had piston valves, Walschearts gear, and the Gresley conjugated motion, for the middle cylinders. This series was named after counties served by the L.N.E.R., as in the case of the engine shown in our picture, No. 2754 *Rutlandshire*. A later series built in 1928, had Lentz rotary cam poppet valves. These latter were named after famous hunts in L.N.E.R. territory, and bore the figure of a fox in full flight above the nameplate. The 'Shires' were mostly used in Scotland, while the 'Hunts' were used around Leeds, Hull, York and Newcastle. Although slender in appearance, by reason of their high-pitched boiler, they were capable of hard work, though they tended to get rough in operation after their mileage after shopping had substantially increased. The poppet-valve engines were fast and free runners, and one of their regular turns for many years was the working of the morning express from Leeds to Scotland, which they took as far as Newcastle. This involved a fast non-stop run of 80 miles from York to Newcastle, which was often done at an average speed of nearly 60 m.p.h. from start to stop. Taking piston valve and poppet valve engines together the 'D49' class totalled 76 locomotives.

166 A Beyer-Garratt 2-6-0 + 0-6-2; L.M.S.R.

One of the great problems of modern railway operating has been to provide locomotives of adequate power without exceeding the limit of weight or length that can be permitted by the civil engineer. An easy, though uneconomical way of providing increased tractive power is to use two engines, though this also doubles the cost of working by having a second crew. The Beyer-Garratt type of locomotive, that has been used overseas in many countries of the British Commonwealth, consists virtually of two separate engines fed with steam from one very large central boiler. Thus two engines can be managed by one crew, though it needs some very heavy stoking to provide the necessary steam. On many engines of the Beyer-Garratt type mechanical stokers are fitted. The L.M.S.R. example illustrated provides the equivalent of two standard 2-6-0 engines (reference 163). These enormous engines were used on the very heavy coal traffic of the former Midland Railway between Toton marshalling yards, near Nottingham, and the London distributional yards for the coal trade, at Cricklewood. It was a long, slow haul, and the Beyer-Garratts put in many years of good service on the job.

167 L.M.S. '5XP' (Baby Scot).

After grouping a sustained attempt was made by the L.M.S.R. to develop a locomotive of enhanced power from the L.N.W.R. 'Claughton' class. Considerable success attended the fitting of enlarged boilers on to a number of the ex-L.N.W.R. locomotives. But the success of the 3-cylinder 'Royal Scots' suggested that a more extensive reconstruction might prove profitable, and a new design was worked out using a synthesis of standard parts. This consisted of a 3-cylinder front-end and motion, on the lines of the 'Royal Scots', but using the enlarged 'Claughton' boiler. The result was a handsome and successful locomotive, strongly reminiscent of the 'Royal Scot' in external style, but with a smaller boiler. The resemblance suggested the original nickname of 'Baby Scots'. At a slightly later time the scrapping of the famous London and North Western war memorial engine *Patriot* led to the perpetuation of the name on a 'Baby Scot', together with the inscription that accompanied the name, and from that time the engines were known as the 'Patriot' class. Eventually the class was 52 strong. They were fast and powerful engines. Some retained the name of the L.N.W.R. 'Claughtons' they replaced; others were unnamed, and a few had names with special associations such as the engine illustrated No. 5538, which was named after Giggleswick School, lying within sight of the Anglo-Scottish main line of the Midland Division, over which this engine regularly worked.

168 **A Southern 'School'.**
Locomotives of enhanced power were required in 1930 for the Hastings line of the former S.E.&C. Railway. It is a most awkward route, with heavy gradients, much curvature, and serious engineering restrictions in the clearances available in the tunnels just south of Tunbridge Wells. Maunsell would like to have used the 'King Arthur' 4-6-0s, but the clearances and weight restrictions prevented this being done. A new design had to be worked out, as quickly and cheaply as possible. The result was once aptly described as a 'three-quarter Nelson'! The cylinders and valve gear were the same as the 'Nelson', but using three instead of four, but the boiler was a shortened version of that fitted to the

'King Arthur'. The 'School' was thus a synthesis of detail made up very economically from existing patterns and tools. No synthesis – a virtual makeshift! – can have been more outstandingly successful. Far from being a special type confined to the difficult conditions of the Hastings line, the 'Schools' came to do magnificent work on the fast Portsmouth trains, and eventually they superseded the 'King Arthurs' on the Bournemouth expresses. They were light on coal, and could tackle loads of 450 tons as a matter of course. They were, without any doubt, the most successful 4-4-0 locomotives ever to run in Great Britain. The engine *Stowe* of this class has been preserved, and is contained in Lord Montagu of Beaulieu's Motor Museum, at Beaulieu, Hampshire.

169 **A Pannier Tank;** Great Western Railway.
The Great Western was always a very large user of tank engines, and from its own diverse early designs, and from the large variety of engines that came into the stock from the local railways in South Wales after the amalgamation of 1923, it owned at one time more than 1,000 of the 0-6-0 type alone. In 1929, from the famous Dean 0-6-0 tender engine (reference 45), there was designed a modern tank engine that could be standardized and built in large numbers to replace the diversity of older engines that existed. Except that the tank engine did not have a superheater the boiler and firebox were the same as those of the Dean goods, and the cylinders and motion were the same. The tank engines had 4 ft. 7½ in. coupled wheels, against 5 ft. 2 in. on the tender engine. The so-called '5700' class was a great success, and no fewer than 790 have been built since 1929. Though officially designated 'light goods and shunting engines', many of them were regularly used on passenger trains, and speeds of up to 65 m.p.h. have been recorded with them. The example shown

in our picture is one of the series fitted with condensing apparatus for working the meat trains through the Metropolitan line tunnels to Smithfield Market. As dieselization spread over the Western Region of British Railways, and many of these engines became redundant, some were transferred to the Southern. A number of them did good work on the empty stock trains into and out of Waterloo, while a batch of them went to Folkestone Junction for working boat trains on the very sharp incline between the Junction and the Harbour station.

170 A Stanier 'Black Five'; L.M.S.

If a competition were to be held for the most generally useful locomotive class ever to run on British metals the Stanier 'Black-Five' would be a very strong candidate for the prize. In principle the idea of a general-utility 4-6-0 of intermediate power capacity, and of such dimensions as to be usable over almost the entire mileage of the L.M.S.R., undoubtedly stemmed from the success of the Great Western 'Hall' class (reference 164). But the Stanier Class 5, 4-6-0, combining the best of both Great Western and L.M.S. practice, proved a remarkable engine, able to take heavy and fast express passenger trains on virtually equal terms with the 'Royal Scots' (reference 160), do heavy goods work, and run up to 90 m.p.h. on the moderate-loaded express trains of the Midland line. As mixed traffic units they were painted black, hence their unofficial designation of 'Black-Fives'. They were used all over the L.M.S.R. system, from Bournemouth to Wick, from Swansea to York, and were universally acclaimed. The design was first introduced in 1934, and at first it was not finalized. The first 70 engines were subject to modification; but from 1935 onwards they were built in large numbers, down to the year 1951. Ultimately there were 842 of the class in service.

171 A Gresley 'P2'; L.N.E.R.

Sir Nigel Gresley, as a true successor to Stirling and Ivatt, in the locomotive 'chair' of the Great Northern Railway, at Doncaster, greatly disliked double-heading. The old Doncaster tradition of 'one train, one engine' persisted with him, and when faced with a serious haulage problem on the East Coast Route north of Edinburgh, where even his Pacifics could not take the heaviest trains, he designed the mighty 'P2' class, of 2-8-2s. These were 3-cylinder machines, with 6 ft. 2 in. coupled wheels, and an enormous boiler. The first two engines of the class had an arrangement of smoke-deflecting screens at the front-end, but the later ones had the same streamlined 'prow' as proved so successful on the high speed 'A4' Pacifics. The 'P2' class, of which six were built specially for service between Edinburgh and Aberdeen, were very successful as weight pullers. While the Reid 'Atlantics' were limited to 340 tons, tare, and the 'Pacific' to 450 tons, the 'P2' class took 550 tons and more with equal success. Unfortunately the conditions that developed during World War II led to their maintenance deteriorating, with consequent troubles and failures; and after Gresley's death they were rebuilt as 4-6-2s, and became less effective. In their prime, however, they ranked as the most powerful engines ever to run in this country.

172 A World Record Breaker; Gresley's Mallard, Class 'A4'.

These world-famous engines represented the consummation of the story of Pacific locomotive development at Doncaster. Into them Gresley put those finishing touches to the already very successful 'A3', in the form of still higher boiler pressure, larger diameter piston valves, and the internal streamlining of steam ports and passages. These features substantially improved the haulage capacity and speedworthiness of the engines, while the very striking form of the external streamlining fairly captured popular imagination. The first four engines were designed for the Silver Jubilee high speed service, and were finished in silver, and when the pioneer engine, No. 2509 *Silver Link* attained a maximum speed of 112 m.p.h. on its very first public trip the fame of the class was assured from the outset. From this spectacular beginning the 'A4s' have gone from strength to strength. They hauled tremendous loads at ordinary express speeds; they frequently topped 100 m.p.h. in ordinary service, and in 1938 engine No. 4468 *Mallard* made the world record for steam traction with a maximum speed of 126 m.p.h. After the first four 'silver' engines garter blue became the standard colour for the class, in L.N.E.R. days. Down to the year 1962 they remained in first class express service, one of the finest of their latter-day achievements being the haulage each summer of the Elizabethan express, non-stop over the 392¾ miles between Kings Cross and Edinburgh, in 6½ hours, an average speed of 60½ m.p.h. over this long distance with a normal load of about 420 tons.

173 **The 'Princess Elizabeth';** L.M.S.R.
After Sir William Stanier had taken up his appointment as Chief Mechanical Engineer of the L.M.S.R. designs were put in hand for new express locomotives that could work the Anglo-Scottish expresses through between London and Glasgow, 401 miles. Hitherto the longest working undertaken by a single locomotive on the L.M.S.R. had been the 299-mile run between London and Carlisle. Stanier embodied the fruits of his long experience on the Great Western in a front-end design very similar to that of the G.W.R. 'King' class; but he put on a very much larger boiler and firebox and used the 'Pacific' wheel arrangement, 4-6-2. The first two engines of this new

class were completed at Crewe in 1933 and named *The Princess Royal* and *Princess Elizabeth*. It was from this latter name that the class derived its affectionate nickname of the 'Lizzies'. After some experimental running, and subsequent modifications to the boilers, the 'Lizzies' became a great success, and did that which was expected of them in long-distance running. To the *Princess Elizabeth* belongs the credit of one of the greatest runs in British railway history, in November 1936, when a special train of 260 tons was worked non-stop from Glasgow to Euston at an average speed throughout of 70 m.p.h. – 401¼ miles in 344¾ min. start to stop.

174 **The 'Coronation' of 1937;** L.M.S.
To celebrate the Coronation of His Majesty King George VI in 1937, the L.M.S.R. put on a new express between London and Glasgow, 'The Coronation Scot', making the 401¼ mile run in 6½ hours, inclusive of a stop at Carlisle. From the experience with the 'Princess Royal' class 4-6-2s it seemed that considerable improvements could be made in a 'Pacific' locomotive designed expressly for continuous running at high speed; at the same time such improvements in performance as seemed possible would also be of great benefit in the working of the ordinary expresses of the line, many of which it was desired to accelerate. The five new engines built specially for the 'Coronation Scot' service were finished in Prussian Blue, and the streamlined form was designed to minimize air resistance at high speed. These engines gave remarkable results. On a trial trip before the 'Coronation Scot' service was inaugurated a speed of 114 m.p.h. was attained, and the return run from Crewe to Euston, 158 miles, made in 119 minutes – an average speed of 79.7 m.p.h. A later engine of the class, streamlined, but finished in the standard L.M.S. red livery

did some notable running on American railroads in 1939, when it was exhibited at the New York World's Fair in that year. The engine that thus crossed the Atlantic was actually named *Coronation*, but the name was transferred from the first of the blue engines of 1937 specially for this visit to America.

175 A 'Green Arrow'; London and North Eastern Railway.

The Great Northern Railway was a pioneer in the practice of running fast goods trains, carrying block loads, with all vehicles fitted with continuous automatic vacuum brake, and with scheduled speeds of about 45 m.p.h., start to stop, over runs such as from London to Peterborough, Peterborough to York and so on, powerful locomotives were needed when these trains were loaded to 40 and 50 wagons. In early L.N.E.R. days the 'K3' type 2-6-0s were used, but Gresley felt that there was scope for a still more powerful class and in 1936 he brought out the first of the 'V2s', No. 4771 *Green Arrow*. It had a shortened version of the standard 'Pacific' boiler, and a leading pony truck like that of the 'K3'. Four engines were built for trial, but such was their success and versatility that when quantity production of the class began they came to be regarded as reserve express passenger engines, and on top form there was little difference between their finest work and that of the 'A3' express passenger 'Pacifics'. In heavy goods service they could tackle anything the traffic department liked to hang on behind them. In passenger service, before World War II, they occasionally deputized for the streamlined 'A4' Pacifics on the high-speed limited trains. In ordinary express service they frequently attained speeds of 90 m.p.h. They were particularly successful in the moderate-speed heavily-loaded passenger traffic of war time. In all 184 of them were built.

176 A Stanier '8F'.

This excellent design formed the heavy-freight equivalent of the Stanier 'Black-Five' (reference 170), but used more particularly in general goods service. The design was introduced on the L.M.S.R. in 1935, but the need for new freight engines was not so great as for passenger and mixed traffic units, and by the outbreak of war in September 1939 only 126 of them had been built. Then orders were placed by the Government for 240 of them for overseas service. They were equipped for oil burning, and did much good work in Egypt, Palestine, Iraq, and Persia. Then, as the war effort at home intensified, and more locomotives were needed for freight traffic, this Stanier design was selected for production as a national standard, and engines of this type were eventually being built at Ashford, Brighton, Darlington, Doncaster, Eastleigh and Swindon, in addition to many more in the various works of the L.M.S.R. At its maximum strength the class, as running on British Railways, numbered 719 strong, including many that were returned to Great Britain after war service overseas. Although primarily a goods engine the '8F' has a fine turn of speed, and when used in emergency on passenger trains they have been known to exceed 60 m.p.h.

177 An L.M.S. 'Jubilee'.

In providing a stud of new standard locomotives for the L.M.S.R. Sir William Stanier built, simultaneously, 4-6-0s for both mixed traffic, and for purely express passenger duties. The mixed traffic units were the very celebrated 'Black-Fives' (reference 170), while for express passenger service he built a 3-cylinder engine, of capacity roughly equal to that of the 'Baby Scots' (reference 167), but with taper boilers. Although more expensive to construct, the taper boilers amply paid off their prime cost by being much lighter on maintenance costs, and less subject to incidental troubles. The new 3-cylinder 4-6-0s were at first unnamed, but in 1935, in honour of the Silver Jubilee of His Majesty King George V, one of them, No. 5552, was specially named *Silver Jubilee*, and many others of the class were named after units of the British Commonwealth. The 'Jubilees', as the class became known, were built to a total of 190 engines. After some slight teething troubles they became first-class motive power units, and worked over most of the L.M.S.R. main lines. Although they were extremely fast engines they seemed to excel at high speed climbing of the banks on the Midland route to Scotland, and some fine records of their performance were obtained on the severe route between Leeds and Carlisle. Originally they were finished in 'Derby red'; but since nationalization they have been painted in the standard British Railways green.

178 'Sir William A. Stanier F.R.S.'; L.M.S.
The first Stanier Pacifics were built at Crewe in 1933 (reference 173) and these were followed four years later by the streamlined 'Coronations'. Although a number of streamlined 'Pacifics' were added to the stock it was found that the additional cost and weight of the stream-lined casing was not really justified, and newer locomotives of the class were built without it. Furthermore the casings were in time removed from the earlier engines. In post-war years a number of aids to improved performance were added to these engines, such as self-cleaning smokeboxes, hopper ashpans, rocking firegrates, and roller bearings on all axles; and in many respects the last two locomotives of this class, built in 1947, represent the highest development of the British express passenger steam loco-motive. It is therefore appropriate that one of these should be named after so

great a steam locomotive engineer as Sir William Stanier. The engine is shown here in the post-war standard livery of the L.M.S.R., black with maroon edging; but since nationalization these engines have borne many colours, from the experimental 'blues' to British Railways standard green, and finally a reversion to 'Derby red'. To one of these engines, the *Duchess of Gloucester*, belongs the honour of having attained the highest power output ever recorded with steam in a dynamometer car test in Great Britain.

179 The Vale of Rheidol Line; a Swindon-built tank engine.
The Vale of Rheidol narrow gauge line was originally an independent concern, but came within the Great Western system in 1923. Today it is the only part of British Railways to be built to a sub-standard rail gauge – only 1 ft. 11½ in. against the standard 4 ft. 8½ in. The journey from Aberystwyth to the Devil's Bridge is an enthralling one from the scenic point of view, but arduous work for the locomotive. The track winds incessantly, on very sharp curves, as it makes its way up the mountainside, and very careful work by both driver and fireman is needed to keep a full head of steam in such conditions. The gradient is 1 in 50 continuously. The smart little 2-6-2 tank engines were designed by the G.W.R. in 1923, specially for the job, and built at Swindon Works. Originally they were finished in plain green with the words GREAT WESTERN in large letters on their tank sides. Since nationalization, however, the engines concerned have all been named, and it is in this present form that one of them, *Owain Glyndwr*, is shown in our picture. It is interesting to find that the Welsh, rather than the English spelling of the name is used. A second engine of the class is named *Llywelyn*, and the third is the *Prince of Wales*. These little engines weigh no more than 25 tons in working order.

180 **Talyllyn Railway;** the original engine.

The Talyllyn Railway has a special place in the history of railways in Great Britain, as being the first to be rescued from closure and disappearance through the activities of a Preservation Society. It is only a tiny little line, 6.6 miles long from Towyn to Abergynolwyn; but the devoted activities of the Preservation Society have resulted not only in the preservation, but the restoration to fully working order of one of the original locomotives, No. 1 *Talyllyn*. This little engine, which weighs no more than 10 tons in working order, was built in 1865 by Fletcher, Jennings and Company of the Lowca Engine Works, Whitehaven. It runs on the 2 ft. 3 in. gauge used on some Welsh narrow gauge railways. When the Preservation Society took charge of things engine No. 1 was in a very run-down condition; but through the generosity of several members of the society she was fully repaired and restored, and in 1959 took the road once more in excellent condition. No speed records are made on the Talyllyn, however. A typical run up the valley, with a heavy train, takes about 55 min. including 10 to 15 min. standing at stations. But it is a district in which no one wishes to hurry, and it is pleasant to trundle along in an open carriage behind so ornate a 'period piece' of a locomotive.

181 **Isle of Man Railway;** a Beyer-Peacock tank engine.

In the Isle of Man railways were laid to the 3 ft. gauge, and from their first opening until the present time reliance has been placed upon tank engines of the 2-4-0 type. The engine shown in our picture is the only one now to retain the original type of boiler, and the characteristic bell-mouthed dome, with Salter valves on the top. The remaining engines of this same design have been rebuilt with boilers having round-topped domes. Originally the engines of the Isle of Man Railway were smartly turned out in a bright green, with much polished brass and copper work, and all are named with local associations. In recent years the livery has been changed to a pleasing shade of brown-madder, still with the adornments of old, and today no stud of steam locomotives are more smartly maintained. Although they are relatively small, having coupled wheels of only 3 ft. 9 in. diameter, they tackle heavy loads of passengers in the holiday season, and with their gay style of painting and profusion of flashing brasswork they make an extremely pretty sight running through the glens, or climbing beside the sea on the northern branch of the line to Ramsey.

182 **Romney, Hythe and Dymchurch Railway;** express locomotive *Hercules*.

Locomotives built to the narrow gauge of 1 ft. 3 in. – roughly one quarter of the British standard gauge – were introduced in the years before World War I for miniature passenger-carrying railways in pleasure grounds, exhibitions, and so on. Their first application on a public railway came when the Ravenglass and Eskdale Railway – formerly of 3 ft gauge, and in Chancery (!) – was converted, during World War I, and two 15 in. gauge 'model' express locomotives were put to work. The Romney, Hythe and Dymchurch Railway was a much more ambitious venture, and every summer it conveys large numbers of holiday makers. Most of the locomotives are 'Pacifics' of a design that could be called a free adaptation of the famous Gresley non-streamlined 'Pacifics' of the L.N.E.R. But in addition to the 'Pacifics' there are two 4-8-2s, designed originally for mixed traffic duties, and for hauling the heavy trains of shingle that are worked from the beaches between New Romney and Dungeness. They are remarkably powerful little engines, and will haul a train of open coaches sufficient to convey at least 150 passengers. With such a load the speed will often rise to 30 m.p.h. Fortunately there are no gradients on the line. From Hythe right out to Dungeness the track is virtually level throughout.

183 'Merchant Navy' Class.
The appointment of Mr O. V. S. Bulleid as Chief Mechanical Engineer of the Southern Railway, was the signal for a strong revival in steam locomotive activity. For some years previously nearly all attention had been concentrated on the extension of the electrified system. In the new 'Pacific' design of 1941 many features were included to combat the gradually worsening conditions of railway operation. The boiler and firebox were designed to use low-grade fuel; extensive use of welding was made in the construction of both boiler and chassis, to reduce weight; and to minimize maintenance work on the running gear the valve gear was totally enclosed in an oil bath. The exterior casing was of striking form, and the final touch of novelty was provided by the Box-poc form of driving wheels. Our picture shows one of these engines as originally built, in the pre-war Southern livery of malachite green. Additional cowling had to be introduced at a later date for smoke deflection at the front end. These engines proved very fast and powerful, but unfortunately some of the innovations, and particularly the valve gear, were troublesome and expensive to maintain, and in recent years the air-smoothed casings have been removed, and a conventional Walschaerts valve gear fitted in place of the totally enclosed gear of special design. The general appearance of the engines today is similar to that of the rebuilt 'West Country' Pacific, illustrated on plate 190, though the engines themselves are slightly larger.

184 A Thompson 'B1' 4-6-0; L.N.E.R.
After the death of Sir Nigel Gresley, in 1941, the new Chief Mechanical Engineer, Edward Thompson, was faced with the need for new locomotives of a mixed traffic character in the middle of the war, with all the restrictions upon tool-making and workshop plant that then existed. The 'B1' 4-6-0 was a very clever synthesis of existing standard parts built into a new engine design of a general utility character. Thus the boiler and firebox was that of a 'Sandringham' class (reference 158); the cylinders those of the ex-G.N.R. 'K2' Mogul (reference 129), and the wheels those of the 'Green Arrow' 2-6-2 (reference 175). In producing a new engine design no major new tools were necessary. The 'B1' class was a great success from the outset, and more than 350 of them have been put into service. They were primarily intended for mixed traffic duties, but when in good trim they have proved capable of very fine express work. During the Interchange trials of 1948, made after Nationalization to test the locomotives of the former private companies against each other, a 'B1' was set to haul a very heavy express train on the Great Western line between Bristol and Exeter: 14 coach trains weighing 500 tons were taken at sustained speeds of 68–69 m.p.h. on level track – a wonderful performance for so relatively small an engine.

185 The Rebuilt 'Royal Scot.'
The original 'Royal Scots' (reference 160) were very good engines for their day. But they included the conventional design of parallel boiler, and straight-sided Belpaire firebox. When the time came for replacement of the original boilers a decision was taken to fit new boilers, having the tapered barrel and other features of detail design that had proved so free from trouble, and so efficient in steam raising on the smaller 4-6-0s of the L.M.S.R. At the same time a more extensive rebuild of the entire engine was

undertaken, providing new cylinders and valves, with the same advanced features of design that had proved so successful ðn the 'Coronation' Pacifics of 1937. The changes made a considerable difference in the outward appearance of the engines, but they made a remarkable improvement in the performance, so much so that in 1948, when the nationalized British Railways conducted a series of test runs between locomotives of the former privately-owned companies, the 'Rebuilt Royal Scots' were able to compete on very nearly equal terms with 'Pacifics' from other railways, although the difference in weight between these 4-6-0s and their competitors ranged from between 10 to 20 tons. Eventually all 70 engines of the 'Royal Scot' class were rebuilt in conformity with this most successful modernization.

186 **Austerity 2-8-0 of 1942.**
During World War II, when plans were being made for the liberation of the countries of Western Europe over-run by the enemy, designs for a general service locomotive were required. Standard British designs, such as the Stanier '8F' of the L.M.S.R. (reference 176), were based on peacetime practice and running conditions, and something more suited to the rough conditions of service in proximity to a battle-field or in countries recently liberated was specified. The design for a massive 2-8-0 was prepared by R. A. Riddles, Mechanical and Electrical Engineer, Scotland, L.M.S.R., but then attached to the Ministry of Supply as Deputy Director General of Royal Engineer Equipment. The first engine of the new design was completed by the North British Locomotive Company, in 1943, and no fewer than 733 returned to service on British Railways after the war. Although built in austerity conditions, for austerity service, these engines have since won golden opinions in ordinary freight service at home. The design features

built into them for the roughest of usage, have rendered them singularly trouble-free, and in many parts of the country they are regarded as the best heavy freight engines that have ever run.

187 **The Peppercorn 'A1'; L.N.E.R.**
Following the great success of the Gresley Pacifics on the L.N.E.R. in years before World War II it was to be expected that post-war development would be based on the same design. During the war years however some trouble was experienced in maintaining the Gresley conjugated valve gear, and post-war designs included three separate sets of motion – one for each of the three cylinders. Arthur H. Peppercorn developed the Gresley boiler, using a larger firebox, and with the modification to the front-end previously mentioned he produced an engine capable of very hard work on the line. The Peppercorn Pacifics were not called upon for such high speeds as those regularly run by the Gresleys in pre-war years, but several instances have been recorded of speeds over 100 m.p.h. A locomotive engineer in the North of England once summed up the characteristics of the Gresley and Peppercorn engines thus: 'The Gresley's are the real "greyhounds" of the stud; but if you have to take 600 tons on a dirty night give me a Peppercorn.' The latter engines first appeared in L.N.E.R. apple-green; but later they were finished in the standard British Railways green, in which guise the engine in our picture is shown.

188 **A 'Britannia' Pacific.**
As a result of the Interchange trials of 1948 the engineers of the Railway Executive of the British Transport Commission, under the direction of Mr R. A. Riddles, the member for mechanical and electrical engineering, designed a series of new standard locomotives embodying features shown to be most satisfactory in the performance of the former companies'

locomotives. The first of these new designs to appear was the Class 7MT 'Pacific'. To emphasize its national rather than regional character the first of these engines was named *Britannia*, while others have been named after famous locomotives of the past, and famous characters in British history, literature, and fiction. The engine illustrated, No. 70037 *Hereward the Wake*, was in regular service in East Anglia. The 'Britannia's' might, in other circumstances, have had as long and distinguished a career as many of their predecessors in British locomotive history. But the decision to supersede steam traction entirely was made in 1955, and replacement of the 'Britannia's' by diesel-electric locomotives began in 1958. During their short career on express work, in East Anglia, on the Western Region, on the Irish Mails, and on the Continental expresses of the Southern the 'Britannia's' did much excellent work, with economic use of fuel.

189 A 'BR5' Mixed Traffic 4-6-0.

On the grounds of general utility and proven excellence in service the Railway Executive would have been fully justified in adopting the Stanier 'Black-Five' as one of the national standard engines. But Riddles and his staff were most anxious to avoid any appearance of favouring one of the former railways in preference to the others, and the new 'BR5' 4-6-0, while closely similar to the Stanier in its boiler and motion was 'styled' like the 'Britannia's' and other new designs, and incorporated a number of new details. The 'BR5' class have proved splendid engines. They have been allocated to depots in many parts of Great Britain, and have been universally welcomed. On the Eastern section of the Southern Region, in particular, although designated 'mixed-traffic' they were used with outstanding success on express passenger services to the North Kent coast resorts. Although

an 'alien' design, so far as the men were concerned, they had the rare distinction of being preferred to their own and well-tried 'King Arthur' class (reference 155). When the latter engines were being scrapped some of their names were transferred to the new 'BR5' 4-6-0s. British Railways adopted the livery of the former London and North Western Railway for its intermediate and mixed traffic types, and the 'BR5' is here shown in the same painting style as former Crewe celebrities, like the 'Precursors', 'Prince of Wales' 4-6-0s, and 'Claughtons'.

190 A 'West Country' 4-6-2.

Following the introduction of the Bulleid 'Merchant Navy' class Pacifics, in 1941, the Southern Railway built a lighter version of the same design in 1945 of which the earlier batches were named after places in the West of England served by the Southern Railway. After 48 of these engines had been put into service the 'Battle of Britain' series followed, named after personalities, aerodromes, and units engaged in the Battle of Britain, in 1940. A final series, bringing the total for the class up to 110 locomotives, was named after a further West Country towns. Like the 'Merchant Navy' class these engines were capable of excellent work; but they suffered from the same defects, and commencing in 1957 a number of them were rebuilt, with conventional valve gear, and with the air-smoothed casing removed. Our illustration shows No. 34028 *Eddystone*, of the rebuilt series, and very massive imposing locomotives they now look. The change has greatly improved their reliability without lessening their capacity for hard work or very fast running. *Eddystone* is shown in the standard British Railways livery. In addition to working over all main lines of the Southern Region some of these engines have done excellent work on the very heavily graded route of the former

Somerset and Dorset Joint Line between Bath and Bournemouth. Of the 110 locomotives of the class a total of 41 have been rebuilt in the style shown in the illustration.

191   A 'BR4' Standard 2-6-0.

The range of new British standard steam locomotive design introduced from 1951 onwards included a 4-6-0 of Class 4 capacity, three varieties of 2-6-0, and three varieties of passenger tank engine all styled in a similar manner to the 'Britannia' and the 'BR5'. The engine chosen for illustration is the very successful Class 4 2-6-0, first introduced in 1953. While bearing an unmistakeable 'family likeness' to the 'BR5', the 4MT 2-6-0 has achieved an individuality of its own. With relatively small coupled wheels of only 5 ft. 3 in. diameter the nominal tractive effort is high in relation to the size of the engine. At the same time the excellent design of cylinders and valves has permitted of the free flow of steam, and made the engine very fast on the road. In earlier days a wheel of at least 6 ft. 6 in. diameter was considered essential for express work; but these small engines run freely up to 75 m.p.h., and form an interesting and impressive example of the last phase of steam locomotive design in this country.

192   The 'Evening Star'.

The last of the standard steam locomotives introduced by R. A. Riddles was in every way the most remarkable and successful of all. There was need for a heavy freight engine having an ability to run on as many routes in the country as possible; and the decision was taken to use a boiler similar to that of the 'Britannia' and the 2-10-0 wheel arrangement. As fast, as well as heavy mineral service was envisaged the coupled wheels were made 5 ft. in diameter. The result was an extraordinary versatile and successful locomotive, of which more than 200 have been built. The versatility of the type does indeed stand as a tribute to the accumulated experience of more than 100 years in locomotive designing in this country, and as a fitting climax to the story. Although primarily intended for heavy goods service these engines are occasionally used on fast passenger trains, and one of them ran at *ninety miles per hour* with the 'Flying Scotsman'. It is fitting that the very last steam locomotive built for service on British Railways should have been to this outstanding design. While the rest of the class are painted plain black, without any lining, the last one, which was built at Swindon, was decked in the 'passenger green' and named *Evening Star*. It was put into service in 1960.

WHEEL ARRANGEMENTS
The Classification of locomotive types:

What is known as the Whyte system provides the most generally accepted method of classifying the various wheel arrangements of steam locomotives. This specifies the number of wheels in the groups of 'carrying' and driving wheels. Thus a locomotive with a leading four-wheeled bogie, six-coupled driving wheels, and no carrying wheels at the trailing end is a 4-6-0. Some of the most commonly used wheel arrangements have a type name. For example a locomotive of the 4-6-2 type is known as a Pacific. Some of the most familiar British types illustrated in this book are shown here:

oOo	2-2-2	—
oOO	2-4-0	—
ooOo	4-2-2	—
ooOO	4-4-0	—
ooOOo	4-4-2	'Atlantic'
ooOOO	4-6-0	—
ooOOOo	4-6-2	'Pacific'
oOOO	2-6-0	'Mogul'
oOOOo	2-6-2	'Prairie'
oOOOOo	2-8-2	'Mikado'
oOOOO	2-8-0	'Consolidation'
ooOOOoo	4-6-4	'Baltic'
oOOO OOOo	2-6-0+0-6-2	'Beyer-Garratt'

The following are some common British types almost entirely confined to tank engines:

OOoo	0-4-4
OOOo	0-6-2
OOOoo	0-6-4

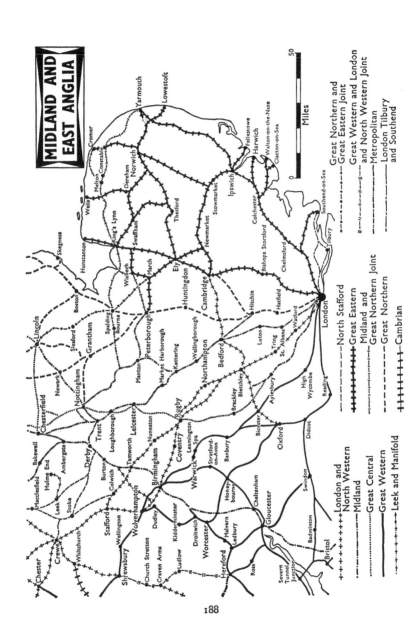

MIDLAND AND EAST ANGLIA

Miles
0   50

Great Northern and
Great Eastern Joint
Great Western and London
and North Western Joint
Metropolitan
London Tilbury
and Southend

North Stafford
Great Eastern
Midland and
Great Northern Joint
Great Northern
Cambrian

London and
North Western
Midland
Great Central
Great Western
Leek and Manifold

INDEX

Figures in heavy type are colour plates.
Figures in Roman are descriptive notes.

189